REPRESENTING THE ROYAL NAVY

To the memory of my mother, Mary Smith

Representing the Royal Navy
British Sea Power, 1750–1815

MARGARETTE LINCOLN
National Maritime Museum, UK

Published in association with the

ASHGATE

Published by
Ashgate Publishing Company
Gower House
Croft Road
Aldershot
Hants GU11 3HR
England

Ashgate Publishing Company
Suite 420
101 Cherry Street
Burlington, VT 05401–4405
USA

The author has asserted her moral right under the Copyright, Designs and Patents Act, 1988, to be identified as the author of this work.

Ashgate website: http://www.ashgate.com

British Library Cataloguing in Publication Data

Lincoln, Margarette
    Representing the Royal Navy: British sea power, 1750–1815
    1. Great Britain. Royal Navy–Public opinion 2. Great
    Britain. Royal Navy–History–18th century 3. Great
    Britain. Royal Navy–History–19th century 4. Public
    Opinion–Great Britain 5. Great Britain–History, Naval–
    18th century 6. Great Britain–History, Naval–19th century
    I. Title
    359' .00941' 09033

Library of Congress Cataloging-in-Publication Data

Lincoln, Margarette
    Representing the Royal Navy: British sea power, 1750–1815 / Margarette Lincoln.
        p. cm.
    Includes bibliographical references and index (alk. paper)
    1. Great Britain. Royal Navy–Influence. 2. Great Britain. Royal Navy–History–18th
    century. 3. Great Britain. Royal Navy–History–19th century. 4. Sea power–Great
    Britain–History–18th century. 5. Sea power–Great Britain–History–19th century.
    I. Title
    VA454 .L65 2002
    359' .00941' 09033

2002066468

ISBN 0 7546 0830 1

This book is printed on acid-free paper

Typeset in Palatino by Pat FitzGerald

Printed by MPG Books Ltd, Bodmin, Cornwall.

Contents

List of Illustrations

All illustrations are held in copyright by the National Maritime Museum, Greenwich

Jacket Illustration

A French Hail Storm, – or – Neptune Losing sight of the Brest Fleet, by J. Gillray (artist and engraver), H. Humphrey (publisher), 10 December 1793. NMM Repro. ID PW3926.

Black and White Figures

Preface

This book examines changing representations of the British Navy from the Seven Years War (1756–63) to the end of the Napoleonic War (1815). There are many political and military histories of the Navy in this period that focus on key battles and personalities. Economic historians and those with an interest in labour relations have studied aspects of naval administration.[1] More recently, there have been studies of the operation of the Navy and life at sea.[2] These works consider the Navy as an organization with specific military objectives, logistical requirements, and operational problems. In contrast, this book considers the Navy as a cultural presence in the public sphere, a presence that circulates through, and is refracted by, specific media in the service of particular social and political interests. In this way the immediate operational aims and needs of the Navy can be seen in relation to the cultural mechanisms which helped to shape contemporary attitudes to its performance. By identifying the presence of the Navy as discourse and image, it is possible to clarify its place in the formation of public attitudes to war and peace, nation and empire, race and gender. The impact of war on society in this period continues to be a relatively neglected subject in spite of important works by distinguished scholars, including John Brewer's account of the emergence of the fiscal-military state, Linda Colley's study of the forging of British national identity in the context of recurring war with France, J.E. Cookson's survey of the British nation under arms,[3] and John Peck's account of how Britain's success at sea was reflected in novels and helped to shape the political, social and cultural character of the nation.[4] Perceptions of the Navy have been generally neglected in cultural studies of the period 1750–1815, and there is no detailed examination of how the image of British sea power was constructed and deployed in the public sphere. This book aims to help re-position naval history, illustrating its importance for inter-disciplinary study, and drawing attention to little-used sources.

The framework of the book is thematic: individual chapters discuss the representation of the attitudes of particular groups towards the Navy, including merchants and financiers, politicians, churchmen, women, doctors and seamen. The seamen themselves obviously had first-hand knowledge of the workings of the Navy, but some of the other groups also contain those who would have had personal experience of naval life, such as naval surgeons, naval chaplains and wives. This grouping allows for a comparison between those who may have seen the Navy at sea, and those who could only imagine what it was like from their vantage points on land. I have omitted some social groups, for example artisans, who lacked the means to express themselves publicly and at length as a distinct group. Within this framework, individual chapters follow a broadly chronological approach to allow discussion of the changing status of the Navy. This structure is designed to show the relation between particular reactions and general cultural and social trends. It allows us to appreciate the interconnections between the different social groupings, gain insights into the growing status of professionalism, and explore aspects of the role of medicine in British imperialism. It also allows us to challenge perceptions of gender roles. The image of women waiting on the shore after the departure of their menfolk has a long history but in this period the traditional image was both reproduced and reworked. An examination of changing attitudes to the Navy over time not only reveals the widespread networks of people, power and communication, but also illuminates trends in social and class relations, and allows us to reflect on processes like commodification and the construction of masculinity.

The period 1750–1815 is rich in materials that allow us to study the Navy as a cultural presence; Britain was often at war and the Navy was high on the public agenda. P.J. Marshall has shown that by the time of the Seven Years War, Britain's rulers were mostly investing empire with a new significance. Empire was seen to be vital to Britain's economic success and standing as a world power, and successive governments began to commit resources to overseas war and colonial issues on a much greater scale.[5] There was a growing understanding that naval outcomes in far-flung outposts of empire had a crucial bearing on the economy and quality of life in Britain. By 1815 it was accepted that national security would stem from investment in naval power and global commerce. In this energetic period from 1750–1815, the Navy was represented in a wide range of media, of which little remained free from the constraints of government propaganda or the commercial exploitation of patriotism. The present study considers a variety of visual and textual sources, from pamphlets, sermons and prints, to civic architecture and funereal monuments. Much of the material is housed in the National Maritime Museum, Greenwich, including manuscripts, paintings, ceramics, prints and caricatures, sheet music, and uniforms. Images of the Navy were constructed by different elements of society, and collectively these images helped to shape public opinion in an era when, as Jürgen Habermas has argued, there had already emerged a new capacity for rational and critical public debate.[6] Habermas locates this 'bourgeois public sphere' between the private domain of the nuclear family (which he defines as including the basically privatized but publicly relevant realm of commodity exchange and social labour), and the public domain of state and court. In theory, entrance to this public sphere was open to all who took advantage of their opportunity to become educated and own property. Habermas overemphasized the exclusion of women from the public sphere and neglected the complexity of social identities but his ideas provide a useful framework for this investigation of public perception.

I should like to thank successive Directors of the National Maritime Museum, Richard Ormond and Roy Clare, for giving me the time to work on this book. I am grateful to the John Carter Brown Library for awarding me the Alexander O. Vietor Memorial Fellowship in 1998 when much of the research for Chapters 3 and 4 was undertaken, and where I benefited from the comments of such excellent scholars as Felipe Fernández-Armesto, John Hattendorf and James Alsop. I am particularly grateful to Roger Knight, formerly Deputy Director of the National Maritime Museum and now Professor of Naval History at the University of Greenwich, for his support in the early stages of this project and for his comments on Chapter 3. Colin White, Director Trafalgar 200, gave generously of his time to read an early draft. The book has also benefited from the advice and suggestions of colleagues at the Museum, and from discussions following the maritime history seminars held at the Institute of Historical Research. Thanks are due to the Museum's library and manuscripts staff for their unfailing help with inter-library loans and enquiries; to Rachel Giles, the Museum's Head of Publications, and to Fiona Renkin, the Museum's Publishing Executive. I am indebted to editorial staff at Ashgate Publishing Limited for their skill and attention to detail, and to the editors of the *Journal for Maritime Research* for allowing me to reproduce in Chapter 4 material published in May 2002 as 'Origins of Public Maritime History: The Royal Navy and Trade 1750–1815', JMR (May 2002). Finally I owe my greatest thanks to my husband, Andrew Lincoln, and to our children, Anna and Sophie, who seem even more relieved than I am that this book is finished at last.

Margarette Lincoln

Notes

1 D.A. Baugh, *British Naval Administration in the Age of Walpole* (Princeton, NJ, 1965) and *Naval Administration 1750–50* (NRS. Vol. 120, 1977); R. Morriss, *The Royal Dockyards During the Revolutionary and Napoleonic Wars* (London, 1983).

2 For example, B. Lavery, *Nelson's Navy. The Ships, Men and Organisation 1793–1815* (London, 1989); N.A.M. Rodger, *The Wooden World: An Anatomy of the Georgian Navy* (London, 1986); B. Vale, *A Frigate of King George: Life and Duty on a British Man-of-War 1807 – 1829* (London and New York, 2001).

3   J. Brewer, *The Sinews of Power: War, Money and the English State, 1688–1783* (London, 1989); L. Colley, *Britons: Forging the Nation 1707–1837* (New Haven, CT, 1992); J.E. Cookson, *The British Armed Nation 1793–1815* (Oxford, 1997).
4   J. Peck, *Maritime Fiction. Sailors and the Sea in British and American Novels, 1719–1917* (Basingstoke, 2001).
5   P.J. Marshall, ed., *The Oxford History of the British Empire*, 5 vols (Oxford, 1998–99), vol. II (1998), p. 1.
6   J. Habermas, *The Structural Transformation of the Public Sphere: An Inquiry into a Category of Bourgeois Society* (Cambridge, 1989); originally published in German in 1962.

Abbreviations

Add. MSS	Additional Manuscripts, British Library
CWPR	*Cobbett's Weekly Political Register*
GM	*Gentleman's Magazine*
NMM	National Maritime Museum
NRS	Navy Records Society
SPCK	Society for Promoting Christian Knowledge

Chapter 1

Introduction

Sea power enabled Britain to dominate world trade and acquire an empire: in the eighteenth century, maritime activity was central to many aspects of society. During this period the Navy was a vital force for national defence, trade protection and imperial expansion. It also had a huge influence on Britons' understanding of their world. This book focuses on one strand of a much larger picture of war and society during a critical period of civic development and national expansion. Yet the Navy had such influence on public life that a study of its representation adds to our understanding of British culture, cultural politics and the ideology of empire.

I

Since the Navy is no longer such a pervasive force in the public mind, it is useful at the outset to consider how 'the senior service' markets itself today when the operations of nuclear-powered submarines are largely secret and surface warships rarely fight pitched battles. Recruiting literature now focuses on the advantages of the Navy as a career, on opportunities for training, travel, and the security of close friendships. The monotony of life at sea is glossed over. An issue of *Navy News*, for example, might choose to focus on high-speed chases against drug smugglers, defence diplomacy and exercises in such distant locations as South America and the Falklands.[1] In an age when young people are reputed to 'want it all, now', the Navy entices school leavers with the possibility that 'you'll very likely have seen and done more by the time you're 20 than many of your friends at home will in the whole of their lives'.[2] Glossy pictures show immaculate ships in calm seas against a variety of backdrops from ice flows to sunsets. While the literature continues to emphasize the traditional role of the Navy – national defence and trade protection – it now also stresses the Navy's role in combating environmental disasters such as oil spills, its activities against terrorists, and its humanitarian efforts to help the victims of flood or starvation. Potential recruits are assured that conditions of service are attractive in themselves and that civilian employers will value the skills they have acquired. The literature carefully appeals both to the material impulses of some potential recruits and to the finer feelings of others who might wish to work towards making the planet a less dangerous place. The two lines of thought are neatly summed up in one naval slogan, 'See the world ... differently'. In contrast, other aspects of the media present a less upbeat view of the Navy. There are few opportunities for naval officers to be interviewed on television compared to army officers, and often they merely appear as cautious – though well-briefed – spokesmen of current government policy. In the aftermath of the terrorist attacks on America on 11 September 2001, the Navy briefly hit the headlines in December when it intercepted a cargo ship in the Channel suspected of attempting to carry terrorist material into London. Its traditional role as defender of Britain's shores seemed once more pertinent as the country faced a new war against terrorism. The press in peacetime is less respectful. 'Rule the waves? These days we're lost at sea' fulminated Jeremy Clarkson, writing for *The Sunday Times*. The Navy 'would struggle to gain control of a puddle', he claimed, while the British have largely lost the sense of being an island nation.[3] Less opinionated pieces in the press also present a view of the Navy 'gone soft'. The Defence Editor of *The Times* reported proudly in 2001 that the Navy was to make its submarine-hunting Duke class frigates 'whale and dolphin-friendly' after discovering that the active sonar used by the frigates had an adverse, sometimes fatal, effect on these mammals. Over £500 million could be spent on developing and installing a new sonar system, and although this would make the fleet more operationally effective, *The* Times chose to give the story an emphasis that was predominantly environmental. The Ministry of Defence was reported as categorically stating that the difficulty faced by whales and dolphins was one of the key issues considered by the Royal Navy.[4]

In contrast, by the mid-eighteenth century, English naval tradition was already strongly focused. It was identified with the defence of liberty, the protection of national religion and with the prosperity of the nation. On the whole, army officers still enjoyed greater social standing than naval officers. Admiral Vernon, on campaign in the West Indies in 1741, gave a speech to rally his officers in which he admitted that they had long been considered 'in a secondary light, as Persons of little Consequence out of our own Element'. Yet he looked forward to the day when all men of political influence, of whatever party, would be forced to acknowledge that the Navy and naval officers in particular were 'the only natural Strength of *Great-Britain*'.[5] In fact, Vernon's campaign had already helped to bring the Navy firmly into the public consciousness. His victory against the Spanish at Porto Bello in 1739 had caught the public imagination, and popular commemorative pottery, first manufactured to mark this event, had been widely circulated. Medals were struck in Vernon's honour and both his birthday and the anniversaries of his victory were marked as festive occasions. A little later, Anson's celebrated circumnavigation of 1740–44, which culminated in the taking of a Spanish treasure ship, inspired enormous confidence in the ability of British seamen to help the nation achieve greater international status. *Rule Britannia*, written by James Thomson, was first performed in 1740 in the masque *Alfred*, a work which encouraged Britain's imperial ambitions. The cultural significance that was being invested in the Navy at this time ensured that *Rule Britannia* immediately struck a chord and became a national song. In 1748, the introduction of naval uniform for sea officers further distinguished the service in the public estimation. A year later, the magnificent Greenwich Hospital was completed as a home for retired seamen and rapidly became synonymous with naval power.

Popular media, including songs and ballads, displayed a burgeoning national pride in naval achievement. Publications aimed at a more sophisticated audience occasionally reflected tension between aggressive and humanitarian impulses and displayed signs of ambivalence regarding the ruthless use of naval power in the pursuit of empire, but these were in a minority. The execution in 1745 of Lieutenant Phillips of the *Anglesea* for surrendering his ship to the French – prefiguring the more notorious case of Admiral Byng in 1757, who was also executed for failing to fight with sufficient vigour – made the character of the naval officer a talking point.[6] Arguably, the event increased public expectation of the Navy while making officers themselves all the more eager to avoid accusations of cowardice. The ordinary sailor, too, began to be seen in an increasingly favourable light. Back in the 1740s, Vernon did much to help this process. His published speeches to his officers contain such flourishes as: 'Remember you have the good fortune to command one of the bravest Classes of Men, such as do not know what Fear is; who will perform that in Sport, which scarce any Reward would induce others to attempt.'[7] Over the years, the ordinary seaman, so often a problematic, potentially disruptive figure, was made safe and acceptable as 'Jack Tar', a caricature that glossed over his moral laxity and capacity for violence. It was this figure that was repeatedly celebrated in popular song, theatre and prints. Although the image of Jack Tar showed a capacity to change over time, and occasionally featured in prints with a radical undertone, it never entirely broke free from the sentimentality with which it had originally been invested.

II

In this period, the Navy became a more attractive career to potential officers. Service as a commissioned officer in the Royal Navy was one of the few professions in which a man without an independent income could maintain himself as a gentleman, apparently working for the public good rather than for private gain. The ethos of command in the Navy became more paternalistic in the course of the eighteenth century, mirroring the sense in civilian society that professionals (as distinct from aristocrats, who were often accused of doubtful morality), were becoming the repositories of social virtues (demonstrating a greater sense of public responsibility). Increasingly, then, the Navy appealed to men of good family and to the younger sons of the landed classes, especially those who needed a career to support them. In wartime, the Navy was a prime means of social mobility: individuals moved up the ranks more quickly as officers fell in battle and those who were fortunate enough to capture enemy prizes could find themselves with enough capital to purchase land. The basic pay for naval officers was not good. Between 1747 and 1807, the pay of a captain of a first rate rose from £28 to £32 4s. per lunar month, and since a captain's pay depended on the size of ship he commanded, those in smaller ships received less. During most of the period, though, Britain was at war and men could hope for prize money. High-ranking naval officers also had access to power structures beyond those operating on board ship. Since important commands were likely to be political decisions, many sought a seat in the House of Commons where they could hope to influence such decisions; consistently in this period around 4 per cent of Members of Parliament were seamen.[8] The rewards given to lesser members of a ship's crew only became a cause of real dissatisfaction towards the end of the century when, in a period of inflation, pay for seamen in the Navy fell behind peacetime wages in merchant ships. After the naval mutinies in 1797, there was an increase in seamen's pay and yet another in 1806. Therefore between 1747 and 1808 an able seaman's pay rose from 22s. 6d. to 32s. per lunar month (net of fixed deductions).

The Navy increased in size and importance. During the Seven Years War there were on average 74 800 men serving in the Navy. This number increased in successive conflicts until at the height of the Napoleonic War in 1805 it had risen to 120 000 – a number caused by a proportionate growth in naval tonnage. The British public was used to the idea of war but had no experience of war at first hand because actual conflict took place at sea or in other continents. In consequence, there was a gulf between the experience of civilians and that of fighting men. While this certainly affected the representation of the Navy, it should not lead us ultimately to underestimate the effect of war on British society. Between one in seven and one in eight British adult males of military age were engaged in the American war.[9] The social impact of the great struggle against France was even more substantial: it is estimated that by 1803 over one in five of the population of Britain capable of bearing arms were engaged in some form of military service.[10] The magnitude of the war effort exacerbated existing tensions in society. The effect of war on most people's lives in this period, including such things as the loss of manpower across the country and the sight of mutilated servicemen, has never been explored to the same extent as for the two World Wars in the twentieth century. But for areas of the country where naval recruitment was traditionally strong, social disruption and trauma were inevitable. In an age of poor communications, many people entered the Navy never to be heard from again. Overall losses at sea from battle and shipwreck were considerable in all conflicts of the period, and an even greater number of seamen died from disease. According to Dudley Pope, during the French Revolutionary and Napoleonic Wars the Navy lost 1875 men in action, 13 600 from shipwreck and 72 000 from disease or accident.[11]

During the 1790s when the Navy rapidly expanded and needed men desperately, only a small percentage of seamen were true volunteers.[12] More than half the average crew was obtained by press-gangs.[13] Warships, isolated from society, formed their own rigid communities subject to naval discipline. At the same time, the seamen, drawn from different parts of the British Isles, forged a common identity which, while they were together, overlaid regional and other local identities. The Navy abroad therefore constituted a projection of 'Britishnessness' which some contemporaries appreciated and were keen to cultivate. Perceptions of the Navy at home, though, often reflected contested definitions of patriotism and the difficulties of establishing a coherent national identity.

Britain maintained its capacity for waging war through efficient taxation. Warship construction and the maintenance of the fleet were both high-cost operations and vast sums were needed for the Navy. The government reaped the benefits of this heavy investment: the growth of Britain's economic power paralleled the growth of its professional navy. Perceptions of the Navy have to be set against the prevalent mercantilist ideology, which assumed that a relationship existed between international trade and the military power of the state that required careful attention. Britain became the dominant naval power largely because it was able to deploy more ships and men than any rival nation. It had the administrative and fiscal ability to organize extended naval operations. The British government was always concerned about available numbers of warships and men, to such an extent that seamen became of greater importance to the nation than any other sector of the labour force. The strength of the mercantile marine was closely related to Britain's supremacy at sea: a large pool of seamen was needed in order to maintain a powerful fleet at sea in wartime, although prolonged conflict in itself led to thousands of landmen and boys being trained for naval service.

At sea, the Navy deployed the nation's largest workforce, since no organization on land required the coordinated efforts of 900 or so men, as did a first-rate warship. But naval operations employed far more men than the numbers actually serving at sea. As has often been pointed out, the naval dockyards were Britain's biggest industrial complexes in the eighteenth century, employing a greater workforce than the largest factories, breweries or mines, and therefore the Navy was one of the largest single employers of civilian labour of the period. Throughout most of the century the dockyards were expanded and improved in order to provide adequate facilities to service, supply and repair the fleet, necessitating administrative structures on a scale that civilian enterprises did not as yet require. The Victualling Office at Deptford, for instance, headquarters of the Navy's Victualling Board, was the first large-scale food manufacturing and catering organization in the country – which is not surprising given that it had to provision thousands of men at sea. The vast dockyards were a reflection of the extent of British sea power and also the government's financial and political commitment to maintaining that power. Certain domestic trades and industries were also geared to supporting armed conflict. For example, the development of iron and copper industries was notably accelerated in wartime.

III

The Navy's impact on all levels of society inevitably took many forms. From the time of Vernon's victories, naval battles were re-enacted at popular shows. As early as 1741 at Southwark Fair there was a 'machine showing the Vernon's siege of Carthagena'. Later, panoramas (or at least very large canvases) of recent engagements brought scenes of war home to a curious public. From the 1790s, in the wake of Nelson's victories, mimic battles between model ships in real water (naumachia) became a popular form of entertainment – often concluding in a thunderous display of fireworks. Such spectacles continued to be fashionable until the end of the Napoleonic War. Models also helped perpetuate the glories of Britain's military victories well into the next century, and the naval monuments at St Paul's were also a visitor attraction.[14] It's worth remembering, too, that art shows were by no means the province solely of the better educated. In the early nineteenth century, for example, the more refined visitors complained that all pictorial exhibitions were now crowded 'with the lower orders of people ... even sailors in their jackets with their doxies on their arms, now elbow the first people of rank at these spectacles with the utmost of familiarity'.[15]

Different ranks of seamen can be linked to different aspects of 'Britishness', but as part of their imperial aspirations in this period the British in general consolidated a national fiction in which the sea was held to be part of their being. This was not simply at the level of a comforting myth of national superiority. The construction of the image of the Navy and seamen allowed Britons to assume that a degree of fair-dealing and a notion of fellowship were two of the qualities at the heart of British national identity. While successive governments invested heavily in maritime affairs to secure political ascendancy, the story of maritime Britain was constructed in positive terms: it helped to bind and unite the nation and it apparently allowed the nation to display its better qualities. In 1808, Sir Arthur Wellesley (the future

Duke of Wellington), described the Navy in Parliament as 'the characteristic and constitutional force of Britain'.[16] It had come through the American war, won successive victories against revolutionary and Napoleonic France, and was now helping to support the army in the Peninsular war. People felt that they owed the Navy a great obligation. Until Wellington's victories began to redress the imbalance, the Navy was always far more popular than the army, whose reputation was always clouded by the public's suspicion of a standing army. The Navy became a national symbol that could be adapted to both government and opposition views about the war. As loyalist and radical groups each struggled to appropriate and define the cultural meaning of the Navy, this effort had a great and prolonged impact on all walks of public life, and was reflected in print, art and state pageants. No cultures are homogenous – as has been noted, there was obviously more than one 'eighteenth-century experience' on offer and different groups in society identified and pursued their own interests differently, however bound by common frameworks. The present study both underscores this message and helps to chart the extension of social relations and networks across different communities. Their interconnections are nowhere better found than in their response to the Navy, which as an agent of state policy aimed to protect national freedoms and consequently the very 'public sphere' in which it featured so largely.

Notes

1   *Navy News*, October 2001, pp. 1, 16.
2   *Your Future in the Royal Navy*, CP5 (prepared for the Directorate of Naval Recruiting by Andrew Clarke, Bristol, May 1999), p. 1.
3   *The Sunday Times*, 2 September 2001, p. 13.
4   *The Times*, 20 August 2001, p. 5.
5   *A Second Genuine Speech Deliver'd By Adm[ira]l V[erno]n on board the* CAROLINA *to the Officers of the Navy After the Sally from Fort St Lazara* (London, 1741), p. 19.
6   For example, the *London Evening Post* no. 2763 (20–23 July, 1745), p. 4.
7   *The Genuine Speech of the truly honourable Adm[ira]l V[erno]n, to the Sea-Officers, at a Council of War, just before The Attack on C[artagen]A* (London, 1741), p. 18.
8   J. Brewer, *The Sinews of Power: War, Money and the English State, 1688–1783* (London, 1989), p. 45.
9   S. Conway, *The British Isles and the War of American Independence* (Oxford, 2000), p. 29.
10 J.E. Cookson, *The British Armed Nation 1793–1815* (Oxford, 1997), p. 99.
11 D. Pope, *Life in Nelson's Navy* (London, 1987), p. 131.
12 See B. Lavery, ed., *Shipboard Life and Organisation, 1731–1815* (Aldershot, 1998), pp. 632–3.
13 R.J. Cootes, *Britain Since 1700* (Harlow, Essex, 1982), p. 103.
14 R.D. Altick, *The Shows of London: a panoramic history of exhibitions, 1600–1862* (Cambridge, MA, and London, 1978), pp. 62, 97, 136.

15 E.B. Neff, 'John Singleton Copley: The Artist as "Realist" and London Impresario' (PhD thesis, University of Texas, 1997), p. 117.
16 See J. Cannon, *The Oxford Companion to British History* (Oxford, 1997), p. 674.

Chapter 2

The Navy's Self-Image

British seamen of the period had a strong sense of their own identity and, by the end of the century, a clear understanding of what constituted a true-bred 'man-of-war's man'. They were tempted to regard landsmen as an inferior species, and used markers of dress, bearing and language to set their own world apart. Yet their self-image was inevitably influenced by popular representations of seamen in a range of media. Though the Navy sought to mould its own identity, it also projected a set of values determined by society, which naturally changed over time. This chapter explores the interaction and tension between these different processes, and considers the Navy's self image in the context of other public representations of the service.

I

For the seaman, work at sea was a form of temporary exile, a way of life necessarily adapted to the needs of working the ship and further limited by the accommodation available. The result was a unique lifestyle that produced men who were recognizably different from landsmen. Physically, ordinary seamen were marked by a distinctive muscle development and by their weather-beaten faces. The hardships they faced as members of a community at sea encouraged a 'clannishness' on land that amounted to an oppositional culture carefully nurtured as a means of asserting a particular identity. In 1776, the magistrate John Fielding famously registered the gap in understanding that existed between seamen and landsmen:

> When one goes into Rotherhithe and Wapping, which places are chiefly inhabited by sailors, but that somewhat of the same language is spoken, a man would be apt to suspect himself in another country. Their manner of living, speaking, acting, dressing, and behaving are so peculiar to themselves.[1]

Sailors grappled with the difficulties of representing maritime culture as much as any group that turned its attention to the Navy or to the sea. Arguably, there was no single, homogenous maritime culture in Britain: seafaring communities varied in different parts of the country and sailors' experience of local culture would in any case be infused by a variety of

9

experiences of foreign travel. It was all the more important, then, for the Navy to establish its institutional identity.

Uniform was an obvious means by which the Navy sought to distinguish itself as a military service. By the mid-eighteenth century, naval officers had become acutely conscious of the relation between dress and status. Finding themselves alone among their European equivalents in not having a distinctive dress, they successfully petitioned the Admiralty and were granted a uniform in 1748. At first the uniform was restricted to commissioned officers and midshipmen; warrant officers had to wait until 1787 for theirs. Between 1748 and 1815, naval uniform underwent no fewer than 20 detailed changes or extensions in order to further differentiate rank. In 1768, for instance, lieutenants complained about the plainness of their uniform and were given white lapels and cuffs. In 1783, Flag-Officers obtained a gold-embroidered full dress coat – though this elaborate garment was abolished in 1787. In 1812, by which time military display had become if anything even more important, all officers except gunners, boatswains and carpenters had a crown added above the anchor on their buttons. In the early years, naval uniform was often worn incorrectly, according to individual taste, although officers generally attached great importance to uniform. William Spavens, a crippled ex-seaman who published his memoirs to earn a subsistence, related the fate of a lieutenant during the Seven Years War who hastily took command of a ship's boat without donning his uniform, sword or cockade:

> The captain then asking him why he came on duty without those badges of his office, he like a Wappineer tar replied, I am as good a man without them as with them. For which contumacious answer the Captain laid him under an arrest, and sent one of his own Lieutenants to succeed him in his command, and kept him prisoner on board his ship till he arrive in port to bring him to trial.[2]

The lieutenant was duly court-martialled for contempt of his office and his superior.

Uniform was a means of enforcing a regard for rank and discipline. Oddly enough, given the need to prevent desertion, no uniform was prescribed for ordinary seamen until 1857, although it would have made deserters instantly recognizable ashore. Instead, from the middle of the eighteenth century until well into the nineteenth, seamen distinguished themselves from landsmen by wearing blue and white and by adopting standard items of dress that varied in shape only with the fashion of the day. Commonly, they wore a blue jacket, waistcoat, checked shirt, neckerchief, blue or white trousers, grey stockings, buckled shoes, and a tarpaulin or straw hat. The resulting homogeneity of appearance marked them as a separate group. The sign of a Portsmouth 'Sea-Draper', put up in 1791, illustrates the Navy's combined use of dress and language to preserve the differences between life at sea and life on land:

> Sailors rigged complete from stem to stern, *viz.*, chapeau, mapeau, flying-job and flesh-bag; inner pea, outer pea, and cold defender; rudder-case, and service to the same, up-haulers, down traders, fore-shoes, lacings, gaskets, etc.[3]

A seaman's shore dress, at any rate, gained him many admirers. Samuel Leech, who went to sea aged 12, records his elation when he was given his first sailor's clothes – a tarpaulin hat, round blue jacket and wide pantaloons:

> Never did young knight swell with loftier emotion, than I did when in sea dress I trod the streets of Gravesend. This had always been my highest ambition. The gaudily dressed soldier never had charms for me; but a sailor, how nice he looked! Well, here I stood, at last, in the often coveted dress; it was the first luxury connected with my life at sea. Pity that each successive step had not yielded me equal delight.[4]

Whatever brave appearance the Navy achieved through the combined effects of approved uniform or distinctive sea dress, experienced seamen appreciated the contrast between the glamour to which the service aspired and the realities of a naval career. This is keenly expressed in Spavens's account when he contrasts the colourful spectacle of a naval review with the very different review of pensioners receiving money from the Chatham chest. To prevent fraudulent claims, pensioners were summoned periodically for inspection. To Spavens, they presented a picture of collective misery:

> At one of these reviews, what a shocking spectacle presents itself to the eyes of the spectator! Here you may behold perhaps 500 mutilated creatures of different ages and appearances … some have a hand, some an arm off; some, both near the wrists, some, both close to the shoulders; other, one at the wrist and the other above the elbow; some are swinging on a pair of crutches; some with one wooden leg below the knee; another above the knee; some with one leg off below the knee and the other above; some with a hand off and an eye out; another with an eye out and his face perforated with grains of battle-powder, which leave as lasting an impression as though they were injected by an Italian artist … . A gentleman once observed to me, he wondered why all or most of the pensioners did not reside near the chest, that they might attend without so much inconvenience! His notion was plausible and well meant; but were such a measure adopted, the cities of London and Westminster, and the whole counties of Kent. Essex, Middlesex, Surry [*sic*], Berks, and Sussex, would be inhabited with little else than a motley company of halt, maimed, blinkards, and cripples: Who then would carry on the manufactures and drive the Lord Mayor's coach?[5]

Spavens knew the subversive potential of his words. He immediately assured the reader that he wished 'to promote, and not to depress the service', and took care to explain that disabled and worn out naval seamen also had resource to the Royal Hospital at Greenwich. But he made a point: the total human cost of naval warfare was partially disguised since the maimed were geographically dispersed.

The narratives of individual seamen are not necessarily representative of a group, but it is noticeable that officers and men generally offered different perspectives when representing the Navy as an institution. This is not surprising: only officers had a permanent connection with the Navy as a service. Ordinary seamen viewed themselves primarily as members of a ship's company and often moved from the Navy to the merchant service as circumstances and individual preference dictated.[6] An officer's own social standing depended on the Navy being held in high regard, and his chances of promotion were mostly determined by his performance in that service. Consequently, officers tended to celebrate the Navy in their published writing or argued for reforms that would enhance its status. Inevitably, there are fewer publications by common seamen. Those that survive are more likely to be critical of naval systems or to complain of individual grievances, even if the authors also exhibit a reluctant pride in some aspects of the service.

A useful starting point in any examination of the writings of officers and seamen is the reason they give for going to sea in the first place, which indicates their initial perception of the Navy, or at least of a life at sea. Many were attracted to sea by other sailors. The conversation of ordinary seamen at leisure seems to have been taken up with tales of adventure and hair breadth escapes. Adam Smith remarked ironically that instead of disheartening potential recruits, such tales seemed to recommend the sea to them:

> A tender mother, among the inferior ranks of people, is often afraid to send her son to school at a sea-port town, lest the sight of the ships and the conversation and adventures of the sailors should entice him to go to sea.[7]

Yet Smith observed that for those who gambled on naval service, the odds were not hopelessly long. In this lottery only a few achieved the highest success but smaller prizes were more numerous: common sailors gained some fortune and preferment more often than common soldiers. And, as Smith noted, 'The hope of those prizes is what principally recommends the trade'. This view, that young men were drawn to seafaring by the prospect of adventure and fortune, is born out by seamen themselves. William Spavens, watching the ships on the Humber in the early 1750s, envied sailors their opportunities of visiting foreign countries: 'I thought of nothing but pleasant gales and prosperous voyages.'[8] John Nicol, who joined the Navy in 1776, had reread *Robinson Crusoe* many times and longed to go to sea.[9] In wartime, prize money was much publicized by naval captains seeking volunteers, and those with a reputation for taking rich prizes had less trouble in finding crews. Later in the century, it became more common to suggest that it was prize money that chiefly attracted men to the Navy, rather than a longing for adventure. The number of prizes taken rarely matched expectations, so increasingly the distribution of prize money to the advantage of high-ranking officers became a grievance. Watkin Tench, a major in the marines, compared the British system unfavourably with the system operating in revolutionary France when he observed it as a prisoner of war.[10] In 1797, following the naval mutinies, an officer openly argued that since prize money alone enticed common men to join the Navy, it should be shared more fairly amongst all ranks.[11] After the shock of the 1797 mutinies, which greatly damaged the trust between officers and their crews, officers were prepared to publish texts, albeit anonymously, which listed the disadvantages of a naval career and suggested reforms. Yet however tough life in the Navy might be, for delinquents more or less commandeered into the service there was at least the possibility that it might provide a fresh start in life.[12]

The appeal of a naval career to potential officers depended on whether Britain was at war or at peace. In wartime, opportunities for promotion and prize money were greater, though the risk of death or injury was higher too. Many joined on impulse only to repent at leisure. A captain who complained in 1773 of the difficulties of subsisting on half-pay in peacetime, anticipated that his readers would reply callously that seamen surely knew what to expect from the service before entering it. He therefore added: 'I hope that none of our countrymen will ungenerously reproach us for a conduct, which, so far as it was our choice, resulted from that vivacity, that restlessness of young men of spirit, which has been the means of raising the British nation to its present pitch of greatness.'[13] This counter-argument indicates that certainly at one time the Navy was popularly represented as a field of opportunity for adventurous youth. The writer reinforced this image though his pamphlet, taken as a whole, illustrates the downside of a naval career. Other officers similarly agitating for better terms of employment represented naval service as a family tradition that ought to be cultivated for the good of the nation:

> What a discouraging circumstance it must be to those, who are desirous of rearing their children for the support of the British bulwark, when they reflect, for their long services – and their lives – that their widows and children may be left to starve upon eighteen guineas a year![14]

The implication, thinly disguised, is that without more support officers will cease to breed their sons to the sea – and the Navy will lose a valuable source of manpower. Since the profession proved attractive to younger sons of the gentry precisely because it required no purchase of a commission but only a modest initial outlay to secure some training, the status of its officers was a sensitive issue clearly linked to pay. Yet by 1816, one ex-seaman turned poet indicated that a father of modest means who sent his son into the Navy had reason to be optimistic, 'Such Fortunes had of late been made | He thought the Navy no bad trade.'[15]

II

In wartime, of course, many ordinary seamen were pressed into the Navy. Thereafter, common sailors experienced severe restrictions on their liberty due to the scarcity of men willing to volunteer for the service, and the need to press men and then prevent desertion. Seamen objected most of all to the institution of turnover by which crews of warships coming in for refit or repair were turned over to ships ready to sail. This was increasingly used from the 1740s and a sailor might spend years without setting foot in England or seeing his family. It was an acknowledged paradox that, in a land which boasted of the liberty of its subjects, the very men who helped to preserve this freedom seemed to have no liberty at all. Astute officers like Vernon, recognizing that it was important not to alienate men from the service and noting that men's health deteriorated if they were kept at sea, repeatedly advised the Government to find some means of obtaining the voluntary service of seamen.[16] No pressing was allowed in America once the British colonies achieved independence, though in practice British captains often continued to impress American seamen arguing that those who had been born British remained so. During the American war, British captains nailing up recruiting posters in those colonies found it more productive to stress that the Navy needed men of merit, who, if they joined up, would be given the opportunity to rise in a service that would respect the freedom of the individual. One such poster for 1777 reads:

> ALL GENTLEMEN SAILORS, Desirous of rendering themselves useful to their Country, let them repair on board His Majesty's armed Ship the VIGILANT, Captain CHRISTIAN, COMMANDER, Where they will be received, and every Indulgence given that their Merit can entitle them to. The said Captain will engage his Word of Honor, that the Persons so entering, shall not be carried out of America without their Consent.[17]

Frequently the British system of manning warships by pressing was contrasted with the French method of keeping a register of seamen who, theoretically, served in rotation. But other British naval officers of the time sought to justify impressment. They argued that the French system of rotating seamen meant that crews were never fully trained as a fighting unit, and that pressed seamen had the same opportunities of advancement in the service as those who joined as volunteers. They pointed out that no commoner could be an officer in the French navy and that without this inducement, seamen were less likely to work their hardest. Such publications depicted the Navy as disciplined but ready to reward merit.[18] If John Nicol's memoirs are to be trusted, some ordinary seamen accepted the need for impressment however much they sought to avoid it as individuals. Nicol, who published his memoirs in 1822, wrote that during the Revolutionary Wars when workmates asked how he could reconcile impressment with the concept of 'British freedom', he always replied, 'Could the government make perfect seamen as easily as they could soldiers, there would be no such thing as the pressing of seamen.'[19] Nicol here seems to have absorbed a key argument of the dominant class and reproduced it in turn to help sustain the social authority of that class, neatly illustrating Gramsci's concept of hegemony.

Nicol's comment on impressment also suggests his own pride in being a 'perfect seaman'. But this skill could be demonstrated only to others at sea; once ashore, sailors ostentatiously sought to impress by their flamboyant shore-going rig. This self-display had such impact that contemporary prints rarely showed seamen dressed in their work clothes and the quality of life on board ship was scarcely appreciated on land. For officers, public ignorance of the business of the sea could have severe disadvantages, as Admiral Byng quickly realized when defending his failure to relieve Minorca in 1756. At his court martial, Byng found it hard to explain how decisions at sea could be affected by a succession of different circumstances. He remonstrated that no commander at sea could provide against all the contingencies of war but for those sitting at home, it was extremely easy 'after the Event of an Action, to point out how and by what Means it might have succeeded better'. That was the core of the problem: armchair critics did not require any specialist knowledge. As Byng complained, 'This Sort of Science requires no other Abilities, than a great deal of Ill-nature and a little Wit'.[20] Here, of course, Byng might be aiming at naval colleagues who chose to put the worst possible construction on his failure to beat the French. But he had more cause to fear public opinion, which was being shamelessly manipulated by a ministry anxious to disguise any failings in its own preparations for war. For example, Byng's numerically-based arguments, which might have been countenanced by prudent naval commanders, were immediately distorted for the popular press by his political enemies. Material such as these doggerel verses, which featured in an amusing print, proved extremely persuasive:

'B—g's Plea'

With thirteen ships to twelve says B—g
It were a shame to meet 'em
And then with twelve to twelve a thing
Impossible to beat 'em

When more to many less to few
And event still not right
Arithmetic will plainly shew
t'were wrong in B—g to fight[21]

Whether or not Byng's conduct in the war was reprehensible, the process of his trial was decidedly unfair. His execution not unnaturally made naval officers extremely sensitive on the issues of cowardice and honour for decades afterwards. Byng's failure to represent his conduct and tactics in a favourable light made his successors more anxious about their success in combat and also more alert to the constructions that could be placed on behaviour and appearances.

Similarly, while seamen revelled in their own distinctive use of language, some saw the need to communicate key aspects of working a ship to a wider audience. The seaman William Falconer, who later became a purser in the Navy, prefaced his poem *The Shipwreck* with an engraving of a merchant ship showing all the masts, yards, sails and rigging to that readers could better understand the poem. This popular work, first published in 1762 and reprinted many times, gives a sympathetic picture of sailors emphasizing both their skill and the dangers they faced. It also made the point that even great skill and specialized knowledge afforded no complete protection: a boatswain and three sailors struggling to furl a sail are lost when a wave dashes them into the sea. But the poem elevated a sea career: the voyage and shipwreck are depicted in epic terms. The experience of the ship's master, who saw his men die one by one, is compared to Priam's grief when the Greeks sacked Troy: 'So pierc'd with anguish hoary PRIAM gaz'd, | When Troy's imperial domes in ruin blaz'd'.[22] Falconer also compiled *An Universal Dictionary of the Marine* before his own death from shipwreck. This successful work gave an accurate record of the practice of seamanship and further helped to communicate to an interested audience the business of the sea. In 1796, William Spavens appended 'An Explanation of Nautical Terms' to the narrative of his life in a similar attempt to communicate to a general reader. His glossary serves to emphasize the amount of 'hauling' and manual labour that was required on board ship but also indicates pride in his knowledge of the more specialized equipment. After Nelson's famous victories, the problem of communication became more complex. Now seamen had to struggle to overcome persistent sentimentalization of the Navy and well as explain unfamiliar sea-phrases. In 1808, one naval officer published *The Cruise; a Poetical Sketch, in eight cantos* in order to give readers a correct idea of naval life: 'Tell us how act a brave, a BRITISH Crew, | But do not o'er the path, the tinsel fiction strew.'[23] In an attempt to communicate 'fact' rather than 'fiction', this work included an index to the footnotes where most of the explanatory detail was to be found.

Naval officers were, in some sense, always in the public eye and their actions invariably elicited comment – often ill-informed and unfair. When Lord Howe relieved Gibraltar in 1782, protecting the outward-bound convoy against a numerically superior Franco-Spanish fleet, he was criticized for avoiding a fixed battle with the enemy. Howe's account of the skirmish (the enemy were content with a long-range, partial action), provoked a sarcastic response from one author purporting to be a retired seaman. He marvelled that after so great an expense in equipping a powerful fleet, Howe's ships 'should skirmish and brush about with their enemy in the manner they have done, dancing like fairies by moon light, or buzzing about like flies in a summer's evening, or like a scene in the opera, ending in fire and smoke.' Still worse, it seemed to this critic that the nation had been 'deceived and bubbled' by Howe's laboured and confused narration of events. His account contained 'parenthesis within parenthesis, like a nest of Chinese boxes, and nothing at the conclusion but a mountebank's pill'. In short, the author denounced the whole episode as 'too ridiculous to be suffered with common patience'.[24] This again illustrates the point that officers had to be careful about possible slurs on their honour. The expectation was that they would do their utmost to bring about a 'close action' when the alleged superiority of British seamen would have the greatest effect. In wartime the success of the Navy was also deeply bound up with party politics. Individual commanders could find themselves immersed in party political intrigue without trying. If they received patronage from politicians in government, for example, those in the opposition would be eager to fault their conduct.[25]

It is not surprising that, given an opportunity, officers talked up the Navy and its function in society. At the beginning of this period, as we have seen from Vernon's speeches, naval officers clearly felt they had some ground to make up. In the wake of the Byng fiasco, Naval professionals sought to establish a tradition for Britain's supremacy at sea. In 1766, there appeared *Britannia Triumphant: or, An Account of the Sea-Fights and Victories of the English Nation from the earliest Times, down to the Conclusion of the late War, under the following noted Commanders, viz ... Drake, Raleigh ... Hawke ... Anson.* It was written by 'a society of naval gentlemen', who argued that from the earliest times Britain had exerted dominion over the seas, and the book included plates of famous admirals, which helped to personalize their achievements. Rather pointedly, their account of Admiral Hawke's victory over the French in 1759 ends: 'Perhaps there never was a naval engagement of such extent, in which no captain was accused, nor even in any degree suspected of misbehaviour or cowardice.'[26] The natural corollary of successive naval victories was to claim the superiority of British seamen. A critic of Keppel's indecisive skirmish with the French fleet in 1778 commented mischievously that since the superiority of British officers and seamen was so established in Europe, 'they can acquire but little honour by an engagement with a ship

A VIEW* OF THE LAUNCHING OF HIS MAJESTY'S SHIP QUEEN CHARLOTTE FROM DEPTFORD YARD JULY 17th 1810.

Figure 1   *A View of the Launching of his Majesty's Ship Queen Charlotte from Deptford Yard July 17th 1810*. Produced on 7 August 1810 by G. Thompson.

of equal force, unless the enemy prove uncommonly brave'.[27] There was continual pressure on officers to represent their actions and their profession to advantage. In response, officers frequently alluded to the nation's dependence on its Navy. The authors of *Britannia Triumphant*, for example, accepted that British naval expeditions were aimed at conquest and settlement. Their account of Boscawen's victories in the isle of Cape Breton contained such details about the island as 'the mountains here may be cultivated to the top' and 'domestic animals, such as horses, black cattle, sheep, swine and poultry thrive well'. The authors concluded by reflecting on the territorial gains of the Seven Years War and anticipating the day when Britain might 'become as famed and more powerful than any empire'.[28] Similarly, the junior officer who in 1768 served up to the public *The Dolphin's Journal Epitomized in a Poetical Essay* was keenly aware that Wallis's circumnavigation in the *Dolphin* had contributed greatly to Britain's national prestige.[29] Officers naturally worried about government attempts to spend less money on the Navy in peacetime. A typical complaint of 1786 reads: 'the neglect, and in consequence the decline of our navy is, of all political evils, the most alarming to this country'. The author warned that naval cutbacks would result in 'a *scarcity* of [that] *most invaluable* but *neglected* description of men, called *sailors*'.[30] Here he hinted at a lack of sincere public interest in the welfare of ordinary seamen, for the most part absent from view and, in inland towns, even an object of curiosity. By 1795, when Mark Moore began his memoirs with a dedication to Lord Howe, he was able to describe the Navy's vital importance to the nation with confidence. He was able to claim that the Navy had always been the favourite service with every honest Englishman. It had been the constant theme of poets, the dearest subject of historians, and both statesmen and patriots had derived their brightest honours from the success of British fleets. Under the protection of the British flag merchants had explored new markets, and enlarged old ones; and the productions of the nation's artisans had been conveyed to the most distant quarters of the globe.[31] The Navy had become an emblem of national identity, or as one captain put it, 'the glory of Britain and the envy of the world'.[32]

This triumphant, patriotic view of the Navy had been encouraged by naval victories, but also by naval ceremonies that took place on land – most obviously the launching of warships. These had become events that united all classes of society. By the 1780s the ceremony of launching a warship had moved from the ship itself to the shore, which made it safer for the dignitaries involved in actually naming the ship and encouraged the royal family to attend more frequently. Ship launches became public spectacles, the more important attracting crowds of as many as 100 000 people.[33] The colour and excitement of these launches is conveyed in many contemporary prints and newspaper reports which helped to convey the patriotic enthusiasm of these dockyard events to an even wider audience (see Figure 1).

Around the same time, the administration of the Navy acquired a prestigious public face. The Navy Office obtained new premises on the River Thames in Somerset House, a block built specifically to house the Government's burgeoning administration and the largest building operation carried out at public expense during the Georgian era. It was intended to be an object of national splendour as well as public utility. The Royal Academy, the Society of Antiquaries and the Royal Society were accommodated in the block facing The Strand; government departments were housed around a large inner courtyard, stretching down towards the River Thames. The Navy Office was accorded the most imposing doorway of all the administrative departments, immediately facing the entrance to the courtyard and so the first to strike the visitor's eye. It was also given the most prestigious stairway. The architect, William Chambers, had control of the design and execution of the whole project, but it is inconceivable that he would not have entered into delicate negotiations with the prospective occupiers of the new building who would have sought to influence the final allocation of space and the key decorative features. The location of the Navy Office reflected consensus about the Navy's national importance. The theme of the Strand front (constrained by existing buildings but still the showpiece of the project), was Britain's relation with the sea. The facade was adorned with motifs that reminded onlookers of the importance of the Navy and sea transport to Britain's national and global interests. In the main quadrangle, a statue of George III leaning on a rudder occupied pride of place. Though 11 years had elapsed since parliament had approved the project, when the Navy Office finally occupied the new apartments in 1786, the status of the maritime aspect of the nation's military power was nobly reflected in bricks and mortar.

III

In contrast with the glowing image of the service which was being constructed, persistent complaints about pay from naval officers throughout the period struck a demoralizing note – though of course once the importance of the Navy had been accepted, it was easier to argue that officers should be better rewarded. Inevitably in peacetime officers complained about living on half-pay but officers could suffer considerable financial hardship even when employed if, as was quite normal, they had only their pay to live on. These complaints give an indication of how, in their lifestyle, officers sought to represent the Navy and Britain too. In 1773, for example, one captain explained that his personal expenses could be substantial: on receiving strangers, especially in foreign ports, he was bound to entertain them generously out of regard for honour of the King, and the dignity of the Navy. But although British people might expect naval officers to indulge their national pride on such occasions, naval officers could not hope that their creditors would have the same public spirit or be less importunate in their demands. The author also pointed out that, by a late regulation, captains were obliged to do honour to their corps by wearing an elegant uniform that was admittedly well suited to their rank, but at the same time very expensive, and ill suited to their pay.[34]

As we have seen, between 1747 and 1807 captains of the most powerful warships saw their pay rise modestly from £28 to £32 4s per lunar month, although they could expect to augment this with prize money in wartime. Naval officers often compared their pay disadvantageously to officers of comparable rank in the army. And while it was understood that after any war there would be a glut of ordinary seamen that would need to be reabsorbed into the labour market, officers presented themselves as inherently incapable of pursuing any other profession in order to supplement their half-pay and support themselves as gentlemen.[35] A common complaint was that officer training equipped men for nothing other than a career at sea. Some officers came from wealthy, aristocratic backgrounds but by far the greater number belonged to poor though respectable families; they had no hopes but their rise in the Navy and no fortune but their sword. One disconsolate officer in peacetime wrote bitterly: 'Our parents had much better made Barbers and Taylors [*sic*] of us, than to have given us a profession which only taught us to look high, to make us more sensible of our fall.'[36] But even in wartime, officers grew increasingly discontented about their pay. After the 1797 mutinies, some showed support for the ordinary seamen who had so resented the pay increase that government had awarded the army while ignoring the Navy. One officer argued that government should have instituted equity in pay and promotion in the Navy 'whereas at present everything is confusion, disorder, irregularity, discontent, and oppression'.[37]

The issue of promotion was also important to the ways in which naval personnel represented the service. For one thing, naval officers thought that they were promoted more slowly than their counterparts in the army. One complained that a subaltern officer in the army was soon made up because he had little more to learn than the exercise of a musket and the manoeuvring of a company, and both could be learnt in three months. But he believed that the case differed widely with a naval officer: it required years of experience, service, and application to fit him for his duty. In an excess of special pleading, the author concluded that, since Britain's empire by sea was the sole security of the nation's liberty, he could think of no more important an object of the nation's care than the cultivation of a naval officer's abilities, and the reward of his services.[38] The Navy was allegedly open to merit but as a rule 'patronage was the spring that drove the machinery of promotion', and the patronage system itself was open to abuse.[39] Some officers who considered that they had been 'neglected' assumed that the nation was deeply interested in their plight and rushed into print. This not only reflected badly on individual officers but on the service as a whole. This state of affairs was well authenticated since in their published works ratings as well as junior officers referred to worthy men who failed to win promotion through lack of influence.[40] Some seamen who had been passed over for promotion complained about 'boys' being made lieutenants before they were the statutory 20 years old. In 1785 one sailor suggested that this practice of promoting youngsters would produce an effeminate navy:

> The very shameful abuse of this article calls loudly for immediate reformation; the whole nation are in astonishment at its *unbounded subversion* ... our navy will become so wretchedly degenerated, that instead of the respectable, manly appearance, which ought to characterize the *true-born* sons of Neptune, we shall possess nothing more that the modern finical manners and habits of macaronies.[41]

The anxiety that incessant competition for promotion could produce in those without powerful interest is highlighted in a series of maudlin letters from a midshipman to a friend in the service. 'We must, if we appear like gentlemen, spend our whole fortune, if it is small, in the chace [*sic*] of preferment, and at last perhaps not arrive at it … . I do not know as yet how I am to be disposed of, I have no prospect of *promotion*; and where I shall exist this year I have not determined on.'[42] The midshipman was killed in 1777 in the war with America and his letters seem to have been published years afterwards by his friend, together with some advice on how to be a good captain apparently written by a father to his son due to take up his first command. The two halves of the book sit oddly together. The midshipman's letters, which tell of disappointment and the struggle against depression in Haslar naval hospital, contrast with the sense of responsibility that is being instilled in the naval father's advice to his son. Yet, they may only be two sides of the same coin, simply revealing the vagaries of a naval career from a personal and potentially subversive viewpoint since in accepting command, there would have been few officers who did not struggle with self-doubt. The issue of promotion seems to have become less contentious over time. In 1808, the author of *The Cruise* devoted one of his footnotes to a matter-of-fact, balanced summary of promotion in the Navy:

> Promotion is by no means monopolized in the Navy by men of high connexions; – there are very few such, comparatively speaking, and every one deserves the situation he holds, through merit. As the actions of these Noblemen are publicly known, it cannot be thought indelicate bringing them forward in this manner. The fact is, there is scarcely an Officer who has not risen through his own exertions. The mass of the Navy is composed of men, whose parents had little or no interest with those in power … they recommend themselves to Captains by serving zealously under them, and thus acquire patronage, ever carrying weight with it. The road to promotion is indeed open to all … witness Cook … and such men reaching the goal would oftener happen, had but [they] sufficient learning to fill higher stations. (p. 83)

Promotion, then, was firmly linked to education and increasingly officers represented the Navy as improving in this respect. Lieutenant Edward Thompson published his letters in 1766 for the benefit of his cousin and other men determined to join the Navy. He explained that not all commanders were gentlemen or men of education; rather they were brave men who had learnt their trade at sea. But officers increasingly needed a range of skills:

> The last war, a chaw of tobacco, a rattan, and a rope of oaths, were sufficient *qualifications* to constitute a lieutenant: but now education and good manners are the study of all: and far from effeminacy, that I am of the opinion the present race of officers will as much eclipse the veterans of 1692, as the polite, the vulgar.[43]

He recommended that would-be officers learn French, Spanish, Italian, and some mathematics to help with navigation. It was necessary, he thought, to be qualified in drawing, fortification, and surveying coasts and harbours. Fencing and dancing were also useful 'light accomplishments'. All this had to be attained before the age of 15 because the new recruit would have to serve six years at sea (unless he went to Portsmouth Academy, which counted as sea time) before he could be examined for lieutenant's rank at the age of 20 or 21. It was not advisable, he wrote, to seek promotion before that time since command of a watch required ability and attention. Thompson was concerned to revise the mistaken notion 'that any blockhead will make a seaman'. To shine as an officer, an individual needed to be 'a man of letters and languages, a mathematician, and an accomplished gentleman'.[44] After the War of American Independence, there was concern that in peacetime the Admiralty wasn't taking the education of junior officers seriously enough or giving them the practical experience they needed.[45] But as David Morrice, a former schoolmaster in the Navy, admitted, the education of youngsters at sea was 'very uncertain, and at best trifling'. It was the captain's duty to see that the boys were taught English grammar, writing, accounts and basic mathematics to lay the foundation for navigation. But though the captain might mean well and even try to ensure that lessons took place, there were many circumstances that conspired to interrupt if not totally prevent his wishes. In bad weather, for example, it was impossible to pay any attention to the boys, especially in frigates. Schoolmasters themselves were often too young and poorly qualified in most subjects except navigation – and drunkenness was a problem. Morrice thought that, however useful alcohol might be to the schoolmaster in drowning care and thought, keeping out the cold, or enjoying the society of their mess-mates, yet it was totally destructive of their authority over the young gentlemen placed under their care and direction.[46]

Certainly from the 1790s some officers complained that the one regular naval academy in Portsmouth Dockyard provided insufficient officer training for a maritime nation. While they argued that it would be good for the country to introduce more formal professional training, they were once again also concerned about the status of the service. One officer commented that if France and Spain had naval academies, 'Why should England then, whose very existence depends on her Navy, so totally disregard the very fountain of everything which makes the service respectable?' He added cynically that perhaps one reason might be that it would lessen ministerial influence by weakening the patronage system of promotion.[47] Academies were viewed as one means of tackling the problem of unjust promotion. Similarly, in 1808 another officer proposed free schools for the sons of seamen in port towns so that they could obtain the learning that would enable them to be promoted fairly.[48]

In contrast, by the end of the century there was little doubt about the effectiveness of the basic training for ordinary seamen on board a British warship. A surgeon who described his voyage in 1805 wrote, 'Our men were regularly trained, as is customary, to the exercise of great guns and small arms'. He thought that it was this attention to drill that gave British warships superiority over their enemies and seamen themselves great 'confidence in their own powers'. Although his ship was captured by the French, he still took pleasure in noting afterwards the difference in the handling of the ship 'in point of discipline and alacrity, as well as seamanship'.[49] No doubt, the surgeon was a biased witness but the drill on British warships had long been praised and used to justify recruiting landsmen in wartime. As early as 1778, a lieutenant had claimed proudly that no nation on earth understood the method of training and making sailors so well as the English, and that six months of discipline and exercise on board an English man-of-war were equivalent in that respect to 12 months on board a ship of any navy in Europe.[50]

A view on this subject from the lower deck is given by an anonymous, disabled sailor who allowed his adventures to be published as a penny tract, presumably as a means of support. He was pressed into the Navy on his return from serving on an East India Company ship as a landsman.

> The boatswain found me, as he said, an obstinate fellow: he swore he knew that I understood my business well, but that I shammed Abraham, to be idel [sic]; but, God knows, I knew nothing of sea business, and he beat me, without considering what he was about.[51]

Presumably, at the end of six months, this seaman was proficient as well as patriotic.

Few officers pretended to be well-read or schooled in literature. In 1768, the seaman who praised Wallis's circumnavigation in verse told readers to expect only 'the rude Production of a Sailors Pen', unadorned with poetical art. His self deprecation is specious since he also thought that the reader would be all the more satisfied to know that his work was 'free from all romantick fiction'.[52] Men who went to sea at a young age may not have been educated in the polite arts but there is no doubt that seamen took the image of the plain, honest sailor – so popular on the stage – and turned it to their own political advantage. For example, in 1779 one author complaining about the conduct of the war with America and purporting to be a seamen wrote, 'It may be asked, who am I, that thus set up myself to instruct my Countrymen. I answer, a plain, open-hearted Sailor, zealous from the Glory of my King and Country.'[53] Ordinary seamen adopted the same pose, sometimes disingenuosly. Richard Parker, ringleader of the mutiny of the fleet at the Nore in 1797, began his defence at his trial with:

Gentlemen,

As I have been at sea from my youth, I therefore hope nothing will be expected from me but a narrative of plain facts. I cannot dress up my defence in the pompous language of a lawyer; could I have procured assistance, I might have been enabled to have expressed myself with more propriety.[54]

Here a popular image – in this case involving the accepted stereotype of the British seaman – operates as an area of exchange or negotiation between the classes.

Negotiation, often involving popular perceptions of what was appropriate to the Navy and due to the seaman, also played a part in naval discipline. Nicholas Rodger cites the episode when Philip Carteret pardoned eight men who jumped ship in 1766 since they meant 'only to get a skinful of liquor, and then to swim back to ship'. Carteret mused afterwards that 'the failings of brave men should be treated with kindness; there was neither malice nor want of honour in their conduct, they were only hurried away by the violence of their passions'.[55] Rodger argues persuasively that officers of the 1750s and 1760s were untroubled by discipline as an issue: whereas later officers expected to command, they had hoped to persuade. Secure in the general acceptance of a hierarchical social structure, they did not feel threatened by the class divisions that played a part in the 1797 naval mutinies. They might find certain men insubordinate, but the lower deck as a whole did not present a threat. By the end of the century, this had changed. With the decline of the old manning system based on patronage, which had meant that officers could often rely on local men volunteering to serve with them, class interests became more dominant, and the pressure of prolonged warfare helped to produce widespread discussion of discipline in the Navy. Views from the lower deck are few. Jack Nastyface did not publish his memoirs of the Napoleonic Wars until 1835 but they evinced a hatred of officers largely because of their unlimited right to punish on board ship. He had the misfortune to serve under the Honourable Sir Charles Paget, a tyrannical officer 'whose name was a terror to every ship's company he commanded', and was so scarred by the experience that he seems to have deliberately set out to present the Navy in the worst light. Alfred Burton, a master's mate under Sir Samuel Hood, was dismissed the service as being unaccountable for his actions, and he also indicated that unjustified flogging was the one thing that seamen hated most about the Navy. The hero of his poem *The Adventures of Johnny Newcome in the Navy* is unfairly flogged by a tyrannical captain, and, though the hero is able to admit that this captain is perhaps atypical, he brooded over the unnecessary disgrace. The experience made him disaffected and eager to leave the service. 'For Gales, and Actions – and all that, | I do not care – but d—m the Cat!'[56] In 1796, the radical John Gale Jones reported that the officer in charge of a ship holding French prisoners near Gillingham considered naval service *'the most abject slavery'*.[57] The disillusioned officer thought that seamen in battle were stimulated not by patriotism but by a sense of danger and fear of punishment.

Jones was an ardent proponent of parliamentary reform and may have been seeking negative views. Certainly, this isn't the picture of navy discipline that most officers liked to promulgate. In the wake of the 1797 mutinies, one officer exclaimed that the violent and unjust severities that used to mark the discipline of the Navy were no more. Though flogging was still necessary in order to preserve discipline and subordination, punishments were now inflicted with a purposeful, albeit reluctant hand. As a consequence, the seaman who used to malign his officer now looked up to him with filial reverence and respect, and regarded his captain as his friend.[58] This officer blamed the mutinies on Britain's political enemies or disaffected Irish seamen and believed that the majority of seamen still adhered to the sentiments he described. In 1800, a captain advised:

> As the captain may properly be called the father or the ship's company … it is his indispensable duty to see himself that the poor seaman be not wrong'd of his due, or the service carried on by *noise, stripes,* or *blows*; a method so inhuman, so unlike the officer, and so contrary to all true discipline, as [desertion] … must be the unavoidable consequence.[59]

This message is echoed by officers time and again during the Napoleonic Wars. Officers represented the Navy as operating under a strict but fair discipline and are as much concerned to fulfil their duty as formerly they were to guard their honour. A handbook for naval officers advised the captain to imagine 'the movements of his ship to be those of a great machine, whose vigour, expertness, utility, and effect, are dependent on discipline'. But the health and happiness of the crew were equally the captain's charge: he was to be 'a friend to good and deserving men; a terror to bad ones; the protector of the weak, and an impartial administrator to the whole'.[60] Officers were shocked at the apparent lack of hierarchy on French ships, where 'men spoke to their superiors as if they had been equals', and preferred instead to adopt a religious rhetoric to describe the relationship between commander and crew reminiscent of the idea of the fatherhood of God. [61]

The published narratives and letters of seamen give rare insights into their perceptions of conditions on board a warship. In 1766, Edward Thompson tried to dissuade a young relative from following in his footsteps, 'If I have met one tar who was uneasy on shore, I have found thousands in a worse situation at sea'. Thompson lists a string of hardships: poor food, particularly in extreme weather (subsisting on boatswain's tallow for four days); lack of sleep ('you must get up every four hours, – for they never forget to call you'); the gloom below decks ('your light for day and night is a small candle, which is often stuck at the side of your platter at meals, for want of a better convenience'). The mental suffering of being forced to hide negative emotions seems keener than the physical discomforts. 'Here are no back doors through which you can make your escape, nor any humane bosoms to alleviate your feelings.'[62] If young officers felt they could not speak freely, the case was the same with ordinary seamen. Jack Nastyface complained that whatever was said about Britain's boasted liberty, from the moment a youth joined the Navy he lost his liberty to speak and act freely: he could *think* but would soon learn to keep his thoughts to himself.

Humane commanders like Edward Vernon had long called for better health care at sea, complaining that 'many of our Ships are moving Hospitals', and other officers did not shrink from describing the fluxes and scurvies that decimated crews on expeditions overseas.[63] Even in 1797, officers saw that conditions of naval service could not encourage established surgeons to compete for places. 'It is a field for young men just past their education, who cannot afford to set up in business.'[64] By the end of the century their comments strongly reflect improvements in hygiene and preventative medicine, and handbooks written by officers for junior colleagues emphasize the importance of cleanliness to health. Nevertheless, John Nicol's account of how he was blinded with opthalmia for six weeks reveals the limitations of contemporary naval medical care. He sat on his sea-chest with a basin of cold water, constantly bathing his eyes. 'If I slept I awoke in an agony of pain. All the time the flux was most severe upon me, and the surgeon would not dry it up, as it, he said, relieved my eyes.'[65]

Some officers described conditions at sea in a positive way, such as the author of *The Cruise* who chose to comment on the ample allowance of provisions in the Navy and compares the coarse-spun hammock to a bed of down, but most ordinary seamen painted a bleaker picture. Samuel Leech complained that:

> A casual visitor in a man of war, beholding the song, the dance, the revelry of the crew, might judge them to be happy. But I know that these things are often resorted to, because they feel miserable, just to drive away dull care.[66]

He compared this behaviour to the superficial gaiety of the slave population in the southern states of America when they were released from work, and sailors often compared themselves to slaves, or used the language of abolition when describing their own situation. Jack Nastyface even described the ritual of prostitutes being ferried on board ships in port to 'the trafficking for slaves in the West Indies', a reminder that thousands of working-class people, in different ways, were sacrificed to keeping the Navy afloat. If the public recognized the suffering endured by seamen, it appears that they preferred to think of them suffering without complaint. The author of *The Disabled*

Sailor, a penny tract published in 1800 when years of war had made disabled seamen a common sight, struggled to reconcile readers to their plight. He prefaced his seaman's tale with, 'It is inconceivable what difficulties the meanest of our common sailors and soldiers endure, without murmuring or regret … . Every day is to them a day of misery; and yet they endure their hard fate without repining.'[67] John Nicol's remarks on being paid off in 1801 strike a more credible note: 'Did those on shore only experience half the sensations of a sailor at perfect liberty, after being seven years on board ship without a will of his own, they would not blame his eccentricities, but wonder he was not more foolish.'[68]

The extent to which Christian practices were observed on board ship depended entirely on the captain. While the Navy was happy to represent itself as helping to preserve Britain's Protestant religion, individuals nevertheless presented navy life as fundamentally irreligious.[69] In the 1750s Lieutenant Edward Thompson explained the difficulties of maintaining a true religion onboard:

> There's not a vice committed on shore, but is practised here; the scenes of horror and infamy on board a man of war, are so many and so great, that I think they must rather disgust a good mind, than allure it … .You will find some little outward appearance of religion, – and Sunday prayers! – but the congregation is generally drove together by the boatswain … who neither spares oaths or blows. In spite of all these you may be good, your church and religion must be in your own breast.[70]

John Nicol, who had been strictly brought up in Scotland, found little to support him in his faith when he went to sea in 1776: 'I had all my life been used to the strictest conversation, prayers night and morning; now I was in a situation where family worship was unknown.'[71] *The Dolphin's Journal*, 1768, indicates how a display of religion might be kept up at key points in a voyage. Prayers were said before setting sail, for example, 'The mighty God, the Pray'r receiv'd | Our Sails we loose, our ship reliev'd' (p. 4). Yet sailors made no attempt to represent themselves as closer to God through the nature of their work, though supposedly this allowed them to experience the power of His creation and many times brought them close to death. This state of affairs does not seem to have altered even by the end of the century. Samuel Leech recalls that the even Sabbath was 'a day of sensuality' on board a warship:

> True, we sometimes had the semblance of religious services, when the men were summoned aft to hear the captain read the morning service from the church prayer-book; but usually it was observed more as a day of revelry than of worship.[72]

Leech was later converted to Methodism so his memoirs may reflect excessive distaste of his former, rejected way of life, but a poem published in 1806 by a sailor indicates that Leech did not mistake the attitudes of ordinary seamen. The sailor recounted the story of a man who fell overboard. His messmates at once threw a chicken coop over the side, hoping that he would cling onto it, but the man sank. At first there was a shiver of fear which affected even the most dissolute, 'Nay damning Jack, whose heaven lay in the bowl, | Sigh'd out, The Lord have mercy on my soul!' But the crew quickly recovered and the captain himself made a jest of the tragedy. The author excused the irreligion of sailors, who 'while they prosper, seldom pray' but when food is short or a gale blows 'then you'll hear them pray, | That Providence would send them some relief'.[73] It seems likely that this attitude was bound up with shipboard concepts of masculinity. Openly religious sailors were sometimes marginalized by their shipmates and men were encouraged to adopt a devil-may-care attitude.[74]

IV

The popular image of the sailor which came to dominate by the end of the century was of a blunt, cheerful lad determined to enjoy the present and heedless of the future. This was the image in Dibdin's sea songs and on the stage where such songs often formed part of the entertainment. Thompson, a naval captain who wrote for the theatre, subscribed to this popular image (no doubt giving the public what it wanted), and seamen themselves seem to have internalized the image and tried to live up to it.[75] We know that sailors liked going to the theatre and that they were an extremely participatory audience whenever plays with a nautical theme were staged. 'In sea-port towns, where Play-houses are frequently to be found, it may be observed, how sailors are perched in abundance in the upper gallery. Music and dancing they are fond of.' [76] Their readiness to storm the stage at key moments is not surprising since music and dancing played an important part in life at sea, and many plays were inspired by contemporary naval incidents. Some sailors even ended up on the stage, where they earned a living by exaggerating their picaresque adventures.[77] Sailors may have formed too receptive an audience and helped to promulgate a view of Britain's 'jolly tars' that actually prevented the public from taking their real hardships at sea all that seriously. It was understood that Britain relied on the Navy for national defence, and the protection of trading and imperial interests. Conditions at sea were not well known to those who had never served on a warship but all could confidently assume that conditions were unpleasant. It made people less uncomfortable to foster an image of the Navy composed of as devil-may-care, happy heroes. Officers valued 'your jolly, merry-making, don't care sort of seamen' because they were good for morale;[78] sailors themselves may have found the fearless image increased their self-respect. Certainly by the 1790s it was common for sailors to exhibit a blind faith in the superiority of the British Navy and a patriotic pride in all things British that showed little sense of the ideological reasons for war with France. For example, one ex-seaman recalled his time as prisoner of war in a French jail. One night the boatswain asked if he was ready to ready to dash out the French sentry's brains to make an escape. '"I don't care", said I "… if I lend a hand … I hate the French, because they are all slaves, and wear wooden shoes".'[79]

In the eighteenth century, the attractions of an increasingly urban, commercial society prompted a discussion of what constituted acceptable masculine behaviour in this more refined social space. Conduct writers developed a standard for urban males, who were increasingly expected to display a capacity for refined conduct in a way that distinguished them from both boorish oafs and effeminate fops. This new definition of manliness was based on display of finely judged politeness that required genuine sociability prompted by natural goodwill. It also required men to control their conversation carefully in order to avoid giving offence. This new idea of refined masculinity was inherently problematic. Some commentators worried about the potentially debilitating effects of a polite education and predicted a decline in the national character that would affect its military capability. Men were therefore increasingly warned of the dangers of becoming superficial, enervated fops and a firm distinction was made between foppery and true refinement that might work to promote national health. Effeminate officers were a prime target for satires on the Navy. Smollet's Captain Whiffle in *Roderick Random*, who took command of his ship wearing a mask and white gloves to preserve his complexion and Attwold's mid-century print *The Naval Nurse, or Modern Commander* are examples (see Plate 1). While the professionalism of the service would suggest that there could have been few such commanders in the Navy, senior officers were always conscious of the possibility of cowardice in action. Since officers alone had the difficult task of overseeing close combat without any vigorous physical task to take their mind off the dangers they faced as obvious targets for enemy snipers, cowardice might be understandable. Perhaps for this reason officers, but also ordinary seamen, were anxious to confirm their masculine identity. Generally, however, because of the hardships they endured seamen provided so great a foil to unmanly fops that commentators automatically recommended a spell as sea as a cure for the over-fastidious.

In the 1770s, and again in the 1790s, there seems to have been particular anxiety about British masculine identity. At Garrick's suggestion, for example, in 1773 Captain Edward Thompson adapted Shadwell's *Fair Quaker of Deal; or, Humours of the Fleet*. First performed in 1710, this comedy was played often up to about 1730 and then not revived again until 1755. A key character is Captain Mizzen, who furnishes his cabin with a picture of Venus and Adonis, a Turkey carpet, and a piano and guitar. We are also told that he works his ship by music. In 1775 a naval officer who complained about the indigence of officers' widows, rejected any suggestion that the answer might be to recruit only men of private means, because 'such kind of sailors will fritter the glorious spunk of an English mariner to the light feather of a Frenchman'. He warned that an infiltration of French manners into the Navy threatened national security, 'The naval manners of France, the Fops of our Navy are hourly adopting; nay boasting of their ignorance, and censuring the youth who presumes to know more than the stem from the stern.' British military power was in danger of being debauched and softened until the country was ripe for invasion, whereas 'a rough, boisterous, gallant sailor has always answered the intentions of the Admiralty, and done his country's service like a man'.[80] The naval captain who wrote *The Cruise*, published in 1808, noted that humour at sea was 'hard and manly, not the least effeminate'. Though he explained that seamen were 'remarkably nice about their hair; – combing, making it shine with clean grease, queuing it down to a considerable length, but leaving a long brush, and platting the sides', yet he is careful to point out that this only distinguishes the British seamen from his French and Spanish counterparts who are 'disgusting from their filth'. He also affirms that the officers deliberately favour 'Such clothes as grace the Man! Not useless Beau!' and that they detest foppery.[81]

The Navy tested the courage and strength of young boys and early placed them in a male environment that made it easy for them to distance themselves from children and young women and identify with older men. Their identity was constructed in terms of this kind of masculinity, and seamen absorbed and reproduced a view of their life that emphasized their strength and manliness in the face of extreme hardship. As Falconer wrote in *The Shipwreck*, 'They scorn the wretch that trembles in his post | Who from the face of danger strives to turn.[82] Jack Nastyface described similar situations. During the Napoleonic Wars when the wind made it impossible for the French fleet to leave port, the blockading British Channel fleet would put into Torbay or Cawsand for fresh supplies. Paradoxically few seamen welcomed this because they were ridiculed by other seamen returning from foreign stations and taunted by girls in these seaport towns. People laughingly told them that they would never get scurvy, 'or that they might as well be by their mother's fire-side, and tied to the apron strings, as merely running in and out of harbour; and nothing hurts Jack's feelings more than being taunted of anything unmanly or inferior'.[83] It is evident, too, that in the close confines of a ship few could escape the critical gaze of others. Officers were very much 'on show' and to some extent their life was one of performance. All were judged by their skill in carrying out their duty and by the balance and self-control they exerted in their social relationships. Handbooks for junior officers, for example, stressed the need for all the ship's officers to fix on one system of delivery when giving commands. These were to be as concise as possible. The officer had to get the attention of the men by some such word as 'prepare' and then wait for them to reply 'ready' before giving the order.[84] This may help to explain why seamen often preferred aristocratic officers since they were more assured in giving commands and instilled confidence.

Physical pain was part of gender training at the time and boys were physically punished more than girls. This partly may help to explain the admiration for seamen who bore the pain of amputation without complaint and who were even able to joke at the event. Jack Nastyface describes the general admiration for one seaman who, finding both legs had to be amputated, cried, 'Now to the devil with all the shoe-makers, I have done with them!'[85] The author of *The Cruise* assumed that every officer could recall instances of men singing a loyal song under amputation, and even wishing that their limb could be rammed into a gun and fired back to the enemy. A disabled sailor concluded his tale with, 'I had almost forgot to tell you, that in the engagement, I was wounded in two places; I lost four fingers off the left hand, and my leg was shot off.'[86] His only regret is that he lost these body parts on board a privateer, not a naval warship, and was therefore ineligible for a pension. Not all seamen fell for the propaganda. One midshipman of the late 1760s complained that he had been bred to arms but deplored the military life. He claimed not to understand why a natural disposition or talent for killing other humans was credited with the name of 'valour' or 'heroism'. 'The whole is a kind of illusion with which the *great* deceive the inferior classes of mankind, in order to make them serve as the instruments of their passions, and especially of their ambition.'[87] The fact that Britain was not engaged in a desperate war at the time of composition might have made the hardships of naval life seem less justifiable.

It was all very well to foster a breed of manly seamen to create a strong navy, but unrestrained and on shore the same men presented a liability. Samuel Leech recalled that 'many [sailors] fancy that swearing and drinking are necessary accomplishments in a genuine man-of-war's-man'.[88] Surgeons and commanders reinforced the paternal relationship they liked to present between captain and crew by representing drunken seamen as children. Admiral Colvill, for example, refers to seamen as children when complaining about drunkenness on Halifax station.[89] Perhaps because seamen could pose a threat to social order on land, they were increasingly represented in prints, ballads and on chinaware, as faithful to their loved one at home. Once again, this image seems to be reciprocated in works by seamen themselves, at least in those written by officers, although the more practical advised delaying firm attachments until they had won promotion and could look forward to peacetime.[90]

V

It was in the interests of officers seeking promotion to seize any opportunity of increasing their reputation and not to ponder overmuch on the dangers and disadvantages of life at sea. Boys in the Navy were encouraged to draw so that they could sketch views of coasts and harbours, and make charts. Those who were skilled might also sketch battle plans, engagements or key events and later offer the sketches to engravers who would work them up in the hope that the 'authenticity' of the finished product would guarantee sales. Such prints often included the words 'taken on the spot' in the title, and sometimes the name of the officer who had made the original sketch. For example, the title of one print reads, 'Lord Nelson's attack on the Danish Line and City of Copenhagen April 2nd, 1801, from a Drawing make on the spot by Captain William Bligh of H.M. Ship Glatton'. Even if the officer were not named, the medium gave a unique opportunity for the Navy to influence public opinion and give the most flattering interpretation of recent actions. Prints had a longer life than newspaper accounts, and contributed more strikingly to a sense of national identity because they were often displayed in public places. These prints also had the effect of raising the status of individual officers who carried captured vessels against the odds, took rich prizes or won important victories, since they too were often mentioned by name.

Naval officers could help to shape their public image by hiring the services of a competent portrait artist. Portraiture was the major genre of this period and did much to create popular naval heroes. Officers often commissioned portraits after they had taken part in important battles, using the wealth they had accumulated in wartime to affirm their social status. Captain Alexander Schomberg, for example, the son of a German-Jewish doctor, had his portrait painted by Hogarth at the end of the Seven Years War in which he distinguished himself in several actions, including the taking of Quebec. Strikingly, the painting shows that he had the lapels of his uniform altered to suit the fashion of the day as they bear little resemblance to the original pattern. The dashing Sir William Sidney Smith had his portrait taken by John Eckstein after he successfully defended Acre against Napoleon in 1799.[91] He was painted in hessian boots, his uniform bristling with pistols, and brandishing a scimitar. Three duly intimidated Turks skulk in the smoke to his left. Officers who had their portraits made on being first promoted, often had the uniform in the painting altered if they were promoted again, which further illustrates the importance they attached to signifiers of rank. The immediate aim of any portrait was to capture the likeness of an individual but portrait painters could claim that they represented the inner person not just the outer appearance. This, in turn, led some to claim that portraiture was a form of history painting. And because elements in a portrait tended to conform to stylistic conventions (for example, naval sitters were usually painted against an imaginary seascape or a representation of some event in which they had played a part), individual portraits could work as representations of naval types, or even connote aspects of the service as a whole. The sitter of course faces forwards, and viewers contemplating the background of the picture are placed at a disadvantage. They gaze at something they often have little experience of, while the sitter appears someone who has confidently mastered that element and lived to tell the tale. It is accepted that portraits are part of a symbolic structure and that, in sitting for a portrait, the individual participates in a production of meanings that cannot be defined simply by standards of likeness.[92] For example, wigs were a male fashion item from the seventeenth century to the beginning of the nineteenth and the issue of whether or not the sitter should wear one was clearly important. Wigs signified virility, respectability and social power, all positive messages; but they also had sexual connotations that could be ambivalent or subversive.[93] When Commodore George Johnstone (1730–87) had himself painted bald, he may well have been making a statement – but he had little to fear from opinion. It is on record that as an MP, 'his total want of fear and his adroitness with a pistol made him a useful addition to his party'.

When a naval officer commissioned his portrait, he often commissioned a complementary portrait of his wife. When hung, these served as proof of wealth and status. The portraits would also have signalled to viewers that the Navy offered an opportunity to attain a respectable position in society. (Unfortunately, maritime museums have generally collected only the male portrait of such pairs and in such cases the total effect has been lost.) Successful naval officers also had their portrait taken to give either to patrons or to powerful men who wished to demonstrate their patriotism by displaying images of Britain's successful commanders. There were still other opportunities for naval officers to promote themselves and shape their self-image. Viscount Samuel Hood presented his portrait to the Company of Ironmongers on being admitted to their order in 1784, which was neatly done since the finished portrait, displayed in Ironmongers' Hall, flattered both Hood and the Company that received it. Yet it was understood that portraiture essentially reflected private individuals and was not the ideal medium in which to reflect public virtue or to represent individuals as a public body.[94] Captain John Bentinck (1717–75) and Francis Holburn (1704–71) had themselves painted with their sons who both seem destined for the Navy. In Holburn's case, the boy was painted in at a later date. Such paintings might be thought a hostage to fortune in that the father would have to feel secure that his reputation would never mar his son's prospects. But presumably also the presence of a son added to the representation of the officer's patriotism. The Bentinck painting was completed in 1775, the year of Captain Bentinck's death. It evokes an uncomfortable response (see Plate 2). Father and son do not quite make eye contact; the boy, in the uniform of Naval Academy at Portsmouth, cradles a model boat and his vulnerable appearance suggests that he has been made a victim to family tradition at too tender an age. The dog, symbol of faithfulness, perhaps signals their determination to serve their country but also helps to illuminate the nature of the bond between father and son. Unusually, they are shown in the Captain's cabin of the *Centaur*, 74 guns, a guardship at Portsmouth, which adds domesticity to the scene while recalling the differences to a domestic scene on land with females present. Yet this picture does succeed in offering the viewer affirmative imagery, conveying a moral message through the interaction of private individuals and the objects which surround them. In this sense, the Bentincks, father and son, come closer to representing the Navy and naval tradition than most portraits of sea officers.

In the 1760s and 1770s there was a great increase in the production of political prints, chiefly caricatures, as the Government came under attack for the way it handled events at home and abroad. Portraiture was naturally implicated in this development and naval officers were depicted whenever their actions were controversial. When Keppel was acquitted at his court martial in 1779, Reynolds at once took the liberty of sending his portrait of Keppel to an engraver so that it could be copied as a print. This helped Keppel to publicize his triumph over a government that had tried to discredit both him and the Whig opposition to which he was attached. Prints were commonly copied from portraits once an officer had made his mark. Officers might have an existing portrait engraved after some noteworthy action, or the portrait might be engraved posthumously. After Captain John Harvey died of the wounds he received in the Battle of the Glorious First of June 1794, an old portrait of 1785 was engraved – even though the print would have been sadly inaccurate since Harvey had lost his right arm in the battle.

The success of the Navy at this period presented artists and also sculptors with an opportunity to raise the status of British art, which was appreciated at the time. When a public memorial in honour of the Navy was projected, John Opie, Professor in Painting at the Royal Academy, immediately saw that the nation, individual artists and the reputation of British art as a whole would benefit. He thought that a public exhibition and subsequent publication of a set of engravings of the work would probably cover its cost with interest. Also 'the rapid dispersion of the prints into all quarters of the globe, would contribute, more than can well be imagined or described, to give an exalted and universal impression of British valour, taste, munificence, and genius'.[95]

There were other visual means of affirming status. If an officer were made a peer, he could commission a coat of arms. These give another perspective on how, through the collective armorial bearings of brave and successful officers, the Navy was able to project an image of itself. Men of comparatively modest origin could earn the distinction of a coat of arms: Admiral Sir Samuel Hood, for example, his brother Sir Alexander Hood and, more famously, Nelson were all sons of country parsons. It is not surprising that members of the minor aristocracy, striving to live beyond their means, resented such instances of upward mobility. Jane Austen may not have been describing an uncommon view in *Persuasion* when she revealed Sir Walter Eliot's prejudice against successful naval officers. The coats of arms of new naval peers generally had a nautical theme and many referred to the battle or event for which the officer had been honoured. Nelson's arms allude to his victory at the Nile. The crest also shows the stern of the *San Josef*, the Spanish warship he boarded from the deck of another prize in 1797. On one side is a supporting sailor armed for war and on the other a lion holding Spanish and French ensigns in his mouth. Sir Edward Pellew was made a baronet for saving the passengers and crew of the troopship *Dutton* which, having been driven ashore, was breaking up in Plymouth Sound. His coat of arms shows the *Dutton* and also features a representation of Algiers, which he successfully bombarded in 1816 thereby ensuring his elevation to viscount. These showy insignia, lacking the gravity of long existence, were emblazoned on the sides of carriages, printed on visiting cards, invitations and writing paper, stamped on wax seals and painted on dinner sets. They were publicized even more widely in the *Naval Chronicle* and no doubt evoked a little envy as well as admiration.

Yet despite seamen projecting their own self-image and their own view of the Navy in various media, they still complained of misrepresentation. Post 1815, when the army was the more popular service, one senior officer complained at length that, because the Navy operated at a distance, the public was both unfamiliar with the service and uninterested in its welfare and concerns. In wartime, he admitted, 'the public is sometimes treated with the meagre notice of a naval victory in the Gazette' but he believed that the consequences of a lack of information were generally damaging:

> In the absence of authentic information, the field is left open to conjecture, and fiction naturally steps in to aid the imagination. Even Dibdin ... repeatedly raises a blush for the nautical ignorance he betrays. The absurdities detailed in graver publications, as to the conduct and character of sailors, would be amusing, were it not for the false, and often unfavourable impressions they create of the service.[96]

In the years after the Napoleonic War, the public image of naval service became increasingly sentimentalized. But arguably there had always been a dichotomy between public recognition of the Navy as an institution and public understanding about the realities of life at sea which seamen's best endeavours could never wholly overcome.

Notes

1   J. Fielding, *A Brief Description of the Cities of London and Westminster* (London, 1776), pp. 28–9.
2   W. Spavens, *The Narrative of William Spavens a Chatham Pensioner Written by Himself* (London, 1998), p. 68. First published, 1796.
3   Quoted by A.F. Scott, *Every One a Witness* (London, 1970), p. 198.
4   S. Leech, *Thirty Years from Home, or A Voice from the Main Deck* (Boston, 1843), p. 35.
5   Spavens, *Narrative*, p. 62.
6   N.A.M. Rodger, *The Wooden World: An Anatomy of the Georgian Navy* (London, 1986), p. 113.
7   A. Smith, *An Inquiry into the Nature and Causes of the Wealth of Nations*, ed. R.H. Campbell and A.S. Skinner, 2 vols (Oxford, 1976), vol. I, p. 127.
8   Spavens, *Narrative*, p. 1.
9   J. Nicol, *The Life and Adventures of John Nicol, Mariner* (Edinburgh, 1822), p. 4.
10 W. Tench, *Letters from Revolutionary France*, ed. G. Edwards (Cardiff, 2001), pp. 33–4.
11 *A Fair Statement of the Real Grievances experienced by the Officers and Sailors in the Navy of Great Britain; with a Plan of Reform … By a Naval Officer* (London, 1797), p. 52.
12 S. Conway, *The British Isles and the War of American Independence* (Oxford, 2000), p. 101.
13 *A Letter from A Captain of a Man of War, to a Member of Parliament* (London, 1773), p. 18.
14 *The Case and distressed Situation of the Officers of the Navy, Explained in a Letter from a Captain of the Navy to a Member of Parliament* (London, 1775), p. 7.
15 A. Burton, *The Adventures of Johnny Newcome in the Navy; A Poem in Four Cantos* (London, 1818), p. 192.
16 See P. Earle, *Sailors, English Merchant Seamen 1650–1775* (London, 1998), p. 195; E. Vernon, *Some Seasonable Advice from an Honest Sailor, To whom it might have concerned for the Service of the C[row]n and C[ountr]y* (London, 1746), p. 72; *A View of the Naval Force of Great-Britain … by an Officer of Rank* (London, 1791), p. 57.
17 A copy of the original is at the John Carter Brown Library, Providence, RI.
18 For example, J.M., a Lieutenant in the Fleet, *The Maritime Campaign of 1778* (London, 1778), pp. 22–3.
19 Nicol, *Life*, p. 205.
20 *The Trial of Vice-Admiral Byng, at a Court-Martial, held on Board his Majesty's ship the St. George. Taken down in Short-Hand* (London, 1757), p. 34.
21 *The English Lion Dismember'd. Or the voice of the Public for an enquiry into the loss of Minorca – with Ad' B—g's plea before his Examiners* (1756), in C.N. Robinson, *A Pictorial History of the Sea Services or Graphic Studies of the Sailor's Life and Character Afloat and Ashore*, 11 vols (London, 1911), vol. III, pt. I.
22 W. Falconer, *The Shipwreck*, 6th edn (London, 1785), III. ll. 682–3.
23 *The Cruise; a Poetical Sketch, in eight cantos, by a naval officer* (London, 1808), pp. viii and 9.
24 Nauticus, *Remarks on Lord Howe's Extraordinary Gazetter* (as published in a morning paper of November 11 1782), p. 6.

25 See *Blake's Remarks on Com. Johnstone's Account of his Engagement with a French Squadron under the Command of Mons. De Suffrein on April 16, 1781 in Port Praya Rd, in the Island of St Jago. A new Edition* (London, 1782).
26 *Britannia Triumphant . . . by a society of naval gentlemen* (London, 1766), p. 159.
27 *An address to the Hon. Admiral Augustus Keppel, containing candid remarks on his defence before the Court Martial. By a seaman* (London, 1779), p. 15.
28 *Britannia Triumphant*, pp. 179, 223.
29 R. Richardson, *The Dolphin's Journal Epitomized in a Poetical Essay* (London, 1768), p. 3.
30 *The Story of the Learned Pig, by an officer of the Royal Navy* (London, 1786), pp. 98, 103. Cf. *An Address to the Right-Honourable the First Lord Commissioner of the Admiralty, upon the Decreasing Spirit, Splendour, and Discipline of the Navy ... by an Officer* (London, 1787), pp. 13, 15.
31 *Memoirs and Adventures of Mark Moore, Late an Officer in the British Navy* (London, 1795), p. vi.
32 *Observations and Instructions for the Use of the Commissioned, the Junior, and other Officers of the Royal Navy ... by a Captain in the Royal Navy* (London, 1804), p. 78.
33 See M. Lincoln, 'Naval Ship Launches as Public Spectacle 1773–1854', *Mariners Mirror*, 83 (1997), pp. 466–72.
34 *A Letter from a Captain of a Man of War*, p. 10. Cf. *The Cruise*, pp. 65, 66.
35 *A Letter from a Captain of a Man of War*, pp. 4, 11.
36 *The Story of the Learned Pig*, p. 91. Cf. *A Letter from a Captain of a Man of War*, p. 11.
37 *A Fair Statement of the Real Grievances*, p. 1.
38 *The Story of the Learned Pig*, p. 97.
39 Rodger, *The Wooden World*, pp. 301–2, 313.
40 See *A New Edition of the Appeal of a Neglected Naval Officer* (London, 1785), p. 1; Spavens, *Narrative*, pp. 73–4; O. Warner, ed., *Jack Nastyface, Memoirs of a Seaman* (London, 1973), p. 116.
41 *Strictures upon Naval Departments by a Sailor* (London, 1785), pp. 57, 58. Cf. *The Story of the Learned Pig*, p. 96.
42 *Sailor's Letters* [signed R- B-] (Nettleton, Plymouth, [1800?]), pp. 8, 9.
43 E. Thompson, *Sailor's Letters written to his select Friends in England during his Voyages and Travels in Europe, Asia, Africa and America from the year 1754 to 1759*, 2 vols (Dublin, 1766), p. 86.
44 Ibid, p. 92.
45 *Strictures upon Naval Departments*, p. 40; *The Story of the Learned Pig*, p. 101.
46 D. Morrice, *The Young Midshipman's Instructor* (London, 1801), pp. 1, 2–3. Cf. *The Cruise*, p. 117.
47 *A Fair Statement of the Real Grievances*, pp. 24, 46. Cf. *A View of the Naval Force of Great-Britain ... by an Officer of Rank* (London, 1791), p. 186.
48 *The Cruise*, p. 113.
49 F.B. Spilsbury, *Account of a Voyage to the Western Coast of Africa performed by His Majesty's Sloop Favourite, in the Year 1805* (London, 1807), p. 6.
50 *The Maritime Campaign of 1778 ... By J.M. A Lieutenant in the Fleet* (London, 1778), p. 22.
51 *The Disabled Sailor* (London, 1800), p. 6.
52 Richardson, *The Dolphin's Journal*, p. 1.
53 *A Letter to the Right Honourable The Earl of Sandwich, on the Present State of Affairs. By a Sailor* (London, 1779), p. 5.
54 *The Trial of Richard Parker ... . Taken in Shorthand on board the* Neptune *by Job Sibly* (Boston, 1797), p. 39.
55 Rodger, *The Wooden World*, pp. 199–200.

56 Burton, *The Adventures of Johnny Newcome*, p. 246. Cf. Leech, *Thirty Years from Home*, pp. 37, 44, 51.

57 J.G. Jones, *Sketch of a Political Tour* (London, 1796), p. 52.

58 *A Fair Statement of the Real Grievances*, p. 50.

59 *Sailor's Letters*, p. 58.

60 *Observations and Instructions*, p. 36. Cf. *The Cruise*, pp. 11, 24.

61 Spilsbury, *Account of a* Voyage, p. 6.

62 *Sailor's Letters*, pp. 85, 87, 175.

63 E. Vernon, *Some Seasonable Advice from an Honest Sailor, To whom it might have concerned for the Service of the C[row]n and C[ountr]y* (London, 1746), p. 136; *Candid Reflections on the Expedition to Martinico, by J.J. a Lieutenant in the Navy* (London, 1759), p. 28.

64 *A Fair Statement of the Real Grievances*, p. 38.

65 Nicol, *Life*, pp. 194–5.

66 Leech, *Thirty Years from Home*, p. 74.

67 *The Disabled Sailor*, p. 2.

68 Nicol, *Life*, p. 32.

69 For example, Vernon, *Some Seasonable Advice*, p. 95.

70 Thompson, *Sailor's Letters*, pp. 89–90.

71 Nicol, *Life*, p. 11.

72 Leech, *Thirty Years from* Home, p. 66.

73 *The Son of Commerce, An Original Poem, in Thirty-four Cantos, Written by a Sailor* (London, 1806), pp. 28, 60.

74 See I. Land, 'Domesticating the Maritime: Culture, Masculinity, and Empire in Britain, 1770 – 1820' (unpublished PhD thesis ,University of Michigan, 1999), p. 224.

75 See Captain Thompson, *The Syrens, a Masque, in two Acts, as performed at the Theatre Royal, Covent-garden* (London, 1794), pp. 12–13; Land, 'Domesticating the Maritime', p. 17. Cf. *The Cruise*, p. 393.

76 C. Fletcher, *The Naval Guardian*, 2nd edn, (London, 1805), p. 157.

77 See M. Moore, *Memoirs and Adventures of Mark Moore*, p. 22.

78 Leech, *Thirty Years from* Home, p. 73.

79 Ibid., p. 6.

80 *The Case and distressed Situation of the Widows of the Officers of the Navy, Explained in a Letter from a Captain in the Navy to a Member of Parliament* (London, 1775), p. 9.

81 *The Cruise*, pp. 134–5.

82 Falconer, *The Shipwreck*, II. ll. 421–2. Cf. II, ll. 416–19.

83 Warner, *Jack Nastyface*, pp. 102–3.

84 *Observations and Instructions*, p. 76.

85 Ibid., p. 115.

86 *The Disabled Sailor*, pp. 7–8.

87 *Sailor's Letters*, p. 4.

88 Leech, *Thirty Years from Home*, p. 65.

89 Colvill to Admiralty, 14 Oct and 25 Oct 1763, (Adm 1/482 PRO).

90 See Richardson, *The Dolphin's Journal*, pp. 3, 16; *Love Elegies, by a Sailor, Written in the Year MDCCLXXIV* (London, 1780), p. 5. Cf. *The Cruise*, pp. 51, 54.

91 Now in the National Portrait Gallery (NPG832).

92 See M. Pointon, *Hanging the Head* (London and New Haven, CT, 1993), p. 112.

93 Ibid., p. 128. For example, Keppel appears to have worn his own hair throughout his life; Rodney was also painted wearing his own hair.

94 See D. Solkin, *Painting for Money. The Visual Arts and the Public Sphere in Eighteenth-Century England* (New Haven, CT, and London), 1993), p. 214.

95 J. Opie, *Lectures on Painting, delivered at the Royal Academy of Arts with a Letter on the Proposal for A Public Memorial of the Naval Glory of Great Britain* (London, 1809), p. 178.
96 [W. Glascock], *Naval Sketch-Book; or, the Service Afloat and Ashore, by an Officer of Rank*, 2 vols (London, 1826), p. vii.

Chapter 3

The Navy and Politics

This chapter investigates the attitude of politicians to the Navy during the period 1750 to 1815 and examines the ways in which politicians manipulated the Navy's image to secure their own ends. The Navy was hugely expensive to maintain and develop, but against the background of intense rivalry with France, successive administrations increasingly invested in naval power. This had been the case since the 1690s but in the second half of the eighteenth century there was a substantial increase of public investment in the construction of warships, improvements to royal dockyards and the recruitment and retention of seamen. Political attitudes to the Navy became more defined at moments of national crisis, especially during periods of threatened invasion when the government's handling of naval affairs became a matter of great public concern. This chapter therefore focuses on invasion scares in particular.

I

The government was bound to be supportive of the Navy since it was recognized as the key to Britain's diplomatic and military strength. There was parliamentary consensus about the value of the Navy as opposed to the value of a standing army, which could be used to keep the peace at elections or even overthrow the constitution. Since Parliament in general (backed by the country gentlemen) upheld the concept of a strong navy, debate and public controversy centred on how well the administration was actually managing naval affairs within this conceptual framework. The amount voted in Parliament to supply the Navy each year was well publicized and acted as an indicator of the government's support for and management of the service.[1] The priority given to naval expenditure is itself an indication of the Navy's status in the eighteenth century – though the opposition might argue vociferously against any increase in the size of the Navy, rarely did they vote against the actual amount requested. The Admiralty was the largest spending department of state, despite intermittent rows about the size of naval estimates. The Navy was held to be the nation's prime defence, and supremacy at sea essential for the protection of British trade. In turn, colonial and oceanic trade proved a significant source of wealth on which the taxation policy of the government depended. Therefore, the majority of ministers accepted that the expansion of trade and the extension of Britain's maritime empire were good for the economy. Strategically and commercially they did not distinguish between the need for a powerful navy to secure global trade and an overseas empire, and the need for a strong navy to secure Britain's strategic position in Europe. This way of thinking happily served the merchant interest, but fundamentally ministers understood that commerce and the shipping industry were necessary aspects of national defence. In wartime, merchant seamen served in the Navy, commercial shipyards helped build the fleet, and trade in general helped to fund the war. Government cannot be said to have had a specific naval strategy but aspects of its other policies had naval implications. Ministers were anxious to 'manage' the public aspect of naval governance so that it reflected well on the administration, and particular Acts relating to the Navy were publicized in ways that reinforced public perceptions of the Navy's importance as an institution. For example, in 1758 the government made available a mechanism whereby men could remit money to their relatives via government channels without charge, and this was widely praised (though little used because few seamen had family ties).[2] In 1773 the government took a decision to allow all captains half-pay in peacetime, hoping to secure continuity and expertise for the Navy. And of course throughout the period Greenwich Hospital, publicized in numerous prints, was a monument to the importance the state attached to the welfare of seamen (though both naval and merchant seamen were compelled to contribute to its upkeep by having sixpence a month deducted from their wages).

The government of the day was held to be responsible for certain areas of naval high command and policy, including strategy, the worldwide disposition and command of fleets, and overall levels of manning and financing of the Navy. The two last were voted on annually in Parliament. During this period, arguably from the time of the American war, the idea of the two-power standard developed with Britain aspiring to maintain sufficient ships to deal with the fleets of France and Spain simultaneously. This policy was expensive and as a result unpopular. Consequently, taxpayers often forced a sense of realism on ministers, tempering their bellicosity. The Lords of the Admiralty were political appointees, subject to the changing fortunes of their party leaders, and were invariably members of Parliament. In this period the First Lord was always a member of the Cabinet. At least one place on the board was held by an active Royal Navy officer, chosen from among the many flag officers who had seats in Parliament. Lord Mulgrave (1744–92), even managed to be on Sandwich's Board of Admiralty and a captain of a ship in the Channel Fleet at the same time. The Admiralty administered the Royal Navy, and with the help of its subordinate civilian bureaus, such as the Navy Board, built, manned and supplied the fleet. On the whole, the Admiralty aimed to resist political interference in what it considered to be vital areas of decision-making – command, appointment and promotion – not always successfully. Naval First Lords, faced with applications for promotion, had stronger reasons for standing their ground than those who were primarily career politicians: they would return to the Navy where their actions would be scrutinized by fellow admirals. The fact that, in the main, First Lords needed to promote officers who would be a credit to them acted as an important check on the patronage system in favour of men of true ability.

As indicated, a number of naval officers were also members of parliament; from 1754 to 1790, for example, a total of 79 serving officers sat in the House of Commons. The highest number (23) entered the House after the 1784 general election but the numbers elected do not seem to have been markedly affected by peace or war. Most were captains when they took up their seat. Discounting those who sat before 1754, the 74 remaining officers included 53 captains. There were also two lieutenants, one commander, six rear-admirals, 10 vice-admirals and four admirals. The two who entered the House as mere lieutenants both owed their seats to their family connections.[3] This disposition of ranks reflected the career pattern of most naval officers who entered their profession as boys, spent the next decade or so reaching the rank of post captain and then had to wait longer for further promotion to rear-admiral. It was in this interim that they entered the House. The aristocratic representation was high – about 25 per cent – but much less than among army officers in the House, of whom 68 per cent were from aristocratic families with the remainder coming from old-established landed gentry. Without exception, all the naval officers who came from noble families were younger sons: a career in the Navy was not a soft option and held no attractions for those who expected to inherit an estate. In the later period between 1790 and 1820, when Britain was mostly at war, some 100 members of parliament were in the Navy, 90 of whom reached the rank of commander. One indication of the growing prestige of the service during the Revolutionary and Napoleonic Wars is that 50 per cent of the 90 came from aristocratic families, with four in every five coming into the House on their family interest.[4] The impact of the naval officers in Westminster was limited since their attendance was constrained far more than that of any other professional group by their duties at sea. Though plain-speaking was a quality naval MPs could surely lay claim to, as it was stereotypically attributed to seamen, most of them never spoke at all in the debates. The average naval officer made an awkward politician, proved a poor speaker and was regarded as out of his element, although there were always sufficient naval officers in the House to represent the interests of the Navy and elucidate technical matters. In the period 1790–1820, the majority supported the government of the day, taking care not to damage their prospects of promotion early in their career. Yet more than 20 were committed to the Whigs and therefore usually in opposition; while another 10 or so vacillated or voted independently. Although naval MPs had little impact in the House, their presence there could certainly be detrimental to the service in time of war. The Navy was highly competitive: service rivalries among senior officers could be continued in Parliament and political quarrels originating there could be carried over into the fleet. If these became public, the ensuing disputes reflected badly on the Navy.

Since the Navy was of such national importance, both naval operations and administration were obvious targets for any opposition, who eagerly charged the government with mismanagement in these respects whenever an opportunity arose. The prevalence of the 'ship of state' as a persuasive trope, with the Prime Minister at the helm, meant that the figure of speech could easily be subverted by the opposition with devastating effect. The policitization of the Navy is reflected in published parliamentary reports, political pamphlets, caricatures, squibs, journals, and even in the nomination of days of general fast and thanksgiving. When popular naval heroes won victories, both the ministry and the opposition would attempt to exploit the Navy's success and claim as much credit for it as possible. There had been precedents in earlier decades. When Admiral Vernon took Porto Bello from the Spanish in 1739, he received the thanks of both Houses of Parliament and was elevated to the status of a national hero in the tradition of Drake and Raleigh, who had also both battled against a Catholic enemy. The phenomenon of Vernon's popularity as a national hero and patriot smoothed the way for later developments involving the use of naval figures for partisan purposes.[5] Vernon was known to despise the fashionable vices of the court and his public persona epitomized the bluff-speaking naval professional who was dedicated to the welfare of his men. Since, as MP, he was later courted by the opposition and spoke out against the evils of privilege and political intrigue that undermined the efficiency of the Navy, some politicians may have wondered if they had been wise to let this genie out of the bottle by encouraging his fame. Yet, following Vernon's initial success against Spain, the theme of imperial expansion assumed critical importance in domestic politics and the Navy became a powerful focus for expressions of British identity.

As is well known, the politics of the period were marked by party conflict. By mid-century, the term 'party' was used variously to describe Whigs and Tories (the latter in continuous decline from the reign of Queen Anne), but also oppositions and more exclusive parties such as the Rockingham Whigs. There was no institutionalized party framework before the 1780s, indeed perhaps not before the 1790s, that was capable of supporting opposition to the government on a regular basis.[6] Politics certainly became more commercialized from the 1760s when radical opposition centred on John Wilkes, journalist and MP for Aylesbury, who directly criticized the King in issue Number 45 of his paper the *North Briton*. Wilkes was committed to the Tower amid a storm of protest, after which he and his supporters proceeded to demonstrate how the press and other means of communicating propaganda could be utilized to engage popular support for a political cause. Conflict with the American colonies also incited debate about parliamentary reform. The American slogan 'No Taxation without Representation' was extremely potent for reformers in Britain who wished to widen adult male suffrage. The debate about American representation in particular offered British urban and mercantile interests an opportunity to press their case for greater participation in the political process, supposedly more commensurate with their power as men of wealth and property.

The press played a crucial role in disseminating information about naval activities and helping to shape popular celebrations or demonstrations that followed engagements at sea. The improvement in communications, specifically postal services in the first half of the century, had facilitated a widespread dissemination of political information.[7] A remarkably large number of people were literate, and since the time of Walpole the press had been an important factor towards the creation of a national political consciousness and an increase in literacy. The growth of new kinds of journalism, notably the review journal, periodical magazine and provincial newspaper, meant that news items might be reproduced or plagiarized to suit several formats, helping to foster debate and polemic. By 1750 there were more than 40 provincial newspapers produced each week and by 1800 more than 70, reaching perhaps in excess of 8 per cent of the population outside London. In the capital, there were about 300 000 papers produced each week from 1780, with most of the dailies having circulation figures of between 2000 and 5000 – a situation which changed little in the early years of the nineteenth century.[8] Different political groups manipulated elements of the press for their own ends and used it as a political weapon, employing hack writers to shape opinion or to counteract the polemical works of their opponents. Though the print runs of pamphlets might be modest, generally 500 copies or so, it was certain that at least in urban areas every copy was read by a great many readers who flocked to coffee houses, inns and taverns to obtain sight of the latest papers. All who could afford a beverage had access to political news and could take part in any discussion on current affairs. In fact, political spies were able to gauge popular opinion by frequenting these places and noting the tone of debate or the response to current pamphlets. Nor were these facilities confined to London; increasingly they were replicated in provincial towns. By the 1780s also, the growth of new forms of commercial organization, especially trade clubs and societies, allowed for the development of a popular market for political propaganda.[9] There was extensive traffic in all kinds of commodities between London and the regions where people keenly imitated metropolitan fashions and interests, often buying cheaper copies. The distribution of satirical prints was socially and geographically wider than formerly thought.[10] Graphic satire, familiar since at least the Wilkes controversy of the 1760s, was disseminated through illustrated magazines, commemorative pottery, and through the inclusion of prints with newspapers sent out by Members of Parliament. (MPs had a franking privilege and were able to send newspapers and political propaganda free of charge to their constituents and supporters.) Handbills and ballads were also cheap and effective methods of circulating political comment. Ballads, printed on single sheets and hawked around streets and fairs by balladmongers who often advertised their wares by singing them, were a key means of bridging the gap between the literate and partially literate. Easily remembered and recited, ballads could be a powerful form of propaganda.

II

The force of all this press activity was clearly demonstrated in 1756–57 when Admiral Byng was court martialled and shot after he failed to prevent the loss of Minorca. One pamphleteer observed in 1757 that 'If I am not mistaken, the Clamour was begun against Admiral [Byng], by the Hawkers and Ballad-singers; everyone must remember *Sing Tantarara Hang Byng*'.[11] It is noticeable that ballads in Byng's defence used sombre rhythms, while anti-Byng ballads were lively, humorous and more memorable – unfortunately for him.[12] During the winter of 1755–56, the invasion scare had prompted popular debate about how best to protect the country from rival powers. Literature on the subject was printed in different formats. For example, pieces that first appeared in the *Evening Advertiser* were collected and published in 1755 as *The Important Question concerning Invasions, a Sea-War, Raising the Militia, and paying subsidies for foreign troops*. Though advertised as fair and impartial, this work betrays contemporary prejudice against standing armies. The Navy is the preferred means of defence, coupled with the use of mercenaries on the continent. Since the author concluded that war would be won by the country that could afford to spend most money, he offered a clear message to government not to economize on the Navy and other measures essential to the nation's liberty. Such contributions to debate only primed the nation for Byng's foray against the French and ensured a highly-charged response whatever the outcome.

In the event, the Byng controversy mushroomed and assumed major political proportions as all levels of society became involved. The Newcastle administration eagerly encouraged Byng's detractors, possibly to deflect any criticism of the ministry for its delay in dispatching a force against the enemy and for the poor state of the fleet. Admiral Byng had already complained privately about these shortcomings and Newcastle feared that he would make them public. French reports of the naval encounter reached London by diplomatic means on 2 June – three weeks before Byng's official dispatches, which did not arrive until the 23rd. In the interval, as contradictory reports of the battle circulated, it seemed to some observers that the public might turn either against the Admiralty or Byng. Two days after having received Byng's official letters, the ministry decided to court-martial him under the naval disciplinary code, the Articles of War. The next day the ministry published a censored version of Byng's report on the battle in the government newspaper, the *London Gazette*. This was cunningly edited to make Byng appear more cowardly and indecisive than he had actually been. The extremity of such tactics indicates the danger that the ministry thought it was in from public outrage over the loss of Minorca. When this shameless use of the *Gazette* was exposed, Ministers justified this censorship on the grounds that the administration was always compelled to suppress detailed information about damage to the fleet that might be useful to the enemy. The argument was clearly spurious because a report of casualties was left appended to Byng's letter, apparently because it served to incriminate him further. The ministry also incited the populace against Byng by advertising the order for his arrest, which was relayed to all the channel ports, so that in July when he returned with the fleet to Portsmouth, a hostile crowd confronted him.

The opposition accused the Admiralty of using Byng as a scapegoat for ministerial incapacity, arguing that the episode demonstrated the government's total inability to conduct a war, and slowly opinion did begin to turn against the ministry, though not until August. Byng himself – wealthy son of a former First Lord and peer, with a passion for collecting fine porcelain – was often presented as proof of a degenerate aristocracy, too enervated by luxury to fight the French. It was suggested that Byng owed his rapid promotion in the Navy to family influence and corruption in high places. Social commentators used him as an example of the apparent moral degeneracy of the governing classes, who in the early stages of the Seven Years War were blamed for poor leadership and the lack of military success. All this time, the natural bravery of the common seaman was extolled as a sop to patriotic zeal and a contrast to Byng's pusillanimous behaviour in the face of enemy fire. The popular theatre reflected and animated this perception. A piece called *The Sham Fight: or, Political Humbug. A State Farce, in Two Acts* attacked both Byng and the ministry, alluding pointedly to the metaphor of the Ship of State. It accused Byng and the government of coming to an arrangement with the French whereby money exchanged hands to fix a sham fight. The bravery of ordinary British sailors, however, was not questioned. For example, one sailor exclaims 'D—n me, I wou'd I were at the Helm of Government, there shou'd be no tickling in the Palm, no twitching o'th'Elbow, nor shrugging of the Shoulder, with their damn'd Frencify'd Grimace.'[13] The implication is that the country has been betrayed. Critics of Byng were also able to subvert long-standing forms of publication and strike a blow at the establishment itself as well as at Byng or the current state of naval command. For example, *The New Art of War at Sea now first practis'd by the English ships, under the Command of the Prudent Admiral Bung* [sic] is in the form of a mock award of the freedom of the City. This broadsheet contains a print showing a battle plan of the fleets and a key. 'A' signifies 'Admiral Byng and his ships at proper Distance from the Enemy'. The proposed gifts to be awarded Byng include 'a pair of neat polish'd Handcuffs for Bracelets', impugning his masculinity as well as his probity.

Byng's exasperated defenders were frustrated and appalled by the level of public debate. One complained that ministers had encouraged public demonstrations in order to shield themselves from blame: 'Money has been given and distributed to the Mob, to dress a Figure in the Sea uniform, to make Fires, and burn him; and thus to keep the Popular eye on B—g only.'[14] A sympathetic broadsheet, *To the People of England*, complained that if anyone of Byng's accusers were asked how they knew him to be guilty, they usually replied 'I have been told so' and had not taken the trouble to read a true account of his trial. Some of Byng's defenders targeted London merchants and artisans, hoping to turn the tide of opinion in the City by winning the support of the more powerful members of society. *A Serious Call to the Corporation of London* called upon the Lord Mayor and Aldermen to petition the King to remove the incompetent ministers who were the true source of the nation's shameful defeat. Some went to the lengths of composing a pro-Byng song to the tune of *God Save the King*, explicitly linking support for Byng to patriotism and firm allegiance to the constitution. The provocative Tory patriot, Dr John Shebbeare, in his *Fourth Letter to the People of England* (1756), which was widely excerpted in the monthlies, attacked the government for failing to send Byng against the French with an adequate force. He presented the loss of Minorca as the latest in a series of blunders that had weakened the nation and diminished Britain's reputation abroad. The various political clubs were active in the debate. For example, a broadsheet entitled *The Wonder of Surry! Or the genuine Speech of an Old* British *Oak*, which satirized the Duke of Newcastle's administration, duly provoked the response *Wonder upon Wonder: or the Cocoa Tree's Answer to the Surrey Oak* (the Cocoa Tree being a London club frequently by Tories and country gentlemen). The irony (albeit heavy) in many of these publications suggests a fairly sophisticated readership, or at least that part of the fun was puzzling out the true stance of individual authors. Byng himself complained that he was censured by armchair admirals who required 'no other Abilities, than a great deal of Ill-nature, and a little Wit'.[15] But, as he stated at his trial, it was also his misfortune to have to try to clear his name 'under the Disadvantage of a popular, and almost national Prejudice'.[16] The whole affair pointed to the force of feeling that British sea power was capable of exciting amongst the common people. Some doubted the integrity of the proceedings: there was a strong movement in the House in favour of commuting the death penalty, and a bill was introduced to allow the officers who had tried Byng to explain their reasons for condemning him. The failure of the bill was possibly owing to the pressure exerted by George III and the Duke of Cumberland, both of whom were hostile to Byng.

Although the controversy clearly focused on Byng, who paid the ultimate price for his caution in battle, the flood of publications prompted by the scandal also led to greater public inquiry about the state of the Navy. Commentators drew attention to the relation of Navy to government, to dubious procedures for promotion, and to questionable naval tactics. It is not possible to trace the authorship of some of these anonymous political works but even pro-ministry publications, chiefly intent on criticizing Byng as an inept commander, by implication call into question the fitness of an aristocratic elite for command. For example, Byng's tardy report to the ministry began with the complacent formula, 'I have the pleasure to desire you will acquaint their Lordships …' and once in the public domain, this was soon ridiculed. One versifier sneered at Byng, 'For thou ingrate, degenerate, and base, | Canst write with *pleasure* of thy own disgrace.'[17] In August 1756, the *Gentleman's Magazine*, a sure indicator of middle- and upper-class interests, carried a piece from a correspondent who suggested that the half-pay granted to sea officers was often misapplied. He argued that those known to be unfit ever again to go to sea should be struck off the list, and those serving at sea who demonstrated that they were not up to the job should similarly be struck off. Even in May the following year, when the publicity surrounding Byng's trial and execution had run its course, readers of the magazine were still invited to consider whether or not naval officers, exempt from the harsh discipline they imposed on common sailors, took their duties seriously enough.[18] This reflects current debate about the competence of senior naval command. From the government's point of view, events took a more worrying turn when the author of a pamphlet in Byng's defence raised the issue of whether or not commanders should accept the orders of a seemingly corrupt government. He asked 'every thinking man in Britain' whether Byng's trial would not have a direct tendency to ruin the service 'by discouraging Men of Parts and Character from engaging in it, and thereby throwing it wholly into the Hands of Fools and Madmen'. And he concluded that only the stupid or insane would accept a commission 'on the ignominious Terms of serving with a Halter about their Necks' just so that the domineering aristocrats in government might be exempt from punishment and even suspicion of guilt.[19] In this way, the loss of Minorca soon led to a perception, which the Newcastle ministry could not contain, that the nation's aristocratic leadership was in crisis. Parliamentary instability worsened until a coalition government had to be negotiated between Newcastle and Pitt: the Byng controversy was one of the few great crises in the eighteenth century when popular demonstrations and political opinion influenced the course of national politics.

Nor was the Admiralty exempt when the various members of the Newcastle Ministry came under fire. Anson, the First Lord of the Admiralty, had married the eldest daughter of Hardwicke, the Lord Chancellor and Newcastle's trusted friend and adviser. Critics of the ministry suggested that Hardwicke had collaborated in Byng's downfall to protect his son-in-law and the ministry's naval strategy.[20] In the ranks of the opposition, where William Pitt was one of Anson's sternest judges, the accusation was that Anson had jeopardized national safety by allowing the Old Corps Whig administration too great a say in naval affairs, thanks to his strong connection to it by marriage. He was charged with scandalously promoting officers who had influence with Newcastle's ministry to the detriment of the service.[21] Byng's defenders also discovered that warships which could have been used to augment his fleet were instead employed in the defence of commerce in the Channel, apparently because the ministry had submitted to pressure from commercial interests.[22] This apparent inability to prioritize had, they argued, led to the loss of a strategic base in the Mediterranean and hindered Britain's ambition to build a maritime empire. These government critics increasingly stressed the cumulative effect of political mismanagement of the Navy, which was depicted as having widespread social effects impacting on the well-being of all sectors of society.[23] The bellicose Pitt, professing a patriot ideology, apparently encouraged Richard Glover, the patriot poet and city merchant, to write a sequel to his famous anti-Walpole poem, *Admiral Hosier's Ghost*. In this later work, *A Sequel to Hosier's Ghost: or Old Blakeney's Reception into the Elysian Fields* (1756), the revered group of British military heroes in Elysium are shown to be utterly shamed by news of Byng's disgrace. The poem indicates how rival politicians were able to use poor naval performance as a means of undermining the government of the day, since Britain's standing abroad was held to be so dependent on its sea power. The Byng affair demonstrated that politicization of the Navy entailed dangers both for its officers and naval administrators.

The Byng controversy also revealed the power of the voice of the common people, although there was obvious political mobilization of the press and people were subjected to waves of propaganda from all parties, Some contemporary publications indicate how ordinary citizens, fired by a patriotic yet anti-aristocratic zeal, could be persuaded that when scandals of such magnitude hit the headlines, the lower ranks were more correct in their thinking than their social superiors. A letter, supposedly addressed to a member of parliament, included this radical threat:

I very well know you have a great Fondness to continue your Seat in Parliament. Your Birth, your Estate, and your Abilities, give you a Right to it: But I would advise you to be extremely cautious of your Conduct in this *Mediterranean* Affair; for should it be so much as suspected or whisper'd in your Borough, that you have in any Shape endeavour'd to defeat the honest and most equitable Demands and Expectations of the People, your whole Estate would not secure your Election; your very Life would be in Danger in passing our Streets; People of all Parties, Ranks, and Degrees, would tell you to your Face, that they don't covet your Money, – that they don't regard your Favour, – nor at all fear your Displeasure.[24]

Byng's defenders addressed their publications 'to the people' and strongly supported the apparent common interest in British sea power. The author of *Impartial Reflections on the Case of Mr Byng* considered that whatever Byng's fate, the controversy had had the good effect of 'strongly rouzing the Attention of the Nation to its naval Concerns' on which the country's political strength and military defence crucially depended.[25] Such focused attention led to greater public scrutiny of government action. The editor of a collection of addresses to George II, concerned with the unsuccessful management of the war and demanding a public enquiry into the loss of Minorca, called his work *The Voice of the People*. He explained that the addresses and the King's response had gone some way towards calming public outrage. Yet he believed the exercise had been necessary 'to revive a spirit of liberty in the nation; to convince those, who were secure in their power, and in a neglect of their duty, that the people were not so indifferent to public good, as to be silent spectators of public ruin'.[26] MPs were liable to be accused of complacency and it was easy to employ scare tactics and raise the spectre of a navy incapable of defending Britain's shores, but criticism from the commercial interest carried weight. One of the addresses in 1756 came from the City of London, who petitioned the King for a public enquiry while also encouraging citizens to contribute to the cost of any necessary improvements to the fleet (after all, any diminution in Britain's sea power affected trade). The City suggested that the Navy should act more offensively against the enemy at sea and allow a militia to shoulder part of the burden of protecting the nation against invasion. In response to these criticisms of government from the middling ranks with a strong commercial interest, an anonymous writer produced a pamphlet, *The Conduct of the ministry impartially Examined*, directly addressed to 'the Merchants of London'. This sought to defend the administration and lay the blame for the loss of such an important base as Minorca squarely on Byng's shoulders. The author flatters the merchant interest, 'You are likewise very capable to pronounce on the real merit of my undertaking; for many among you are men of liberal education'.[27] Evidently, the government could not tolerate such powerful critics without tactfully seeking to rebut their arguments.

Some criticism was focused on the ministry's conduct of the war but the public reputation of naval officers suffered too. Even in distant India Admiral Watson, weakened by fever, reflected in 1757 on the uncertain basis on which an officer's career stood. Perhaps thinking of his recent brilliant campaign in support of General Clive, he concluded, 'how much more hazardous it was for him to err on the cautious, than the desperate side'.[28] Ironically, Watson soon afterwards succumbed to the climate. Publications that professed to monitor contemporary manners and principles notably stigmatized military officers with idleness, luxury, immorality and irreligion. A more charitable reviewer of 1758 wondered, 'whether sea-officers in general are not as intent upon annoying the enemy, as upon picking up prizes',[29] but the effect on officers of the Byng affair was considerable and endured for many years.

III

As already indicated, popular politics became more sophisticated during the 1760s when the Wilkite movement made full use of the various channels of political communication. By the 1770s, the public's demand for political news had grown to the extent that newspaper editors found that their circulation figures dropped if they neglected to include reports of parliamentary debates. These were often concerned with naval affairs, and the annual debate about the size of naval supplies to be agreed by the House was generally lively. The roles performed by the Navy had broad support in the House across the various factions so that the amount of the naval estimate was rarely a matter of major dispute in itself. Instead, the annual debate could range widely over naval matters and it was this element of spontaneity that attracted press coverage. This was certainly the case in 1774 when the North administration, facing war against the American colonists, was keen to secure a stronger navy in order to deter France and Spain from entering hostilities. At the same time, North was aware of the expense of a full naval mobilization, which might have the additional disadvantage of actually provoking the French. Naval debates were often tense affairs, because if the Navy were ever in need of greater investment to counteract areas of weakness, no ministry would wish to present the case in such terms, not least because it would encourage enemies to take advantage.[30]

In the summer of 1778 there was yet another invasion scare (which continued into the following summer) when France, as feared, did enter the American war on the side of the colonists. Full mobilization had begun early in the year when conflict with France was seen as imminent. Opposition MPs who had formerly denounced any augmentation of the Navy for a detested conflict with the colonies now criticized the government for failing to have enough ships ready at the commencement of a new war with Britain's traditional enemy. Press gangs were extremely active and government supporters in many towns tried to increase the numbers of volunteers by offering bounties to seamen and landmen, too well aware that the Navy had failed to mobilize properly in 1775–78. The distinguished admiral, Augustus Keppel, was given command of the Home Fleet – rather surprisingly since he was an energetic member of the Rockingham opposition, obviously unwilling to use force to keep the North Americans within the empire, and no friend of Lord Sandwich, First Lord of the Admiralty. Keppel sailed from Portsmouth to shadow the French fleet at Brest and captured two enemy frigates. Papers on board the captured ships indicated to Keppel that the French fleet was considerably larger than his own and so he prudently retreated. Loyalists at home were critical and the popular press unrestrained in its condemnation of his retreat but some elements in society were anxious to put a face-saving gloss on the situation. The ballad *Admiral Keppel Triumphant or Monsieur in the Suds* insinuated, contrary to fact, that the French tried to escape Keppel's fleet off Brest. Written for a popular audience, the ballad suggested that, having seen the force of British guns, the French retreated under cover of darkness. It concluded on a positive note by wishing Keppel future success, and probably helped to excite public expectation of what the Navy might soon achieve.

Keppel finally encountered the French off Ushant, but again the public was disappointed by an inconclusive battle when they had hoped for a decisive victory. In fact, to this day the French claim that they were the superior side. As public opinion in Britain was poised for outright criticism, key protagonists began to think of covering their backs. Sandwich must have been disposed to trust Keppel when he first offered him the command but the admiral himself had always been more reserved. His political friends had warned him to be cautious and he only accepted the commission after certain conditions had been met. Keppel had been present at Byng's trial, and perhaps had good reason to be circumspect. Now, after the disappointing engagement off Ushant, inevitably both parties were full of mutual distrust. Sandwich wondered whether Keppel had deliberately been less than zealous in battle in order to throw discredit upon the administration and its naval strategy. Keppel for his own part wondered if he had not been set up, as his friends had warned he might be. His junior in the battle, Sir Hugh Palliser, had signally failed to bring up his damaged ships in time to pursue the French, and Palliser was both Sandwich's key aide at the Admiralty and a staunch government supporter. Matters were not helped when the affair was reported irresponsibly by a press eager to make political capital and by the time that Parliament reconvened in late autumn, trouble was confidently anticipated. At this time there were 30 naval officers in Parliament; some owed their seats to government nominations while others owed theirs to

Figure 2 *Counter Commemorating Admiral Keppel's Acquittal by Court Martial, 1779.*

private or family interest and could vote as they pleased. Since an officer's prospect of promotion was enhanced as an MP, politics and naval affairs were closely linked. But naval MPs did not unite politically as a professional group due to the differing circumstances of their nomination, and they were often absent from the House in wartime. In this affair, they could be expected to take different sides and in both Houses angry clashes led to demands for a public enquiry. After Palliser demanded that Keppel be court-martialled, the affair became personalized. The public, following the debate, had the delicious prospect of being able to take sides according to party and military performance at the same time. The Navy, too, was split: some sided with Keppel and others with Palliser.

Keppel's trial in February 1779 became a kind of public entertainment. His ill-health won him the concession of being tried on land instead of on board ship, as was usual. Given that the case was reported in detail in the press and then in the monthlies, the public was able to follow each twist in the drama. Leading Rockingham Whigs and their wives ostentatiously travelled to Portsmouth to support their naval champion, providing a colourful display that reinforced Keppel's political allegiances and encouraged criticism of the ministry. By staging processions through the town that served to emphasize the importance of 'the People', they hoped to contrast their overt patriotism with the apparent timidity of a government that had so far failed to win real success in war. The aristocratic presence of Keppel's supporters in the courtroom prompted the gawping townspeople of Portsmouth to fill the remaining seats and added zest to newspaper accounts. When Keppel was acquitted, there was a procession around the town when supporters proudly wore the light blue ribbons of the Rockingham Whigs. Such activities incorporated familiar, ritualistic elements, included the use of symbols and allowed ordinary people, even those who were ineligible to vote, to feel they were participating in the political process. Later that evening, once news reached London, the unfortunate Palliser's house was looted. The mob proceeded to tear down the gates of the

Admiralty, and break the windows of ministers and Admiralty lords, until the military had to be called to disperse the rabble.

Against the background of this trial and acquittal, Keppel's performance at Ushant was praised more than he deserved. People clearly wanted to be able to celebrate British sea power after a period when it had been judged to be little more than a tool of ministerial policy, routinely enforcing customs laws in American waters. In 1773, for instance, Benjamin Franklin had taunted the British, accusing them of converting 'the brave, honest officers' of the Navy 'into pimping tide-waiters and colony officers of the customs'.[31] Now, just as commemorative medals had been struck to celebrate Vernon's victory, so Keppel's action at Ushant and later his acquittal at court martial were marked by medals and counters, some medals made in the form of badges to be worn on hats and coats. Keppel's portrait by Reynolds was also promptly engraved to take advantage of the moment, and bought by hundreds who wished to show their allegiance to his cause. Josiah Wedgwood made a killing in 1779 and 1790 with his speedily produced portrait medallions of Keppel. Those with disposable income could also buy earthenware plates, wall plaques and table linen, all commemorating the admiral's success. As we have seen in Chapter 2, Keppel found supporters among those with merchant and trading interests. Among the urban middling classes there was broad support for radical politics since the opposition's emphasis on accountable government and independence seemed to promise better support for commerce and trade. Keppel's trial was viewed as a political matter and an indication of incompetence and corruption at the heart of government. For example, a bronze counter commemorating Keppel's acquittal has the admiral's bust on the obverse, and on the reverse the figure of Justice, represented as a woman with a sword in her right hand and scales in her left. At her feet sprawls a figure representing Envy and the legend reads 'Justice Triumphant and Malice Defeated' (Figure 2). The Whig poet, William Mason, also wrote an ode to British naval officers after Keppel's acquittal in which he praised their 'honest fame' compared to the sycophancy of 'Hireling Courtiers' and peers.[32]

In his defence at his court martial, Keppel had carefully claimed to be acting in a wider political capacity than was ordinarily the case with naval commanders. He was not, he argued, to be considered 'merely as an officer with a limited commission, confined to a special military operation to be conducted upon certain military rules'. Instead he was placed 'in a political as well as a military situation' and part of his instructions, he alleged, originated from the Secretary of State as well as from the Admiralty Board.[33] With hindsight, we can see that it was dangerous for the Navy to be so closely involved with politics, especially in wartime. Arguably, the role of the Navy was to carry out Parliament's bidding without question but after the Keppel-Palliser affair, there were sections in the Navy who openly aligned themselves with a political party to the detriment of discipline and morale – which remained poor in the Channel Fleet for the rest of the war. Senior officers at the time were particularly anxious that Palliser's action would prove a dangerous precedent, encouraging junior officers to accuse commanders of misconduct. The fact that newspapers were ready to report the accusations of subordinate officers who also held high civil office (as Palliser had) posed another threat. It had been demonstrated that public opinion was a powerful force and any prospect of a fair trial could be denied the accused if such cases were immediately reported in the popular press. Some commentators attempted to counteract the effects of Keppel's popularity and to point out the dangers of encouraging factions in the Navy along party lines. The author of one address to Keppel, purportedly a seaman, jeered at the admiral's recent performance at sea, 'strangely urged by a designing party, your importance seems to have been *much over-rated* in the late condition of your future service'. He further hoped that since naval officers were of such vital importance to the nation, they would 'never allow their minds to be prejudiced against any branch of administration'.[34]

The memory of Byng's fate certainly helped to colour contemporary reactions to this affair. Keppel, in his defence at his trial (taken down in shorthand and published with his permission), mentioned that government publications seemed to threaten him with the fate of Admiral Byng.[35] But with the American war going badly, Britain's government could not afford to send out a signal that its naval command was less than competent. On his acquittal, Keppel received the thanks of both Houses of Parliament who particularly complimented him on 'having gloriously upheld the honour of the British flag' in the battle off Ushant.[36] Before the Keppel-Palliser affair, the North ministry had been in a strong position with public opinion broadly behind the government in its opposition to the claims of the American colonists. The apparent disloyalty of the opposition MPs who celebrated American successes had been roundly condemned. After Keppel's acquittal, Charles James Fox, on the opposition benches, was more effective in his attacks on Sandwich. He called for the papers relating to government intelligence of the size of the French fleet, to see if the Ministry had been guilty of sending Keppel to sea with too small a force. The motion was defeated on the grounds that it was tantamount to betraying government secrets but a week later, on 3 March, Fox returned to this point in another attack on Sandwich. Keppel, placed in a difficult position, demurred. He could not betray the secrets of government to give his relation, Fox, the support he was looking for. But he did say that he felt that it was inconsistent with his honour to serve at sea again while men in whom he could place no confidence presided at the Board of Admiralty. Lord Howe also declared his resolution to decline all future service so long as the present ministers continued in office. He and his brother had been through a similar experience to Keppel and had returned from the war in America in 1778 to find that they were under pressure to defend their conduct there. Clearly the North Ministry could not control its admirals but, while Fox successfully put North on the defensive, he failed to topple the government for its conduct of the war. However, with eminent admirals who sat in Parliament, including Augustus Hervey and Lord Howe, siding with Keppel against the government and refusing to serve at sea, it was an anxious time for the North administration.

Given the widespread, personalized reporting of naval debates in wartime, naval officers who were MPs could take centre stage in both actual engagements at sea and in the thrust and parry of related debates in parliament. This accentuated the sense of war as a performance, in some sense, particularly since the more lively debates, including Fox's attack on Sandwich, were reported in the papers speech by speech – often with contextual asides that seem almost the equivalent of stage directions: '[Here the house grew very clamourous].'[37] In the House, key protagonists were able to articulate their versions of patriotism and their own interpretation of the progress of the war. In this way parliamentary reports were a crucial means of mediating the war to a wider public. North's ministry lost the confidence of the country at a time when the odds facing Britain were overwhelming and national security a matter of pressing concern. Contemporaries also linked success at sea to much-vaunted British liberty. For instance, one publication, apparently written by a French naval officer and translated from the original, argued that Keppel's official report of his engagement off Ushant was the work of a pamphleteer and only published under Keppel's name. The author contended that the battle was actually a French victory and in a footnote dared to link British pusillanimity to the political condition of its citizens:

> A foreigner arrives at London: in that city which, as every one knows, is *perfectly free*, he meets ten times in an hour, *press-gangs* pursuing passengers, in order to make them soldiers or sailors, by dint of bastinadoes: the next day he goes to Portsmouth, embarks on board a ship, and there finds half those involuntary heroes chained down in the hold; two days after he lands at Brest; the sailors who arrive there unguarded and unconstrained, are disputing the honour of being first embarked.[38]

It did the government no good to have British 'liberty' unfavourably compared with the regime operating in France. True patriots, for example, believed that Britain's free constitution was a blessing that 'must for ever render the naval force of Great-Britain greatly superior to that of her neighbours'.[39]

Yet within a comparatively short space of time, some commentators were providing a more balanced overview of recent events. The author of *The Conduct of the Admirals Hawke, Keppel and Palliser, Compared* adopted a plain, rational style. He concurred with the officers at Keppel's trial that the accused was no coward but then suggested that neither had Keppel shown the same determination in battle that Hawke had manifested when he won his decisive victory against the French at Ushant in 1747. As for Keppel's performance in 1778: 'All that can be said was "the English fleet, while it did engage, was not beat: – this is the honour, and all the honour, due to that day's service".'[40] He was also critical of Keppel's refusal to go to sea again under Sandwich's direction. It was Keppel's duty to serve the King, if not the ministry, and party prejudice seemed to have betrayed him into insubordination. In fact, whereas victorious admirals were commonly accorded the status of folk heroes because they were perceived to be more trustworthy than self-serving politicians, Keppel's recent conduct could be interpreted as part of a general corruption of manners. Ironically, it exposed him to the same criticism of corrupt leadership that was being directed at the Ministry. Other popular publications seized on the implications of having a politicized navy. A mock sermon advised that the anniversary of Keppel's engagement off Ushant should be held as a day of fasting and humiliation. It marked the day when the British flag was tarnished thanks to the obstinacy of the First Lord and the commander of the fleet, who then held different political principles but who were now linked together for the destruction of their sovereign and total ruin of their country. The publication mocked Keppel's determination to cover his back by obtaining precise orders before sailing yet still failing to act decisively when he met the French:

> 8. And after certain days, when the Chief Captain [Keppel] came up with some small ships belonging unto the enemy, he wrote unto *Jemmy Twitcher* [Sandwich], and said unto him, 'What shall I do?' And before he could get an answer he wrote again, and said, 'I have found their great ships, and, moreover, I have done nothing!'
> 9. And there was great marvelling thro' the land
> 10. And he said, 'when it was Noon, I put off fighting until Night; and when it was Night, I postponed it even until the Morning! And when the Morning came, there were none there; they were all OFF, they had departed even unto their own homes.'
> 11. So the side men cursed him for a blockhead, and the prudent men laughed him to scorn, and the brave men d—d him for an ass, and the fool said, 'What a kettle of fish is here!'[41]

The propaganda produced as a result of this affair was geared to a range of audiences from every rank of society, aiming to inform, persuade or amuse but whatever its immediate target, ultimately it did little to enhance the reputation of the Navy.

In 1780, news of Admiral Rodney's relief of Gibraltar, following his interception and defeat of a Spanish Squadron near Cape St Vincent, brought great relief to the North Ministry. The Westminster election of 1780, held soon afterwards, was bound to excite interest. Fox stood for the Whigs (although not all Foxites were Whigs), Lord Lincoln was the ministerial candidate and Rodney stood for the Tories. The constituency of Westminster, where there were about 17 000 male householders eligible to vote, was always hotly contested. This was too large an electorate to be bribed or be unduly under a single influence. Voters in Westminster increasingly valued their say in public affairs and often stood against the powerful influence of the court, making the election an important test of public opinion. Rodney spent great amounts of money on contemporary elections to further his own political and social ends. A contemporary print, biased against the ministerial candidate, shows Rodney, now a national hero, on the hustings in Covent Garden with the other candidates.[42] Rodney is sponsored by Neptune, which may allude to his recent military success and therefore his role in helping Britain fulfil its destiny as a naval power. He holds a drawn sword in his right hand, and in his left a scroll referring to his success at Gibraltar. Fox, sponsored by Britannia, is the central figure and clearly the independent, patriotic choice as a 'man of the people'. Rodney's role is complementary and presumably had a particular appeal to loyalists who valued bravery and decisive action in battle. In the event, Fox was elected and represented Westminster to the end of his life. Typically, other electioneering pieces – such as punch bowls, figurines and mugs, which featured naval officers, as appropriate – would be produced for popular consumption. George III's growing interest in the Navy since his visit to Portsmouth to view the dockyard and the fleet in 1773, meant that those who wished to align themselves with King and country could do little wrong if they demonstrated support for the Navy by purchasing such items. (The royal visit was itself an indication of the politicization of naval affairs since at the time he persuaded the King to go to Portsmouth Sandwich was being starved of funds for the Navy by North.) On the other hand, those who unreservedly donated money to supply the Navy might be accused of undermining democratic government by reducing the dependency of the Crown on Parliament.[43] The East India Company notably gave ships to the Royal Navy.

In 1782, all parties sincerely celebrated Rodney's decisive victory against the French at the Battle of the Saints. In the period immediately before that, commentators had compared the state of the Navy with its strength at the end of the Seven Years War with extreme dismay. Now Rodney's victory encouraged Tories to protest against the efforts of the 'new Whig' government led by Rockingham to achieve peace with America. The victory sanctioned panegyrics on British seamen, with the usual swipe against aristocrat degeneracy: 'No body of men has added so much to the national glory: none have so little degenerated from the spirit of their ancestors.'[44] Contemporaries saw nothing incongruous in moving from a celebration of Rodney's success in biographical terms to a political commentary on the conduct of the ministry.

Though this victory enabled the government to sue for better peace terms, the seemingly calamitous loss of the American colonies administered a powerful shock to British public life. Those who had favoured conciliation from the start were disaffected; those who had supported the use of force were disappointed; and most felt the impact of the huge cost of the war. Commentators remarked on 'the sort of despair' that prevailed with many. One zealous author, hoping to counteract the general trend, pored over government statistics, focusing on the numbers of enemy vessels taken in order to prove that Britain was actually successful against each of her enemies even before Rodney's great victory. He based his claim for the authority of his data on the fact that within the army and Navy there were checks against the least misrepresentation, thereby unwittingly emphasizing the divisions in the military – 'There are I fear in all our fleets and armies, officers who would be glad to contradict the publick account given by their Admiral or General.'[45] In the peace that followed, the Navy would not be immune to calls for reform, but for most the effect of the propaganda surrounding the Navy in the 1780s only confirmed the influence of public opinion in British politics.

IV

There were several invasion scares after the outbreak of the French Revolutionary Wars, most notably perhaps in 1798, and the concurrent wave of patriotic sentiment helped to quash the various forces of political reform prevalent in the 1790s. Yet opposition to the war could be strident, especially in the months before the Navy won success. In these circumstances, naval officers were the butt of politicized ridicule. The attacks on Lord Howe in newspapers and prints were so severe before his victory on 1 June 1794, that he was seriously thinking of resigning his command of the Channel Fleet.[46] A particularly vicious print published by S.W. Fores shows Howe in a 'fog' of indecisiveness and suggests that his cruises against the enemy are so much time and money wasted (see Plate 3). Another by James Gillray, called *A French Hail Storm, – or – Neptune losing sight of the Brest Fleet* (see cover illustration), also shows Howe incapable of engaging with the French. The hail of gold coins which blinds Howe suggests that he is open to corruption. Although the great victory of the Glorious First of June was greeted with euphoria, the British people soon grew tired of the war; when Robespierre fell and the Directory assumed government in France, they clamoured for peace. Pitt resisted such demands as long as he could but in December 1795 and in 1796 peace negotiations were opened; however, they came to nothing and war was renewed. Radicals were more concerned to hit back at 'tyrannical' government in Britain than to oppose the war with France and aspects of military preparation lent themselves to their arguments. The radical writer John Thelwall interpreted the action of press-gangs who disrupted his lectures in Yarmouth as stemming from an unjust oligarchy rather than from frigate captains anchored nearby. In a subsequent publication he depicted the Navy as a tool of a repressive government.[47] In similar vein, the political reformer John Gale Jones applauded the decision of the citizens of Chatham to ban military officers from their assemblies. This offered some protection from 'military coxcombs' who could threaten civilians with martial discipline if they met with any objection to their arrogant behaviour.[48] Of course, one of the most unsettling dissident developments of the decade was the growing discontent in the Navy. The catalyst for the 1797 naval mutinies was dissatisfaction over pay but some historians have detected a political dimension in the mutinies at Spithead and the Nore. In the summer of 1797, when inflation was high, the peace party again persuaded Pitt to renew negotiations with France. All over the country, people clamoured for peace at any price; many opposition papers published poems and songs eliciting sympathy for sailors' families and particularly for war widows. But once again peace negotiations broke down.

In March 1798, the Duke of Bedford in the House of Lords called for the dismissal of the government for its mismanagement of the war. Lord Grenville's speech rebutting the accusation was written down in substance by individuals present and published. Presumably the resulting pamphlet was intended to help consolidate support for ministerial policy but there was a ready market for this kind of political material at moments of national crisis. Significantly, Grenville contended that his opponent Bedford had entirely omitted to mention Britain's naval triumphs – which the ministry could surely be held responsible for, as opposed to the operation of foreign armies over which it had no control. He enthusiastically claimed for himself and his ministerial colleagues a share of the credit for these naval victories, though he admitted that the chief praise should go to the Navy.[49] Just as Keppel's mediocre performance in 1778 had helped to unsettle the government, so Britain's naval victories in the 1790s helped to bolster the authority of politicians in office. The Duke of Bedford's motion was defeated by 113 votes to 13, and an alternative motion advocating solidarity in crisis was adopted without division.

Pitt had been generally disbelieved when he contended that the failure of the 1797 peace negotiations was the fault of the French, so it was fortunate for government propaganda that, in 1798, it was once more rumoured that the French planned to invade England. In the wake of the naval mutinies, and now facing renewed threats of invasion, loyalists exploited the image of the Navy to help raise funds to support the war. One such author appealed to the middle and upper classes for contributions, and interestingly included women as well as men in his address. He was careful to use the traditional image of a patriotic Navy serving the cause of British liberty, and tried to excite readers' annoyance and exasperation by alleging that the French misrepresented the British Navy as 'a gigantic buccaneer who tyrannizes over the sea'. He mischievously claimed that the French confidently expected any invading army of theirs would meet with the cooperation of thousands of Britains who had formerly agitated for political reform or mutinied in the fleet.[50] Such scare tactics strengthened his point. Readers would understand that, in contrast to French insults, the subversive elements in British society and particularly naval society did pose a severe risk to national security. The piece is finely balanced so that any censure of the Navy appears to come from the enemy alone. The author proceeds to repudiate the criticism by complaining that the French are simply envious of British commerce and 'the invincible superiority' of the Navy. But all the time he is playing on the fears of those classes who had most to lose if the Navy proved unequal to the task of defending Britain's shores or protecting her trade. The two were linked, since it was clear that if the Navy proved unable to protect commerce, Britain would soon be in need of revenue to continue the war.

When Sir C.W. Rouse Boughton, MP, similarly addressed a parochial meeting at Chiswick to raise voluntary contributions for the defence of the country, he used naval exploits, notably the relieving of the Siege of Gibraltar in 1782, to show the character of the British nation. This victory, which famously displayed the humanity of the British seamen who saved hundreds of Spanish sailors from the sea, was often celebrated in popular entertainment. (Later in the war, The Sadler's Wells Aquatic Theatre offered the spectacle of the Siege of Gibraltar with men-of-war, floating batteries and 8000 cubic feet of water.) Rouse Boughton tried to reassure his audience by recalling the brave exploits of earlier naval commanders who had rescued the country from alarm when invasion had threatened. He poured scorn on the gigantic invasion craft that the French were supposedly constructing, 'how such unwieldy machines are to be navigated ... as we see them described in our print-shops ... I can in no way comprehend'. But though the Navy had always protected the country from invasion, Rouse Boughton warned that it could not be relied upon if the people themselves were found wanting. His audience would not have missed the familiar allusion to the religious argument that God would only fight on the side of the righteous, 'For Providence will not favour the sluggard'. The address was printed in pamphlet form to calm fears and encourage support for the war effort.[51]

To assist loyalist propaganda, accounts of recent British victories at sea (first published in the government paper, *The London Gazette*) were compiled and reissued for a popular readership as *The British Navy Triumphant!*.[152] Improvements in financial procedures relating to the maintenance of the fleet were also publicized to the government's greater credit.[53] The revenue generated by the convoy tax indicated to contemporaries that, despite various obstacles to trade, Britain's commerce continued to flourish even in wartime, just as it had done after 1759 in the Seven Years War when British supremacy at sea reduced disruption of trade to a minimum.[54] The convoy tax was a small percentage on the value of goods exported and imported, with some exceptions, and a modest tonnage duty on all ships arriving at or sailing from any port in Britain. It allowed revenue officers to calculate that British exports in 1798 exceeded former estimates by at least 70 per cent. These excellent trade figures were published, partly to boost morale during what appeared to be the most perilous war in which the country had ever engaged.[55] Britain, it was argued, drew the means for carrying on the war partly from the growing manufacturing base and the increasing trade of her people, and partly from commerce which, protected by the Navy, benefited foreign countries at the same time that it added to the prosperity of British citizens. By way of contrast, the government represented France as extorting money to pay for war supplies by taxing its citizens oppressively and ransacking each country it overran. Such conservative propaganda, in which the Navy played a crucial part, was generally successful since most people in Britain seem to have accepted that it was in their best interest to strive to protect the status quo. The impact on society of Nelson's great victory at the Battle of the Nile, late in 1798, indicates the extent of the relief felt in Britain at the temporary respite from threatened invasion.[56]

The most serious invasion crisis of the Revolutionary War took place in 1801, and by 1803–04, when there was yet another major invasion scare, the financial burden of the war against Napoleon had become enormous and was keenly resented by large sections of the population. Commentators understood that what the country needed was a decisive naval victory: 'A war of mere cruising fatigues both the navy, the army and the nation, and is apt to produce trifling circumstances that vex out neutral neighbours without advancing our own service.'[57] To some political writers, it was already clear that in order to preserve a lasting peace Britain would have to find means of preventing France from adding a preponderant navy to her continental power. In an anticipation of the nineteenth-century concept of *Pax Britannica*, it was mooted that Britain, on account of its high level of naval power, might seek international recognition as the guardian and guarantor of a liberal system of maritime commerce between nations.[58] But the immediate threat from Napoleon, as he prepared for his 'Grand Design' or invasion of Britain, ensured that such ambitions were shelved for the moment. Napoleon assembled thousands of flat-bottomed boats at Boulogne and up to 130 000 troops and 7000 horses for cavalry and artillery. On the other side of the Channel, the British built coastal defences and frantically amassed volunteer troops (400 000 signed up to defend the country), while the Navy focused on blockading the French port of Brest. Naturally the government had to present its preparations for war in a positive light and bolster people's faith in national institutions, the Navy in particular. Even when raising a bill to enable the King to demand military service from British subjects more easily, the Secretary at War took care to eulogize the Navy as 'the most powerful in the world, and capable of sustaining a conflict with that of the whole world'.[59] William Wilberforce, MP for Yorkshire and close friend of Pitt, was perhaps being more honest when he explained that, although the Navy would do what it could, 'we must not depend on our navy, for preventing invasion'.[60] The enemy might well slip past the fleet, given certain weather conditions, so it would be prudent to secure additional defences to protect the country from invasion. At this time, both the Navy and army expanded enormously: in April 1804, the *Gentleman's Magazine* reported that Britain could boast 77 012 seamen and 11 990 mariners. By publicizing the escalating numbers of men in service, thanks to supplies granted by Parliament, the government helped to reassure the public while affirming its own power and displaying an ability to respond to the crisis.

In an age when foreign news was largely dependent on dispatches and reliable images hard to come by even if they professed to be 'taken on the spot', popular fears were easily manipulated. As in previous invasion scares, printsellers again found a ready market for illustrations of improbable French invasion craft (see Plate 4), one of which was even reported to be capable of transporting 60 000 men and 600 cannon. But popular forms of entertainment might also be a means of raising morale. In 1803, for example, the Theatre Royal, Covent Garden (identified as a Tory establishment), offered 'a new historical comic Opera' called *The English Fleet, in 1342*, written by Thomas John Dibdin. The piece invited the audience to take comfort from the fact that England had roundly defeated the French in earlier conflicts. It featured prize-loving, loyal British tars (a stereotype that the theatre had done much to help create, though the image was far from static), and in the finale openly encouraged young men to join the Navy. Gillian Russell has pointed out how familiar kinds of texts such as playbills could be parodied for political purposes during invasion scares. A broadside from 1803 dismisses the planned invasion of England as 'A FARCE in One Act' featuring 'Principal Buffo, Mr BUONAPARTE Being his FIRST (and most likely his Last) Appearance on this Stage'. In 1804 the broadside was included in the first number of *The Anti-Gallican*, as was the speech of Rolla to the Peruvians from Richard Brinsley Sheridan's play *Pizarro*. This successful play, first performed in May 1799, concerned the fate of the Peruvian Indians at the hands of the colonizing Spanish, but contemporary audiences were encouraged to interpret the play as a commentary on the situation of the British people, threatened by tyrannical France. The speech of Rolla, the Peruvian general, struck a particular chord with British audiences as it compared the Peruvians (fighting for religion, liberty, a popular monarch and domestic peace) with the Spanish (fighting for plunder, extended rule and tyrannical power).

Sheridan, a Foxite Whig MP who had earlier criticized Pitt's war policy, actually produced in *Pizarro* an ambivalent work that could either be taken as the radical response of a Whig patriot to the prospect of tyrannical rule or as loyal support for the established monarchy. *The Anti-Gallican* chose to interpret the Rolla's speech as wholly 'appropriate to the situation of the country', and it was also reproduced as a handbill by the loyalist publisher, Asperne.[61]

Popular fears were reflected and heightened by the press, and newspapers of various political affiliations played a significant part in contributing to public perceptions of the Navy. The progress of wars in various continents, news of prizes taken in battle, and the movement of shipping generally could take up as much as one-third of the contents of contemporary newspapers, and a much higher proportion when Britain was at war.[62] During the invasion crisis, of 1803–04, newspapers often seem to climax in a crescendo of rumour and exaggerated report. The reporting of naval affairs in Tory and Whig newspapers naturally differed considerably – although, as the newspaper business was extremely lucrative, it is unlikely that the press was overly susceptible to direct political manipulation. At this stage in the war, successive governments used the press to bring home to the nation, perhaps for the first time, that success depended on civilian as well as military effort. At the outset of the crisis, pro-government papers like *The London Chronicle* and *The True Briton* carried George III's proclamations encouraging seamen to volunteer for the Navy and recalling those seamen who, after the Peace of Amiens, had chosen to serve foreign princes and states. These items reinforced the gravity of the situation, underlined the Navy's role as prime defender of the country and suggested that men could most effectively demonstrate their bravery by joining the service. *The London Chronicle* was able to indicate its own loyalty by printing such pieces while effectively helping the government's war preparations. When invasion threatened, Whig newspapers also aimed to appear resolutely patriotic. They had always praised the bravery of British seamen, even when registering dissatisfaction with the war. Now that Napoleon's territorial ambitions had become clear, their support for the Navy could be presented more unequivocally. *The Morning Chronicle*, universally held to be the recognized organ of orthodox Whigs, registered deep anxiety at any sign that individuals were inciting the kind of discontent in the Navy that might lead to a repeat of the 1797 mutinies. An editorial on 25 January 1803, complained that a certain weekly newspaper had seemed to justify naval mutiny while attempting to discredit St Vincent, First Lord of the Admiralty. *The Morning Chronicle* had some responsibility to the party and, though outspoken in its criticism of the Administration, was generally restrained in expression. Now the editorial prudently suggested that, while such inflammatory material might be appropriate in political debate, it was hardly useful in public; in the current state of emergency, such comments bordered on treason. The writer complained, 'It is indeed a singular circumstance to find the traitorous authors of the *Argus* at Paris, and the *hyper-patriotic* agents of the war faction in London, labouring by the same falsehoods, to excite or inflame discontent in the British Navy'.[63] The same issue also denounced all 'anti-impressment stories', which currently sensationalized the work of manning the Navy. The paper denied that it had ever justified mutiny itself and even regretted that seamen had received a salary increase since pay should never be the reward of military exertion.

The Morning Post, an exponent of bolder and more liberal politics than most papers on the Whig side, was even more indignant at complaints about press gangs:

> We cannot conclude on this subject, without directing the public censure against some Newspapers which daily whine over the pressed men. – 'The miseries of war;' 'the poor sailors dragged away;' 'the Mansion-house surrounded with their wives and daughters, wringing their hands, their eyes streaming with tears, lamenting their relatives torn away by the press gangs,' &c &c. Is, then, the situation of sailors on board Kind's ships so deplorable? Are not their wages, food, and clothing, far superior to those of most mechanics and labourers? – Where is the cruelty in sending men to sea who have been bred to it, and live by it; who are never so happy as when they are on it? Who are those wives and relatives so piteously bemoaned? Probably strumpets and sharpers, watching to fleece the simple tars of their wages. Is there anything in the present system of pressing more severe than formerly? Then why all this Corresponding Society cant but to sow disaffection in our Navy, discontent among the lower classes of society, and to weaken the efforts of Government in preparing for the defence of the country?[64]

Such comments on naval preparation allowed the Whig paper to enhance its position as a responsible organ, compared to even more radical papers. Yet, apparently objective reports relating to the Navy in *The Morning Post* could still have an unsettling effect. For example, a little over a week earlier, on 2 March, the paper had reported a serious disturbance at the Portsmouth theatre. Ironically, a performance of a play entitled *Hear Both Sides* had been interrupted by a row of young naval officers much the worse for drink. The constables were sent for but the naval officers had side arms and resisted. One threw a lighted candle into a box where ladies were sitting, at which point the military were called. The seamen yelled 'Fire!' and in the confusion several escaped. The ladies climbed out of the boxes and onto the stage, which was protected by spikes. A lieutenant who followed them unfortunately wounded his leg on one of the spikes and the injury was reported to be dangerous. *The Morning Post* was hardly a neutral force for patriotism. This report reminded readers that the Navy ashore could be dangerous force for social instability and the disturbance pointed to the tensions of a highly militarized society in wartime. While there is no suggestion of approval of such civil disorder, there is no outright condemnation either. The naval officers are clearly not obedient, loyal pawns of government but independent-minded men able to break the bounds of convention, and the theatre offered a public location where this point could be made. Similarly, the paper was being mischievous when, the next day, it refuted all reports that the wife of Colonel Despard was under the protection of Lady Nelson. 'We have the authority to state that the circumstance is wholly untrue, and we much fear that the rumour has been propagated by the enemies of the virtuous and amiable Viscountess.'[65] Nelson, who had fought alongside Despard nearly 25 years previously, had been called as a character witness at his trial for treason by the defence. The evidence was overwhelmingly against Despard and he was duly executed. Afterwards, out of pity, Nelson did solicit from the government a pension for Despard's wife, though without much hope of success. *The Morning Post*, while protesting the loyalty of the Nelson family, nevertheless managed to insinuate that even naval heroes were hardly passive tools of the Crown. No doubt there was also an intended side-swipe at Nelson's domestic arrangements since he and Lady Nelson had been estranged since 1801.

By April, *The Morning Post* was criticizing Addington's administration for its slow naval preparations. With Admiral Jervis (Lord St Vincent) as First Lord of the Admiralty, naval operations had been further politicized by his ill-timed and unsuccessful reform efforts. Again, in this crisis *The Morning Post* adopted an indirect method and quoted another newspaper:

> The *Grenville Gazette* represents our Navy as in a most deplorable condition. That paper (the ORACLE) of yesterday, says, instead of Mr. ADDINGTON's promise being fulfilled, that fifty ships of the line would be ready in a month, not one-third of the number is now manned, and ready for sea, though it is five weeks since the KING's Message was delivered.[66]

The Morning Chronicle was typically even more circumspect while also casting doubt on the capacity of the Admiralty. It quoted a ministerial paper, *The Sun*, which had earlier reported that there were imminent changes in the Administration, and added, 'A change at the Admiralty is we believe, anxiously desired by the whole Naval Service'.[67] Less than a month later, *The Morning Chronicle* was safely able to report the Admiralty's own inept defence of its recent performance. Captain Markham, a member of the Board of Admiralty, stood up in the Commons to deny recent aspersions about the state of the Navy. The Navy, he argued, was more than adequate to cope with the force of any power in Europe, and in home waters, too, it was amply sufficient to meet any French invasion fleet. Unfortunately, he then claimed that Napoleon's flotilla 'consisted of nothing better than fishing boats, and existed only in the minds of a few Gentlemen on the other side [of the House]'. This ridiculous bravado met with laughter and Markham hastily explained that his words were 'the licence of the seaman'. The Chancellor of the Exchequer rose to support Markham and further deprecated criticism of the Admiralty in the popular media which adversely affected the war effort. 'The conduct of the Board of Admiralty has been represented in the public prints in a manner which has a direct tendency to dispirit the country at home, and which could not have any good effect abroad', he thundered.[68] Clearly, any would-be critic of the Navy or the Admiralty would have to tread a fine line between patriotism and productive reform. From May to July, however, the official reports of the Commissioners of Naval Enquiry were published. These had been set in train before the invasion crisis and inevitably recommended tighter financial procedures and more careful auditing. The Whig press did not neglect these reports. On 17 June, *The Morning Post* covered the ensuing debate in the House in some detail, leaving readers with an overriding impression that abuses in the administration of the Navy were rife.

The Times, a comparatively recent addition to the dailies, had already become chief supporter of the government among Tory papers. It relayed military news that had already appeared in the official government *Gazette* and boosted public moral by seizing every opportunity to praise the bravery of British seamen, 'a subject of national wonder and gratitude'.[69] National crises of course enabled newspapers to enhance their reputation by careful positioning. When opposition journals accused ministers of 'playing the passions of fear' in order to discourage criticism, *The Times* was quick to deny that it had ever been party to this.[70] With insight, on 24 October, it also complained that the Navy was an easy target for attack by the opposition:

> There is a certain miserable, pettifogging spirit, that is always on the alert to employ any misrepresentation, or to seize on any circumstance that may form ingredients for the abuse of the present Government; and as the naval service is more various in its operations, and more removed from observation, than any other department of the State, it may consequently be attacked with less risk of immediate detection. These puny advocates now insist that the apprehension of invasion necessarily proceeds from a want of confidence in the Board of the Admiralty; because, if that Board employed the power it possesses, with skill, knowledge, and activity, invasion would be impracticable. (p. 2)

The Times insisted that Britain's naval force had never been stationed or arranged with more effective judgement. Indeed, it claimed that critics of the government knew that orders had already been issued concerning the stations of the squadrons due to watch the enemy coast during the approaching winter. On 17 November, *The Times* again leapt to the defence of the Administration, rebutting a morning paper of the previous day that had asked, 'Do the Admiralty ever mean to build Sloops of war and Cutters to protect our Convoys?'. *The Times* argued that the confidence at Lloyd's and the general rate of insurance under the present government offered the best answer to that question. Whether *The Times* obtained this line of defence directly from Markham or whether Markham took his cue from *The Times* is hard to tell. Certainly Cobbett's *Weekly Political Register* scorned Markham for using the same argument when he defended Admiralty policy in the following March against accusations of incompetence and corruption.[71] But now that Napoleon was pursuing an imperial policy, and war with France could no longer be laid at the door of radical revolutionaries, anti-Gallic criticism was once more used to target Britain's own upper classes and an apparently self-serving establishment, as it had been earlier in the eighteenth century.

All through the winter of 1803–04, newspapers of all political persuasions responded to public fears of imminent invasion by reporting all news relating to Admiral Cornwallis's blockade of Brest. Two adjectives were invariably used to describe Cornwallis: 'gallant' and 'persevering'. On 3 January, *The Morning Post* paid tribute to 'the gallant Admiral' claiming that he had won the lasting gratitude of the nation and that a splendid victory could not have more effectively demonstrated the superiority of the Navy than his arduous resistance against the elements. *The Times* assuaged fears about the loyalty of the Navy by intimating that the ability of Cornwallis to weather ferocious storms in the Channel not only testified to his expert seamanship but also to the perfect discipline of his crews. Predictably it also paid tribute to the efficiency of the Admiralty, who, it argued, must be keeping the fleet in good order or ships would not have withstood the tempestuous weather.[72] Any movement of Cornwallis away from his station near Brest was reported with concern, and whenever he was forced into port by bad weather, the time his ships took to repair was also newsworthy. By mid-January, Cobbett told his readers: 'It is confidently reported that ministers are now meditating a grand attack upon the French armaments in Boulogne, which it is supposed cannot be effected without the loss of fifteen hundred or two thousand seamen.'[73] Since this item contains both positive and negative aspects, neither of which is elaborated, its effect on readers is beyond calculation. Yet since we can assume that they would have considered both the ability of government to organize such an attack and the necessity for so many seamen to be sacrificed, the total effect must have been unsettling.

Given the consistent and repeated praise of Cornwallis, the attack on the government's blockade policy in *The True Briton* at the beginning of February 1804 marked a turning point. Months of bad weather and the consequent damage to the fleet, led observers to doubt the wisdom of maintaining the blockade against France. 'We put ourselves to a great expence [*sic*] on a

Service, dangerous in some degree, and the most irksome of all others to our gallant tars, while the Enemy remain in safety, and are comparatively sustaining no expence whatever'. *The True Briton* considered that the French would never come out of port to fight unless greatly superior in numbers and that 'we should, for a time at least, give up the blockading system – we should invite the Enemy to Sea'.[74] The power of newspaper coverage of naval operations was suddenly very apparent. On 11 February, in his *Weekly Political Register*, Cobbett reported:

> The *Press* is of so much importance, its influence is so powerful, in almost every department of public affairs, that, however low, insignificant, and worthless are the persons, in whose hands any portion of it may happen to be, it is itself never an object to be disregarded; especially when its efforts are made in the form of a *newspaper*. (cols 193–4)

In the same issue, Cobbett joined *The True Briton* in condemning the government's blockading system:

> Great praise has been bestowed, and, perhaps, very justly bestowed, on the perseverance of the Admiral, who, amidst all the gales that we lately have had, has, with so little intermission, maintained his station off the harbour of Brest; but, it is in the opinion of those, most likely to be accurately informed upon the subject; and, it is said to be that of Admiral Cornwallis himself, that the system of blocking Brest, as it is now conducted, will shortly destroy a considerable portion of our navy. The ships are hurried out, half fitted and stored; in a state, in which British men of war would not formerly have been sent to sea. It is stated, upon authority, in which perfect reliance may be placed, that several of the ships, after the late gales, had scarcely a whole sail on board and, the consequence may be, the loss of one or more or all of them, in the event of their being overtaken with a gale, upon a lee shore. (col. 184)

Cobbett reported that some officers now thought that, instead of blockading Brest, it would be better to have a squadron always ready to pursue the French should they leave port. The blockade tied up 60 000 sailors and was a great waste of resources. Here he was reflecting the differing opinions of naval officers on the effectiveness of a close blockade – a debate which had been on-going since the Seven Years War. On 18 February, Cobbett followed this up, under the heading 'Lord St. Vincent and the Navy', by attacking all St Vincent's dockyard economies and painting a gloomy picture of the state of the Navy. A little later in the month, *The True Briton* made the government look ridiculous by reporting how one merchant shipbuilder had been fined £1000 for being late completing a frigate though he had proved that the cause had been government demands on his men to attend drills as volunteers. Similarly, the government had brought a complaint against a rigger who was able to claim that ships in the river had not been rigged because his men had been pressed for the Navy.[75] The discussion was continued in the correspondence columns of the *Political Register* even after 15 March when, at Pitt's instigation, the Commons debated the state of Britain's naval defence.

Pitt contended in this great debate that the Navy was less prepared for meeting the threat of invasion in 1804 than at earlier periods during the French Wars. In particular, there was a dearth of gunboats that would allow the Navy to attack the French force in Boulogne. He criticized St Vincent's reforming measures in the dockyards and in summary defended the practice of building warships in merchant yards in times of need, though many complained that they produced poor quality ships. The Treasurer of the Navy, George Tierney, an ex-Whig who had moderated his reformist views and joined Addington's government, intimated that Pitt was mad to question the strength of the Navy and worry the nation at large in a time of crisis. Naval MPs contributed to the debate: Admiral Berkeley, for example, supported Pitt, while Sir Edward Pellew backed the Admiralty and refused to accept any criticism of the Navy's ability to repel an enemy force. Pitt's motion was defeated by 201 votes to 130, but the government was irreparably weakened and convinced it should leave office. Newspapers reported the debate in great detail, often speech by speech like a form of theatre, particularly the Whig press and *The True Briton* (the most reactionary of Tory newspapers). Soon it was the subject of general conversation and people could sit in judgement on the issue. *The Times* loyally argued on 17 March that, although Pitt had warned of the inadequacy of country's defence and the approaching ruin of the British Navy, his evidence had been inconclusive and no charge had been proved. Similarly, on 12 April, when *The Times* reported on the numbers of ships and armed vessels in service, it claimed that the figures had been manipulated to make the government look worse and that an immense number of gunboats in different coastal ports had been omitted.

The issue of how the government depicted the Navy, and especially in relation to the French naval force, now became a matter of desperate importance. *The Morning Chronicle* of 17 March, for example, took exception to the Ministry's apparent overconfidence. Such unthinking bravado could be expected of bragging seamen and bombastic popular entertainment, but a more strategic approach might be expected of government:

> If any thing more than another alarms us respecting our present situation, it is this feeling by which Government seems to be animated … at the beginning of this war we knew that almost all naval men had a profound contempt for the French flotillas. By degrees that over-weening contempt has given way to more just and rational notions. It is natural enough for our seamen to despise any part of the enemy's naval force, and most of all the diminutive navies in Boulogne. It is natural also, for professional men, too, to contemn [sic] that which deviates from the ordinary standard of professional excellence, and

from the ordinary course of their experience. It is quite natural to hear sea jokes at the expence [*sic*] of the enemy's Musquito fleets ... . All this, to be sure, is mighty fine, and perhaps the scene might be displayed on the cistern at Drury-lane Theatre, to the infinite delight of the galleries ... . But will Ministers contend that there is no danger to be apprehended from the Musquito fleets at Boulogne? (p. 2)

The paper argued that the French invasion force was something to be feared and accused Addington's ministry of complacency, inactivity and corruption. Cobbett in his paper commented that many had compared the spirit of party and prejudice that showed itself on this occasion to the controversy that had surrounded Keppel.[76] Those who wrote pamphlets defending St Vincent against Pitt notably advertised their works in *The Morning Post*, hoping to reach Whig readers. The pamphlet war was short-lived but incisive. Political writers attacking St Vincent depicted the Navy as poorly-equipped, thanks to the parsimony of the Admiralty, and demoralized by the long blockade (which was fatiguing and held no prospect of capturing rich prizes). Those who defended St Vincent dissuaded critics from making any reference to the effect the blockading system might have on the morale of seamen, fearing to induce the same mutinous behaviour that threatened national security in 1797.[77] But the fact that the Navy gained neither laurels nor riches through blockade meant that the government could be ridiculed and undermined for an expensive but ineffectual naval strategy. Pitt had shrewdly opened his naval defence debate by agreeing with Wilberforce that 'the naval defence of the land is our national passion, in which we indulge all the excesses of instinctive pride'.[78] If that pride were given little to sustain it, discontent soon followed. By May, Pitt was back in power and newspapers had again demonstrated their capacity to dominate public debate.

The pressure was on the new administration to display a contrasting incisiveness, and any scheme to destroy the enemy flotilla in Boulogne was considered. In October 1804 a project was formed to destroy it under its own batteries by means of new-fangled 'catamarans' containing explosives. These 21 foot-long twin hulls were lead-lined and carried about 40 barrels of gunpowder each, to be detonated by a clockwork timer. The catamarans had to be towed into position and were then allowed to drift against enemy shipping. Five were used in the attack, together with conventional fireships. The first reports of the attack in the British press hugely exaggerated its success. On 5 October, *The Times* reported 'dreadful havoc' among the French fleet and about 40 enemy ships destroyed. By 8 October, the paper was quoting the 'official' account given in the government *Gazette*, which referred to the attack as an 'experiment', and switched tactics to complain that if the strength and ardour of the Navy were frittered away in such inglorious combats, discipline would be harder to maintain. Subsequently, on 11 October,

The Times tried to regain its authoritative voice and claimed to have been attacked by opposition papers for daring to report the truth of the event. Actually, *The Morning Chronicle* was quicker to note that preliminary reports of the attack had overestimated its success. It too worried about the deleterious effect of the project on the mind of the British sailor and poured scorn on the ministry's attempts to claim the attack as a perfectly successful 'experiment'.[79] The government now used every opportunity to associate itself with naval success and in this way to control the political and cultural meanings of the service. Ministerial newspapers publicized the monuments that were being built to naval heroes who had disinterestedly served their country and fallen in recent victories. Similar publications which helped to put the government in a good light included descriptions of the public monuments to naval heroes being prepared for St Paul's or Westminster Abbey, which had been voted by Parliament since the time of the earlier invasion crisis in 1798.[80] As 1804 came to an end, the repeated threat of invasion began to lose its power. The expected disaster never came: the French fleet failed to gain control of the Channel and make it safe for the troop-carriers. In disgust, Napoleon broke up his camp at Boulogne and marched eastwards to smash the latest hostile coalition – this time of Britain and Russia, formed to liberate the North German states.

For the remainder of the war, politicians continued to shape the public profile of the Navy to bolster the war effort, instil a sense of what it meant to be British and reassure the nation that successive administrations had the situation under control. The speeches of Members of Parliament on important issues concerned with the Navy continued to be published. For example, Lord Viscount Melville's speeches, made towards the end of his life, on the scarcity of naval timber and the need to establish armed troop ships were printed and sold. Priced 2s and 2s 6d, they were intended chiefly for a discriminating audience but helped to win support for his arguments and raised the profile of the author and his party. After Trafalgar in 1805 and with the onset of the Peninsular Campaign, the efforts of the army gradually became of more pressing public concern. But the political writing of the previous half-century had done much to associate the Navy inextricably with ideals of Britishness and Britain's place in the world. A succession of high-profile controversies concerning the Navy and naval figures established cultural images, discourses and a representative symbolism surrounding the officers, seamen and the service itself. This cultural representation was shaped at various levels, and this process as well as the outcomes of particular controversy gave the public a sense that their opinions carried weight in this arena and did much to help politicize the nation.

Notes

1   For example, *GM*, 38 (1768), 74.
2   N.A.M. Rodger, *The Wooden World: An Anatomy of the Georgian Navy* (London, 1986), p. 134.
3   Sir L. Namier and J. Brooke, *The History of Parliament. The House of Commons 1754–1790*, 3 vols (London, 1964), vol. I, pp. 143–5.
4   R.G. Thorne, *The History of Parliament. The House of Commons 1790–1820*, 5 vols (London, 1986), vol. I, pp. 313–14.
5   K. Wilson, 'Empire, Trade and Popular Politics in Mid-Hanoverian Britain: the Case of Admiral Vernon', *Past and Present*, 121 (1988), pp. 74–109; pp. 88–9.
6   J. Brewer, *Party Ideology and Popular Polities at the Accession of George III* (Cambridge, 1976), pp. 62, 76.
7   Ibid., p. 7.
8   H. Barker, *Newspapers, Politics and English Society, 1895–1855* (Harlow, Essex, 2000), pp. 32, 47.
9   J. Brewer, 'Commercialization and Politics', in McKendrick et al., eds, *The Birth of a Consumer Society: The Commercialization of Eighteenth-Century England* (London, 1982), pp. 197–262.
10   D. Donald, *the Age of Caricature. Satirical Prints in the Reign of George III* (New Haven, CT, and London, 1996), p. 19.
11   Quoted by J. Brewer, *Party Ideology and Popular Politics*, p. 156.
12   Cf. *More Birds for the Tower, or who'll Confess First* (London, [1756?])
13   *The Sham Fight: or, Political Humbug. A State Farce, in Two Acts*, 2nd edn (London, 1756), p. 23. Similarly, a ballad on Byng's execution, *The Sorrowful Lamentation and last Farewell to the World, of Admiral Byng* (1757), declares that he brought odium on himself, his family and the country but does not say that he disgraced the Navy.
14   *The Citizen*, 21 September 1756 in *A Collection of Several Pamphlets, very little known … relative to the Case of Admiral Byng* (London, 1756), p. 42.
15   *The Trial of Vice-Admiral Byng, at a Court-Martial, held on Board his Majesty's Ship the* St. George *… Taken down in Short-Hand* (London, 1757), p. 34.
16   *Admiral Byng's Defence, as presented by him to the Court, on board his Majesty's Ship* St George, *January 18, 1757*, p. 1.
17   'On a modern Character, and recent Transaction', *London Magazine*, 25 (1756), p. 446.
18   *GM*, 26 (1756), 373; and 27 (1757), 202.
19   *Some Further Particulars in Relation to the Case of Admiral Byng* (London, 1756), p. 70.
20   *The Wisdom of Plutus* (London, 1757), p. 11.
21   *Three Letters relating to the Navy, Gibraltar, and Port Mahon* (London, 1757), pp. 3, 4.
22   Cf. *An Appeal to the People: Containing the Genuine and Entire Letter of Admiral Byng to the Secr[etary] of the Ad[miralt]y* (London, 1756), p. 40.
23   See *The Block and Yard Arm. A New Ballad, on the Loss of Minorca, and the Danger to Our American Rights and Possessions. To the Tune of Whose E'r Been at Baldcock* (London?, 1756).
24   *Some remarks on the late Conduct of our Fleet in the Mediterranean. In a letter to a Member of Parliament. By an Englishman* (London, 1756), pp. 39–40.
25   *Impartial Reflections on the Case of Mr Byng, as stated on an appeal to the people, etc and a letter to a member of parliament, etc* (London, 1756), p. 45.
26   *The Voice of the People: A Collection of Addresses to His Majesty and Instructions to Members of Parliament by their Constituents upon the Unsuccessful management of the Present War both at Land and Sea* (London, 1756), p. vii.

27 *The Conduct of the Ministry impartially Examined. In a Letter to the Merchants of London*, 2nd edn (London, 1756), p. 3.

28 E. Ives, *A Voyage from England to India in the Year MDCCLIV and an Historical Narrative of the Operations of the Squadron and Army in India under the command of Vice-Admiral Watson and Colonel Clive* (London, 1773), p. 177.

29 *GM*, 28 (1758), 249.

30 See *GM*, 45 (1775), 4, for a report of the naval debate of December 1774.

31 Quoted by N.R. Stout, *The Royal Navy in America, 1760–1775* (Annapolis, MD, 1973), p. v.

32 W. Mason, *Ode to the Naval Officers of Great Britain, written immediately after the trial of Admiral Keppel, February the Eleventh, 1779* (London, 1779).

33 *The Proceedings at Large of the Court-Martial, on the trial of the Honourable Augustus Keppel …* (London, 1779), p. 123.

34 *An Address to the Hon. Admiral Augustus Keppel … . By a Seaman* (London, 1779), pp. 74 – 5. Cf. *A Letter to the right Honourable The Earl of Sandwich, on the Present State of Affairs. By a Sailor* (London, 1779).

35 *The Proceedings at Large*, p. 125.

36 See *GM*, 49 (1779), 18.

37 Ibid., 430.

38 *Letter from a Sea-Officer of France to the Honourable Admiral Keppel* (London, 1778), p. 31.

39 J. Sinclair, MP, *Thoughts on the Naval Strength of the British Empire* (London, 1782), p. 16.

40 *The Conduct of the Admirals Hawke, Keppel, and Palliser, Compared* (London, 1779), p. 8.

41 *A New Form of Worship for the 27th of July* (n.d.).

42 Anonymous etching, *Westminster Election 1780*. Published by P. Mitchell and J. Harris (1780), British Museum, London (BM 5699).

43 *An Address to the Landowners, Merchants, and other Principal Inhabitants of England, on the Expediency of entering into Subscriptions for augmenting the British Navy* (London, 1782), p. 4.

44 A. Tweedie, *The Naval Achievements of Admiral George Lord Brydges Rodney. To which is added thoughts on the conduct of the late minority, now the present Ministry of Great Britain* (Edinburgh, 1782), p. 3.

45 *Proofs that Great Britain was Successful against each of her Numerous Enemies before the Late Victory of Sir George Brydges Rodney* (London, 1782), p. 2.

46 J. Greig, ed., *The Farington Diary by Joseph Farington, R.A.*, 8 vols (London, 1922–28), vol. I, p. 63 (18 July 1794).

47 J. Thelwall. *An Appeal to Popular Opinion, Against Kidnapping & Murder, Including a Narrative of the Late Atrocious Proceedings, at Yarmouth, Second Edition, with a Postscript; containing a Particular Account of the Outrages at Lynn and Wisbeach* (London, 1796), pp. 6, 52. Quoted by E.V. Macleod, *A War of Ideas: British Attitudes to the Wars against Revolutionary France, 1792–1802* (Aldershot, 1998), p. 119.

48 J.G. Jones, *Sketch of a Political Tour* (London, 1796), pp. 57–8.

49 *Speech of Lord Grenville in the House of Peers, on the motion of the Duke of Bedford for the Dismissal of Ministers, Thursday, March 22, 1798* (London, 1798), pp. 10–11.

50 *An Appeal to the Head and Heart of every Man and Woman in Great Britain, respecting the threatened French invasion* (London, 1798), pp. 9, 13.

51 *Substance of an Address to a Parochial meeting held at Chiswick, in the County of Middlesex on Tuesday, the 20th Feb. 1798* (London, 1798), pp. 23, 24.

52 *The British Navy Triumphant! Being copies of the London Gazettes Extraordinary; containing the accounts of the Glorious Victories obtained through the blessing of Almighty God, over the French Fleet …* (London, 1798).

53 See G. Rose, *A Brief Examination into the Increase of the Revenue, Commerce, and Manufactures, of Great Britain from 1792 to 1799*, 2nd edn (London, 1799), pp. 44–53.

54 See D. Hancock, *Citizens of the World. London Merchants and the Integration of the British Atlantic Community, 1735–1785* (Cambridge, 1995), p. 238.

55 Rose, *A Brief Examination*, pp. 76–7.

56 See M. Czisnik, 'Nelson and the Nile: The Creation of Admiral Nelson's Public Image', in *The Mariner's Mirror* (February, 2002), pp. 41–60.

57 *Plan of National Improvement … to which are added … Bonaparte's grand project to conquer Great Britain and Ireland* (London, 1803), pp. 136–7.

58 Ibid., p. 142.

59 *The Annual Register* (London, 1803), p. 165.

60 *The Anti-Gallican; or Standard of British Loyalty, Religion and Liberty; including a Collection of the Principal Papers, Tracts, Speeches, Poems, and Songs, that have been published on the Threatened Invasion; together with many original pieces on the same subject* (London, 1804), p. 26.

61 G. Russell, *The Theatres of War. Performance, Politics, and Society, 1793–1815* (Oxford, 1995), p. 146; *The Anti-Gallican*, pp. 8, 16, 165.

62 K. Wilson, 'Imperialism and the Politics of Identity', in A. Bermingham and J. Brewer, eds, *The Consumption of Culture 1600–1800. Image, Object, Text* (London and New York, 1995), p. 240.

63 *The Morning Chronicle*, 25 January 1803, p. 2.

64 *The Morning Post*, 12 March 1803, p. 4.

65 Ibid., 2 March 1803, p. 2.

66 Ibid., 9 April 1803, p. 3.

67 *The Morning Chronicle*, 4 April 1803, p. 3.

68 Ibid., 5 May 1803, p. 2.

69 *The Times*, 10 October 1803, p. 2.

70 Ibid., 15 October 1803, p. 2.

71 *Cobbett's Weekly Political Register*, 17 March 1804, col. 391.

72 *The Times*, 24 December 1803, p. 2.

73 *Cobbett's Weekly Political Register*, 14 January 1804, col. 64.

74 *The True Briton*, 1 February 1804, p. 2.

75 Ibid., 29 February 1804, p. 2.

76 *Cobbett's Weekly Political Register*, 24 March 1804, cols 418–22.

77 See *A Brief Inquiry into the Present Condition of the Navy of Great Britain, and its Resources* (London, 1804) and *A Reply to a Pamphlet intituled 'A Brief Enquiry into the Present Condition of the Navy of Great Britain'* (London, 1804).

78 *The Times*, 16 March 1804, p. 4.

79 *The Morning Chronicle*, 8, 9; and 15 October 1804, p. 2.

80 *The Times*, 4 September 1804, p. 3; P. Hoare, *Academic Correspondence, 1803, containing … a description of the Public Monuments voted by the Parliament of Great Britain, to the Memory of Naval and Military Officers, since the Year 1798* (London, 1804).

Chapter 4

The Navy and Trade

The commercial and trading classes, broadly merchants and manufacturers, understood that the interests of trade were in general best served by peace. Though they did not always speak with one voice, they looked to the Navy to safeguard the vital shipping lanes on which their wealth depended, controlling piracy and upholding Britain's mastery at sea. At times mercantile pressure groups were more belligerent, demanding action against foreign nations who encroached on British trade, and at such times anti-government propaganda was remarkably successful in identifying mercantile demands with the national interest. This body of propaganda appealed to urban middling groups who had a stake in trade, not just to overseas merchants but also to wholesale and retail dealers at every level. For much of this period Britain was at war. In wartime certain types of merchant profited greatly from an expanding Navy – most obviously those who won government contracts to supply sea provisions, transport naval stores or carry mail between key ports. The support that the British merchant class and wider trading interest gave the Navy in both peace and war was therefore complex and variable, and publicly expressed in a range of media.

I

The distinction between merchant and manufacturer was not always clearly drawn, even at the end of the century.[1] A merchant was understood to be a wholesale trader who had dealings with foreign countries. Merchants might underwrite their ventures by investing in land, government securities, transport initiatives and industrial concerns. Speculators could not always be distinguished from bankers and merchants, and some merchants had manufacturing interests. The merchant class consistently improved its social position during the course of the eighteenth century. The economy as a whole was growing at a modest rate: between 1700 and 1770 the output of English industry consumed at home increased by 14 per cent and agricultural output by 17 per cent. In the same period, though, the output of English industry exported to foreign and colonial markets rose dramatically by 156 per cent.[2] Contemporaries registered the phenomenal growth in the export sector of the economy and appreciated its significance for national prosperity. From the mid-century, the British public was intensely aware of the threat from France, and this influenced debate about the position of British commerce and the role of government in supporting it. In the aftermath of the inconclusive War of the Austrian Succession (1740–48), France was pursuing a policy of military revival, and Britain had no doubt that control of the seas was essential to protect trade and, ultimately, to preserve an independent Britain. From the 1750s, commerce and national interest came together in ways that promoted patriotic unity. Colonial trades in particular brought in valuable customs revenue and were an important factor in the financial system that enabled Britain to wage war. Merchants exploited this link to enhance their own social standing and to smooth the paths of business. In 1754, Jonas Hanway – traveller, Russian trader, pillar of the merchant community and pioneer of the umbrella – summed up the priorities of his class in a comment addressed to Anson as First Lord of the Admiralty: 'The splendour of this monarchy is supported by commerce, and commerce by naval strength.'[3] Hanway stressed the need for a powerful navy to counterbalance the growing strength of France and to compensate for the decline of Dutch naval power, which was less able to support British interests in Europe than formerly. Though there were conflicting opinions about the just deserts owed to wealthy merchants and their benefit to the community, by the 1790s it was possible for a contemporary to write that trade 'is in the highest reputation among the English who may be called, eminently, a trading nation'.[4]

A strong merchant marine was essential to the Navy since in wartime it was a source of manpower. The merchant Wyndham Beawes expressed a widely held belief in 1761 when he described the interdependence of trade and the Navy. It was the nation's 'fundamental Maxim', he thought, that 'Trade is the Nursery of Sailors, that Sailors are the Soul of the Navy, that the Navy is the Security of Commerce, and that these two united, produce the Riches, Power and Glory of *Great-Britain*'.[5] The easy logic of this argument insinuates that the interests of trade and the interests of society are one. Adam Smith, amongst other contemporaries, cast doubt on such reasoning and depicted the merchant class as ultimately self-serving but astute enough to persuade others to the contrary.[6] Certainly, the interdependence of trade and the Navy in some areas offered merchants opportunities to reiterate arguments publicizing the apparent coincidence of their own interests with those of the nation. Particular trades were looked upon as nurseries of British sailors and a source of naval strength. These included the coal trade from Newcastle to London, trade with the West Indies, and the British fisheries – particularly the deep-sea fisheries such as the Greenland whale fishery and the Newfoundland fishery.[7] Promotional events connected with these trades might involve admirals and prominent merchants taking the platform together. Speakers generally extolled not only the mercantile value of such undertakings but also the encouragement they would give to the Navy, and the social benefit they would have in occupying the idle poor. Such events were variously reported and helped to project an image of the Navy as inextricably linked to trade and charitable activity.[8]

It was well known that Newfoundland fishing vessels needed more hands than were simply necessary to navigate them. Masters and owners invariably sent servants and others to help work the boats, and it was argued that these landmen were at length trained up to the sea. Experienced Newfoundland fishermen, if pressed for the Navy, immediately made useful seamen and merchants exploited this in their negotiations with the government. In 1793 a committee was appointed to enquire into the state of trade in the Newfoundland fishery. The Chief Justice of Newfoundland testified that merchants from the West of England with an interest in the fishery maintained 'a high Language respecting their own Concerns, and the Merit they suppose they have in carrying on a British Fishery'. Despite such patriotic talk, the Chief Justice believed that it was chiefly self-interest that drove merchants to complain that the fishery was ruined at this time. Faced with competition, they wanted the government to secure for them the freedom to act as they pleased in the fishery for their own profit.[9] Similarly, when British merchants petitioned Parliament in 1792 for the exclusive right to supply the kingdom with sugar grown in the British sugar islands, they used statistics that would carry weight with those who regarded the merchant service as a prime resource for the Navy. Merchants claimed that the inhabitants of British West India 'annually purchase goods amounting to above £2 000 000 supplied out of the commerce of the British Empire; furnish commodities which annually pay more than £2 000 000 in British Taxes; employ a merchant navy which maintains 20 000 seamen and 250 000 tons of British Shipping'.[10] British sugar refiners, on the other hand, who wanted to import additional French sugar, turned the merchants' relationship with the Navy to their own advantage when arguing against a monopoly. They wanted to know how it was that the English sugar trade, which had more capital invested in it than ever before, firmer credit, and 'better naval Protection and Assistance' could be at a complete stand, or at best, just keeping pace with home consumption. Government, apparently, was supporting the interests of the sugar merchant at the expense of the public, and the refiners argued that such a monopoly was damaging.[11] Yet despite intermittent controversy, such arguments remained remarkably consistent throughout the second half of the eighteenth century. In 1805, the historian David MacPherson still claimed boldly that 'the best use of the Navy is to protect the commerce of the country out of which it sprung, and by which it is supported'.[12]

Merchants understandably always represented their own endeavours as vital to the national interest and publicly looked to the Navy, as an agent of government, for support. The Navigation Acts, enforced by the Navy after 1660, were of central importance. They were designed to give an advantage to English commerce and handicap its competitors by ensuring that colonial trade passed through England to the benefit of the economy and the revenues of the Crown. Merchants were keenly interested in how the Navy was regulated. For example, in 1761 the merchant Wyndham Beawes appended to his *Merchant's Directory* an abstract of the 1749 Act (22 George II Cap. 33) which had amalgamated all current laws relating to the Navy into the Navy's disciplinary code or Articles of War. These included items that a merchant would need to know, such as the instructions to officers and seamen appointed for convoy duty. Merchants were most successful in lands where their ships and goods had preferred or exclusive access. Armed naval support was necessary for certain trading ventures and communities of merchants were able to put pressure on government to assist them. Merchants could expect naval support for those areas of their operation that were understood to be in the national interest; for example, British warships were stationed off Newfoundland to police those waters under Admiralty law. Merchants also obtained support from the Navy during serious trade disputes. In the mid-eighteenth century, there was trouble between Dutch and British merchants in the slave forts on the Gold Coast: the Dutch imprisoned natives living under British protection and took some of the territory belonging to British forts. In 1751 Lord Howe arrived with a warship and a sloop under his command. This *'noble* and *gallant* commander', according to one merchant's account, behaved with the greatest justice and integrity. He examined all the original papers relating to the causes of the dispute, and only after this process did he demand that the Dutch General release the prisoners. The Dutch immediately complied.[13] Merchants also looked to the government, and ultimately to the Navy, to obtain redress for acts of piracy against British ships. For example, in 1749 cruisers from Algiers seized the *Prince Frederick* packet boat carrying not only the Lisbon mails but also goods and jewels worth £25 000 (the property of several London merchants). Augustus Keppel, in command of the Mediterranean Squadron, was sent by the government to demand restitution. The Algerines apologetically explained that the treasure had already been divided amongst many and was impossible to recover. They suggested a new treaty so that packets and express boats would not be targeted in future. Keppel proceeded to negotiate this treaty in the King's name with the Dey of Algiers. Many merchants remembered Keppel's prompt action in this instance and supported him in 1778 when he was court-martialled for allegedly failing to attack the French fleet with sufficient vigour. When Keppel was acquitted at court martial, Josiah Wedgwood famously wrote at once for a picture of the admiral that he could copy, regretting that he had not 'had it a month since, and advertis'd it for pictures, bracelets, rings, seals, &c'.[14]

Merchants were able to influence Parliament by obtaining and presenting memorials and petitions. If London merchants took the lead in procuring a petition to Parliament, other trading and manufacturing towns would follow, but the influence of British merchants tended to be effective on political issues only when supported by various ministries. Merchants representing the West Indian interest were particularly successful in getting their voice heard. Sugar was the most lucrative commercial enterprise in the eighteenth century and consequently a cause of political concern. Through carefully orchestrated petitioning and propaganda campaigns, these merchants procured a series of measures in their favour. For example, in the War of the American Independence, they put considerable pressure on government to increase the naval defence of Jamaica.[15] Successful merchants were numbered among members of parliament, and commercial interests were generally well represented there.[16] Rich individual merchants also advanced money to the government, an arrangement facilitated by the fact that in Britain the seat of government happened also to be a great mercantile city. They might remit government funds abroad so that armies could be paid and provisioned, and they performed other financial services for the state, including handling subscriptions to national debt flotations.[17] This increased the influence of some prominent merchants on government policy.

Those merchants who won government contracts for supplying the Navy or the army profited enormously. During the Seven Years War, for example, Wyndham Beawes noted the business opportunity: 'the Navy in Time of War takes yearly for Victualling from ten to twelve thousand Firkins of Butter, and about five or six hundred Tons of *Suffolk* cheese, though in Time of Peace the Consumption is not above one fourth of either'. It has been estimated that in no shorter period could a merchant make a greater amount of money than by executing government contracts in wartime.[18] But though it would benefit no merchant to denigrate the British Navy as an institution, merchants and businessmen were sometimes critical of the way government represented the Navy. When, in 1756, ministers tried to deflect criticism for the loss of Minorca by inflaming public resentment against Admiral Byng, the City of London published an address emphasizing that the parlous state of the Navy should be a greater cause of public anxiety than the alleged failures of one man. The City petitioned the King for a government inquiry, encouraged citizens to place large donations at the Navy's disposal, and instructed London MPs to enquire why Minorca, a possession 'of the utmost consequence to the commerce and naval strength of Great-Britain', had been protected by so small a squadron.[19]

In the eighteenth century, a political radicalism emerged in the City of London that could be fanned into stronger flames whenever there was a popular cause. If the Navy itself was divided, for example, the City might take sides too, as in the controversy surrounding Keppel's command of the fleet at the Battle of Ushant in 1778, an inconclusive action against the French rather than the outright victory the country had been hoping for. Sir Hugh

Palliser, Keppel's junior, had been unable to get the damaged ships in his division back into line, and was therefore partly responsible for the unsatisfactory conclusion of the battle. Though Keppel made no formal complaint at the time, he commented privately: the story got into the newspapers and was exploited by the Whig opposition. Keppel's friends suggested that the Earl of Sandwich, First Lord of the Admiralty, had been behind Palliser's actions with the aim of ruining Keppel's career. In the House of Commons, Keppel then turned his sights on Palliser, hinting at cowardice. Palliser felt he had to respond to this public slight on his honour and retaliated by accusing Keppel of misconduct and demanding a court martial. At this point, Palliser's action was generally condemned since his charges carried the death penalty and seemed far in excess of the circumstances of the affair, but there was no way he could back down. Both men were eventually court-martialled and acquitted; however, while Keppel's reputation temporarily benefited from the ordeal, Palliser's acquittal was tainted with censure and he was forced to resign his seat in the Commons. The episode aroused much popular feeling, not least because politics were involved: Keppel was a staunch member of the Rockingham Whigs and had refused to fight the American colonists until France came into the war; Palliser favoured the Tories. Keppel also had many friends in the City because of his politics and his earlier support of merchant interests. On his acquittal, the West-India planters and merchants planned a magnificent entertainment for him, and also presented him with a formal letter of thanks for his constant attention to the protection of their fleets.[20] On 12 February 1779, a resolution was passed at Guildhall to award Admiral Keppel the freedom of the City of London. The Lord Mayor and aldermen commissioned a presentation box made of oak covered with gold mosaic work, and publicized the event by distributing a pamphlet describing the box and enumerating Keppel's services to his country, and particularly to trade. These services included, in 1751, his demand for restitution from the Dey of Algiers whose ships had been preying on British merchant shipping; in 1755, his protection of trade in Virginia; and in 1778, his action off Ushant against the French. The terms in which the City of London honoured Keppel, in the immediate aftermath of his acquittal, acted as a public reminder of the Navy's key role as protector of British trade and the City's own role as critic, if not arbiter, of professional conduct in the Navy.

In 1780, less controversially, the Guildhall awarded Admiral Rodney the freedom of the City, presented in a gold box, for 'his late very gallant action against the Spaniards' after he relieved the siege of Gibraltar. The *Gentleman's Magazine* indicated the level of publicity this attracted, noting that when the City of London gave Rodney the freedom of city, a pointed epigram appeared in the newspapers:

Your wisdom, LONDON's *council*, far
Our highest praise exceeds;
In giving each illustrious tar
The very thing he needs.

For RODNEY, brave, but low in cash,
You *golden gifts* bespoke:
To KEPPEL, rich, but not so rash,
You gave *a heart of oak*.[21]

Clearly, the publicity surrounding such presentations raised the profile of the giver as well as the receiver and in this case, whatever the City intended, as the epigram suggests, the difference in presentation boxes led to subtler differentiation between the achievement of the two admirals. Later, Rodney's decisive victory at the Battle of the Saints in 1782 led to more pointed comparisons, as Keppel's unnecessarily vainglorious behaviour had already lost him support. After all, Keppel, who had been made a viscount and First Lord of the Admiralty in 1782, had been greatly honoured for what amounted to an unsatisfactory battle at Ushant while Rodney arguably deserved more than the baronetcy he received for his two decisive victories.

II

When war threatened, the competing pressures of politics and economics often produced a confused response from the merchant community. Though merchants might agitate for vigorous military action when foreign nations trespassed on British overseas trade, war could seriously disrupt a merchant's business. In wartime, freight and insurance rates for shipping rose – although increases in premiums need to be set against the inflated prices of imported commodities, which often compensated the merchant for his outlay. The wages of merchant seamen also rose and shipping crews were liable to be pressed for the Navy.[22] While the 'nursery of seamen' argument was useful to merchants in peacetime, its corollary in wartime – namely the re-allocation of men from the merchant marine to the Navy – soon jeopardized business interests and exasperated merchants. For example, in 1800 one merchant rebuffed a reassuring government pamphlet extolling the increase in trade even in wartime by complaining that this had been achieved at the expense of 'maritime tyranny'. He believed that the 80 000 British seamen compelled to serve in the Navy would be 'quite as morally, and much more advantageously, employed, when all the ports of Europe were open to our merchant ships, or in the Greenland, Newfoundland, or Pilchard Fisheries'.[23] In wartime, too, supplies of manufactured goods might be unreliable as the armed forces made increasing demands on available manpower. Merchant ships were at risk from the enemy's navy and privateers, while the need for merchant vessels to sail in convoy caused delays. Merchants themselves sometimes contributed to these delays by attempting to hold back the sailing of convoys when their own goods were not ready for shipment by the official date.[24] The convoy system itself might entail some loss in profit since markets could be glutted when ships all arrived in port at once. Certainly, in trades where it mattered, the convoy system offered less opportunity to obtain high prices by being among the first into port with the new season's crop. In wartime, merchants also worried that their ships might be requisitioned as troop carriers, in which case they would not only suffer a loss of earnings but also additional wear and tear on their vessels, kept at sea for longer than the usual period.

In wartime, during an unprotected press (when only those categories of merchant seamen protected by Act of Parliament were exempt from impressment into the Navy), merchant ships were liable to be left unmanned. At such times, merchants were strongly tempted to thwart the efforts of the government and do all they could to protect their seamen by concealing them or even sending them into the interior of the country. This was one of the many objections raised to the system of manning the Navy by impressment. The merchants' evasions were often public knowledge, so prominent men ran the risk of seeming unpatriotic in times of crisis even though public opinion was always ambivalent about manning the Navy by impressment (for, although perfectly legal and apparently unavoidable, it seemed to infringe civil liberties).[25] Merchants had certain other reservations about the contemporary system of naval recruitment. Fleets were never up to strength at the beginning of a war, so commerce was left unprotected and a prey to privateers for perhaps the first year of hostilities. Merchants missed business opportunities at that time, as they were not sure which routes were safest or how best to use their capital. Furthermore, they had to overpay their seamen as well as possibly bribe the naval press to leave them alone.[26] For all these reasons, in wartime it was in the interest of merchants to help the Navy solve its manning problem. During the War of American Independence, the Mayor of London declined to back the Admiralty's call for warrants to press seamen in the city. Instead, at a subsequent council meeting, it was agreed to vote a bounty of 40s to every able seaman and 20s to every ordinary seaman who volunteered for the Navy.[27] Other towns materially affected by the war eagerly offered bounties to seamen joining the Navy – In Hull, the corporation and Trinity House, composed of the town's leading merchants and gentlemen, consistently demonstrated their support for the war in this way. During the French Revolutionary War, and especially after Lord Howe's victory of the Glorious First of June 1794, the principal merchants and trading companies in London, redoubled their efforts in an attempt to bring the war quickly to an end. Aware of the national importance of the British Navy and the expense of prolonged conflict, they advanced considerable sums to the government in order to pay for naval equipment. They also set up funds for giving bounties as an encouragement to seamen and able-bodied landmen to enter the fleet so that the Navy might follow up Howe's victory. In one case, a fund of £10 000 was raised and many hoped that this would reduce the dependency of the fleet on impressment.[28] In 1795, the issue of naval recruitment became so critical that the government contacted the mayors of principal seaports, including Bristol and Hull, and asked them to consult with local merchants and shipowners to find the most effective ways of increasing the number of seamen. These initiatives were reported in the press, confirming the importance of the Navy to merchant interests. Certain shipowners tried to give Pitt money rather than men, but it was men that the government wanted.[29]

As indicated above, the chief means of defending trade in wartime was convoy protection. During the war with the American colonies, even transports to America had to sail in convoy. Generally, at the outbreak of hostilities, merchants lobbied the Admiralty to provide ships for convoy duty. This process was often reported in the local press, and when merchants received satisfactory assurances from the Admiralty, subsequent newspaper reports added to the status of the merchant class and won greater approval for the Navy. But though the government offered naval protection for convoys, at times there were insufficient escort vessels available. On these occasions, petitions on behalf of the merchant interest resulted in bad publicity for the Navy and the government. In 1776–77, for example, Glasgow shipping was almost unprotected by naval escort in the Clyde Estuary and Irish Sea, as was shipping around the islands of the West Indies. The Navy was overstretched, engaged first in transporting an army to North America and then provisioning the army once it was there. The unsuccessful petitions in 1777 of Glasgow Town Council and the Conventions of Royal Burghs for Admiralty assistance against 'the alarming depredations made by rebel privateers' brought no effective relief. The Admiralty explained that 'it would be impossible for their lordships to station a ship for the protection of each port, more especially while so great a part of the fleet is stationed in America and the Indies'.[30] This exchange was reported in the Scottish newspapers, as was a similar one in 1778, so agitation on behalf of Glasgow's trading interests only publicized the Navy's inadequacies and limited resources.[31] In the crisis period of June–July 1777, the merchants of Port Glasgow, Greenock and Glasgow agreed to subscribe £3000 to equip three armed ships. Again, this initiative was reported in the press: 'We hope soon to be able to protect our trade without the assistance of government, who it seems, cannot spare us any frigates at present.'[32] The publicity surrounding the muddled exploits of this force, and the reporting of various skirmishes between local armed merchantmen and enemy privateers, distracted local readers from the larger naval canvas. Time and again the Admiralty discovered that as merchants made it their business to investigate the condition and force of the Navy, so they were as ready to complain when their property was insufficiently protected as they were to help pay for that protection in the first place.

Losses of merchant shipping in wartime could be appallingly high. In 1780 *Lloyd's List* carried this terse paragraph:

> The Lieutenant of the Thetis, arrived this Day at the Admiralty with an Express, giving an Account that in the Lat. 36.40, Longit. 15W. of London, the East and West-India Fleets that sailed on 29th July, fell in with the combined Fleets of France and Spain, who captured the whole Fleet, except two of the West-Indiamen, and the Convoy.[33]

Losses of £1.5–2 million were involved in this instance (in excess of £75 million by today's values). There was an outcry against the Navy, but the small escort force employed would have been powerless against the enemy's combined fleet. Faced with such criticism, the Admiralty in turn complained that merchants often sent their ships to various parts of the world for an early market without waiting for protection. Valuable cargoes were captured and, even more important to the Admiralty, numbers of British seamen were incarcerated in enemy jails where they could be of no service to the Navy. To prevent this, and to raise additional revenue, a convoy tax was finally imposed in 1798. It was a small percentage on the value of goods exported and imported, with some exceptions, and a small tonnage duty on all ships arriving at or sailing from any port in Britain. The government praised merchants and manufacturers for the 'zeal and public spirit' with which they accepted this tax, for though in some cases it proved less than the cost of insurance saved by its operation, merchants had to make an advance of capital and suffered some inconvenience with regard to the shipping of goods.

The restrained way in which the shipping interest reported naval events in wartime helped to consolidate a respectable, dependable image. Characteristically, *Lloyd's List* (a twice-weekly publication of shipping movements produced by Lloyd's coffee house, headquarters of marine insurance in London), reported war news in the same brief, matter-of-fact way that it recorded the whereabouts of merchant shipping; even its report on Trafalgar ran only to 250 words. Its wartime reporting made no judgements and gave only those details relevant to shipping business. This professionalism added to the status of the mercantile and trading interests and conferred greater weight to their response when they did act on the events of war. Merchants and shipowners would have had a sympathetic understanding of many of the everyday problems faced by the Navy –

problems of navigation, manning and supply, which they also faced, although on a different scale. Merchants also had some understanding of the demands of conflict at sea, given the number of privateers sent from British ports to prey upon enemy commerce in wartime. This knowledge was not canvassed overtly or inserted into highly descriptive accounts of naval actions. Instead, it simply gave authority to their factual reports.

In wartime, merchants might seek alternative employment for their ships and compensate for loss of trade by arming their vessels for privateering, another instance of the interdependence of the two services. This happened particularly in London, Bristol and the ports along the English Channel.[34] During the Seven Years War merchants in Bristol lost so many of their trading vessels to French and Spanish privateers that in retaliation more Bristolians obtained letters of marque for their remaining ships than in any other eighteenth-century conflict. English privateers might even find themselves directly assisting the Navy. From 1759, the Navy tried to stop the American colonies continuing their trade with the French sugar islands in the Caribbean and thereby supplying the enemy. Though American vessels were by definition 'friendly', English privateers found them as profitable as French merchantmen, and in the last three years of the conflict reputedly seized 200 ships from Salem, Massachusetts, alone.[35] Merchants could earn substantial wealth in the form of prize money from the capture of enemy ships, though investment meanwhile was directed away from their longer-term trading interests.[36] On the other hand, in wartime merchants themselves might suffer from zealous naval officers seeking prize-money. In 1779 Lieutenant James Warden, commander of his Majesty's Cutter of War, the *Wells*, seized a Spanish ship with a cargo destined for a London merchant in part-payment of a debt. Although the ship was only a quarter of a mile from the Kent shore when she was taken as a prize, the merchant had to appeal to the high court of the Admiralty before he obtained redress.

Minor inconveniences aside, British commerce was clearly dependent on the Navy and it was in the merchants' interest to support it. The Society for the Encouragement of Arts, Manufactures and Commerce, established in 1754, included a number of prominent merchants. The activities of the Society were informed by a perception that other European countries were actively supporting their own commerce and manufactures, and by a desire not to be left behind. It had several council members and subscribers in common with the Marine Society, a charitable institution founded two years later which sent poor boys to sea. Several measures taken by the Society for the Encouragement of the Arts were directed towards the support of the Navy. For example, members tried to encourage the cultivation of hemp in England and Wales, and also in North America, so that it could be used for sailcloth and cordage in order to reduce the Navy's dependence on Russian hemp. (Even in 1808 merchants were still worried about this and suggesting that

Indian hemp could be used.[37]) Members offered prizes for innovations that would directly benefit the Navy, including 'the best and cheapest Composition which shall effectually secure Ships Bottoms from Worms', and 'the best Machine or Engine for extracting Water out of Ships' to reduce the time crews spent manning the pumps.[38] In 1792 a series of prizes was offered for planting oaks and for determining the best method of raising oaks for timber. These premiums were reported in the press and helped to create an aura of responsible citizenship around the merchant interest, at the same time indicating that the Navy was critically important and worthy of the consideration of the best technological brains in Britain.[39] Even when the Society published papers about agriculture, these often reflected an underlying concern about resources for the Navy. One correspondent suggested that vines should be grown in North America as 'Both wine and fruit are bulky, and would consequently employ many thousand tons of shipping annually: this would be another great advantage, as it would necessarily encrease [*sic*] the number of our seamen'.[40] Another indication of the mutual dependence of trade and the Navy is found in a guide to the East India trade by Robert Stevens, a merchant based in Bombay in the 1760s. The guide gives sample receipts that should be taken from naval officers in return for stores or repair work supplied to them in the East Indies. It also includes the form of a bill of exchange which could be drawn on the commissioners of the Sick and Hurt Board in London to defray the expenses of receiving sick or injured seamen from British warships in India.[41] (The Company was a lifeline for the Navy in the East, providing secure bases, stores and storehouses for naval equipment. Their yard at Bombay was the only British docks overseas at this time, and as this dockyard expanded, it provided the infrastructure the Navy needed to sustain operations in Indian waters.) In the 1780s, the East India Company actually funded Royal Navy warships, which were given 'Indian' names that advertised their generosity.[42]

Britain's Navy was expensive and imposed a heavy financial burden on the nation which was substantially funded by commerce. North America was the most important market for British exports in the later eighteenth century, particularly of domestic manufactures.[43] The perceived connection between trade and Britain's standing as a world power helped to complicate relations with the American colonies in the years preceding the War of American Independence. It also contributed to British fears as the war went badly. Since at least the time of the Seven Years War, Britons had linked pre-eminence in trade to the very preservation of Britain's constitutional liberty – certainly in celebrations of British sea power:

> It being the *British* Trade that chiefly supports and supplies the *British* Power, therefore *Britain* ought always to look upon every Encroachment upon her Trade, by a powerful Rival, as greatly dangerous, not only to her Laws and

Constitution, Liberty, and Property, but to her being a Kingdom.[44]

Nevertheless Adam Smith believed that the expense of the North American colonies far outweighed any advantages to Britain; and some merchants agreed with him.[45] A large, and therefore expensive, naval force was needed merely to guard the North American coasts and the West Indies from the smuggling of other nations. The military estimates for the British government's 1763 budget had been the largest in the nation's peacetime history. The Admiralty had bid for the largest navy the country had known in peacetime, and it included a North American Squadron of 26 ships and 3290 men – the largest component of the Navy after the Home Fleet. During the war with America, merchants with trading links to America found that they had conflicting interests: should they protect their trade with the colonies, or support the sovereignty of Parliament? The question was eased by the fact that some had already found alternative markets in Europe for their goods. Merchants were therefore by no means uniformly against war with the colonies, though there was much heated discussion as to whether they should support colonists or not. At Bristol, Newcastle upon Tyne, Colchester and Nottingham, the petitioners who opposed the government's American policy in 1775 have been identified as mostly shopkeepers and artisans, whereas the greatest number of coercive addressers were drawn from the ranks of the gentlemen and merchants. (The London merchants fully supported the government.) Of the identifiable addressers, one-third were merchants, though only a small fraction of these traded to North America. Many of the merchants were extremely wealthy and others were directors of moneyed companies who stood to profit by the war. On the other hand, 66 per cent of the pro-American petitioners were lesser wholesalers, retailers, and craftsmen.[46] Recent studies have confirmed that the division between those who supported the war and those who opposed it was largely related to social and economic status.[47] But we do know that the American war was extremely damaging to British trade in general, although some escaped its full effect.

West Indian merchants were particularly incensed by the smuggling of French sugar into Britain during the American war, as in previous wars. Ships in this illegal trade operated under pretended letters of marque and 'seized' cargoes of sugar, or they were provided with flags of truce and freely entered French ports in the West Indies – ostensibly only for the exchange of prisoners. Since the war was going badly for Britain, it was scarcely in the power of British cruisers to interrupt this collusive traffic, let alone suppress it.[48] Those with interests in the West Indies had long publicized the contribution the sugar islands made to Britain's economy and to the maintenance of her naval supremacy.[49] From the outset of the conflict with the colonies, West India planters had repeatedly called ministers' attention to the importance of their trade in the maintenance of Britain's Navy and the support of war;[50] they could be fiercely critical of the Navy if they felt that their security was being neglected. For example, merchants with interests in the Dutch island of St Eustatius were outraged by Admiral Rodney's performance in the Leeward Isles when, following his capture of the island, his fleet remained inactive while he contrived to auction off the possessions he had confiscated. The merchants suggested that Rodney's avarice and attention to personal fortune had compromised his defence of the national interest in those waters, and denounced his actions as 'disgraceful to the honor [*sic*] and humanity of the nation'.[51]

At the end of the eighteenth century, in the face of criticism from those opposed to the slave trade, West Indian merchants and planters reiterated the usefulness of the trade as a 'nursery for seamen', claiming that it employed about 25 000 seamen annually. The Liverpool African trade, in proportion to the number of hands it employed, was hailed as 'the most productive nursery for seamen that belongs to the commerce of this country'. In the same work, the discipline meted out to slave gangs on the plantations was justified by comparison to military discipline. The author argued that in any group there would always be delinquents in need of punishment and pointed to the floggings necessary to keep sailors and soldiers in order.[52] The representation of the Navy as dependent on floggings, the press-gang and turnover of crews without shore leave, even in a land of 'boasted liberty' was therefore used as a defence of slavery. As the abolitionist movement gained ground, the West Indian merchants made more of the contribution of their trade towards a strong navy. In 1807, after the latest coalition against Napoleon had failed, the merchants argued that the West Indian colonies supplied a great part of the Navy which guarded the country from invasion, and that their trade affected ports around the country, not just the metropolis, encouraging many to adopt a seafaring life. The intimate connection these merchants drew between British naval power and the state of the West Indian colonies encouraged them to demand that the Navy act to exclude rival enemy colonists from selling to foreign markets since they themselves could no longer maintain prices in an overstocked home market and needed access to this foreign trade.[53] Their self-interested manipulation of the relationship claimed between the West Indian trade and the state of the Navy was evident, but perhaps effective in some quarters: as the merchants and planters pointed out, if they did not prosper, a greater proportion of the cost of the war would fall on the landed classes.

One way in which merchants supported the Navy was to donate to naval charities. Not only did such charity indirectly support their own business, it made them appear patriotic and enhanced their status as wealthy, responsible members of society; most philanthropists needed to be seen as gentlemen. In 1756, London merchants set up the Marine Society. Jonas Hanway, a founding member, reasoned that as merchant service was 'the permanent nursery of seamen', Britain needed, if anything, a surplus of mariners or there would be insufficient in time of war. He argued that wealthy merchants and naval commanders were particularly obligated to place vagrant boys in schools where they might be strictly brought up and well instructed in good morals so that their behaviour overseas might be to the nation's credit.[54] In this way, merchants were positioned as benefactors and the Navy represented as a 'worthy cause' that had a tangential use in that it was a repository for the dregs of society. Merchants in the cities of Bristol, Liverpool and York followed London's example, not least perhaps because when seamen were pressed into naval service, merchants found their own ships short of men. These societies provided training and relief for the children – often orphans – of men in the merchant marine, as well as preparing vagrant boys for naval service. In times of crisis, as in the invasion scare of 1779, they might give sums of money to the Marine Society so that the charity could equip more boys for the sea. Hanway argued that there was no better way to show benevolence and a love of one's country at such times than by considering the welfare of seamen.[55]

Merchants supported Trinity House, a body set up to support shipping, whose responsibilities included the maintenance of coastal navigation aids. They also took an interest in charities dedicated to improving the health of seamen. In Liverpool, for example, where the dispensary was situated close to the docks, 60 per cent of the 360 subscribers in 1796 were merchants and shopkeepers. Bristol also supported a sailors' hospital near the docks in Hotwells which, although almost no records of its existence survive, was almost certainly set up by commercial or merchant interests.[56] Merchants turned the issue of preserving health in the Navy to their own advantage. Clearly there was a strategic danger for Britain if warship crews in hot climates were struck down by tropical diseases: insufficient men might be left to man the ships and bring them home. Merchants intent on expanding Britain's African trade were able to argue that sailors engaged in this traffic were the most useful for manning the Navy since they were inured to living on salt provisions in hot as well as cold climates. To prevent future catastrophes in wartime, merchants recommended that only 'seasoned' men who had already voyaged to the tropics should be pressed for expeditions to the East or West Indies, not men who had worked exclusively in the coasting trade and on short voyages. As there were no known cures for many tropical diseases, the merchants' arguments, though disingenuous, may have carried some weight.[57] Charitable support for the Navy increased towards the end of the century. Some merchants even thought that their class had a responsibility for caring for retired seamen. In 1801, the merchant John Broadley, noting the poverty and radical unrest caused by the long war against France, proposed that the commercial interest should at least look after the 'commercial poor', finding any work for them, however unprofitable, in preference to consigning them to the workhouse. He included the 'poor old weather-beaten Tar' as a 'legitimate child of commerce':

> He conducts and protects it, and when he can no longer go aloft, he shall chuse a birth [*sic*] where he likes ashore, shall have his full allowance as long as the ship will swim, and when the timbers give, still shall the colours fly, and his last breath shall cheer *Old England*.[58]

Subscribers to Lloyd's, an association of marine underwriters given a formal committee in 1771, had supported naval charities since 1782, when £6000 was raised for the widows and orphans of the men drowned in the *Royal George* after it capsized at Spithead. Subsequently after major battles, Lloyd's relieved widows and orphans of killed and wounded seamen. It was in the interest of those engaged in marine insurance that the seas should be safe for merchant shipping, but the charitable activities carried out by Lloyd's were by no means obligatory.

This charitable giving often resulted in the creation of artefacts for display, or at least gifts that were well publicized. For example, bodies representing commercial and manufacturing interests awarded presentation swords to naval officers for bravery or as a mark of respect. In the 1790s, another society representing commercial interests, the Committee for Encouraging the Capture of French Privateers, presented swords or silver plate to naval officers in order to encourage the protection of merchant shipping. After the Mutiny of the Nore, 1797, the Committee of Merchants of London awarded a pair of silver gilt and enamel hilted smallswords to Captain William Daniel and his son, Lieutenant W.H. Daniel. The Committee had been formed to thwart the designs of the mutinous seamen and Lieutenant Daniel, serving under his father who was Regulating Captain at Gravesend, managed to seize several mutineers as they were coming up to the Thames to attack Gravesend. In 1806, Vice-Admiral Duckworth was presented with a gold-hilted 200-guinea sword, together with the Freedom of the City of London, after he had completely defeated a French squadron off San Domingo. Such rewards generally commemorated gallant action against the odds and so perpetuated an image of the Navy as heroic and exciting. The reality of life for thousands of seamen engaged in convoy duty or blockading the French was probably very different.

In 1803, merchants, underwriters and other subscribers to Lloyd's agreed to set up the Patriotic Fund through which they could grant sums of money to soldiers and seamen wounded in action, bestow annuities upon the widows and dependants of officers and men who had been killed, and reward merit. The Fund soon became a national undertaking, operating through an established network of country members and local notables who activated

Figure 3 *Admiral Lord Nelson, KB and the Victory of the Nile.* Produced by Francis Lemuel Abbott (artist), Percy Roberts (artist and engraver) and George Riley (publisher), 25 March 1799.

the parishes, but recognized subscribers to Lloyd's were always actively involved in the new scheme, which continued throughout the war. The Fund was intended to strengthen national determination to win victory. It aimed to give 'every encouragement to our fellow subjects who may be in any way instrumental in repelling or annoying our implacable foe, and to prove to them that we are ready to drain both our purses and our veins in the great cause which imperiously calls on us to unite the duties of loyalty and patriotism with the strongest efforts of zealous exertion'.[59] This patriotic design was applauded in many circles and the Fund grew steadily as subscriptions came in. Yet there was opposition from those who felt that it usurped the function of the Crown, which alone should be the source of honour and reward. William Cobbett, for example, attacked the Fund in his *Weekly Political Register*, prompting a correspondent to defend it in *The Times* of 23 August 1803 as a striking monument to 'British spirit, British generosity, and British benevolence'.[60] By association, these values were linked in some measure to Lloyd's itself, as well as with the bravery of individual officers. Yet again, in March 1804, there were more fears of 'cronyism' when the Common Council of the City of London, without official information, proposed a vote of thanks both to Admiral Cornwallis for maintaining the blockade off Brest, and to other officers commanding in different stations in Europe. Critics of the government were suspicious of collusion. The feeling was that the merchant and trading interest had overstepped the mark and that, worse still, their actions seemed to lend unwarranted approval to the government's conduct of the war at sea.[61]

The Patriotic Fund's awards of merit to officers who distinguished themselves in the war took the form of money, a piece of plate or a sword (although, as demands on the Fund grew, the presentation of plate was stopped in 1809). There were four classes of swords: £30 swords, intended for mates and midshipmen; £50 swords, for lieutenants; £100 swords, for captains and flag officers; and Trafalgar swords (a variation of the £100 design) presented to captains who had been at the battle (see Plate 5a). The difference in the swords was in the decoration of the blade and scabbard, which was more elaborate with the increase in value. The design of these swords was further intended to encourage national unity and strengthen national resolve. Should anyone miss the point of the iconography, an explanation was pasted to the inside lid of the mahogany case in which the swords were presented.[62]

By 1809, merchant interests were becoming ever more anxious that the long war was proving detrimental both to trade and to seamen's enthusiasm for taking prizes. A correspondent to Rudolph Ackermann's magazine, the *Repository of Arts* (1809–28), suggested that seamen needed a 'generous *stimulus*' to rouse them to action if they were expected to put their life on the line. He asked, 'Would it not be wise, generous, and politic, in the great body of merchants to create a fund by subscription for this purpose, and to offer liberal premiums to the officers and crews of British armed vessels in general for the capture of privateers?'.[63] The letter essentially presents a businessman's view of the Navy. The writer acknowledges Britain's unparalleled supremacy at sea and gives full credit to sailors' love of their country but clearly believes that money makes the world go round and a seaman's pressing wants will make him the more zealous if there is hope of gaining extra money through his exertions.

As indicated earlier, awards were generally well publicized throughout the period. When the City of London honoured Rodney in 1781 after his victory at the Battle of the Saints, the event clearly drew a crowd and became a news item:

> Six aldermen and 12 commoners, preceded by the city-marshal, waited on Lord Rodney at his house in Hertford-street, who might be said to make his public entry into the city, being met by a body of sailors, who took out the horses, and drew the carriage in which his lordship rode, to the London Tavern, where an elegant entertainment was provided, at which were present many of his lordship's friends. In the evening many houses were illuminated.[64]

Raising or contributing to subscription funds was one of the most popular ways of showing support for the war effort. Various subscription funds were publicized in ways that celebrated naval heroes as well as drawing attention to the charity of prominent financiers or merchants. For example, in 1799 a print was produced by the artists Francis Lemuel Abbott and Percy Roberts to celebrate the victory of the Nile and draw attention to Lloyd's Nile Subscription Fund (see Figure 3). The stipple engraving includes a portrait of Nelson above an illustration of the battle. Below there is an elaborate inscription: 'This Portrait of Admiral Lord Nelson and View of The Situation of the English and French Fleets … are zealously Inscribed to J.J. Angerstein Esq. And the Gentlemen who have so humanely, strenuously, & successfully exerted themselves for the relief of the Widows and Orphans of those Seamen who bravely fell on the above occasion.' Angerstein was a prominent Lloyd's underwriter and adviser to Pitt, who chaired the committee that formed the Nile Subscription Fund.

Awards made by the Lloyd's Patriotic Fund were carefully publicized, raising morale and contributing to the war effort. On 26 August 1803, for example, *The Times* carried a report of a general meeting of the Fund at which it was decided to reward the officers and men of the *Loire* who had successfully cut out the French brig *Venteaux* from under the batteries of the Isle de Bas. The Fund itself kept full records of its meetings; which were printed and sold to the general public until 1811 when this was discontinued as an economy measure. Significantly, the printed reports were not a literal copy of the minutes of meetings but were revised for publication by a subcommittee set up for that purpose. The reports presented the Navy in the best light and suppressed unpalatable details. For instance, the report for 25 September 1804 records that Lieutenant Craig of the Royal Marines had been awarded £20 per annum for life following the loss of his arm at St Domingo when his musket burst. It makes no mention of the fact that the accident happened as Lieutenant Craig was trying to prevent six men from deserting to the French, though this fact is recorded in the minute book. In 1805, when one such report was printed, the *Gentleman's Magazine* extolled the respectable merchants and others who had raised such sums of money and noted that the reports described 'some of the most noble and extraordinary deeds of enterprize and valour', thereby increasing the market for them.[65]

III

Merchants had access to ready money and a network of contacts. They were well placed to initiate projects that aimed to commemorate wartime exploits and many such initiatives resulted in highly visible monuments that were capable of reaching different levels of society. Very few such monuments were set up without an ulterior motive. For example, the East India Company erected a marble statue in Westminster Abbey at a cost of £1000, to honour Admiral Watson after he died in Calcutta in 1757. The government had sent Watson to India in 1754 when there seemed to be a real risk that French forces under Dupleix would displace the English company and gain control of the country. The monument in the Abbey records how Watson took Gheriah in 1756, then freed Calcutta in January 1757 after the Nawab of Bengal had seized the British fort there and consigned prisoners to the so-called Black Hole. It also commends Watson for his victory at Chandernagore in March 1757 when the naval bombardment of the French fortress proved decisive. During the whole of the famous Two Hundred Days in which the British made themselves masters of Bengal, this engagement, won at appalling cost, was the only convincing battle. The monument to Watson helps to remind onlookers that the Navy played a vital role in securing India (although today it is Robert Clive who is more usually associated with this success). The inscription carefully points out that while Gehriah was conquered from the Indians, Chandernagore was taken from the French, thus implying that rival European powers would have taken advantage of the situation in India had not Britain acted as it did. The representation of Calcutta as a helpless woman elicits sympathy, adding a veneer of moral righteousness to the conquest as if the tragedy of the Black Hole (where women as well as men suffocated) partly justified Britain in seeking to control both territory and trade in India. The woman appears to be white and European, which rather suggests moral blindness. The statue was publicized in the London press and in the

Figure 4 *Statue to the Memory of Admiral Lord Nelson at Birmingham*, Gentleman's Magazine, *May 1812, facing page 417.*

Figure 5 *The Monument of Lord Nelson, Erected in Guildhall London.* Produced by J. & J. Cundee (publishers), 1813.

Gentleman's Magazine, and of course did honour to the East India Company as well as to Watson.[66]

In 1798, merchants were also predominant in the campaign to set up a naval monument at Portsdown, near Portsmouth. The site was chosen because it would be near 'the first seaport of Great Britain ... and, in a military view, the most important on the face of the globe (near the high-road to the capital of the British empire)'.[67] The monument was to commemorate victory against enemy fleets and to act as 'the sacred *palladium* of our laws, our religion, and our liberties, not to perish nor be overthrown but with the downfal [sic] of Great Britain itself'.[68] A contributor to the *Gentleman's Magazine* described a recent meeting at the Royal Exchange when merchants had agreed to back the project. He eulogized their generous donation in terms that indicated Britain's status as an imperial power, the role of trade in contributing to that status, and the patriotism of key members of the merchant community. Yet a less confident note infiltrates his description. The correspondent hoped that such patriotism would set an example to other levels of society and help to unify the country in a national effort, yet at the same time his metaphor alluded to the inertia that needed to be overcome:

> The whole assembly appeared to have been animated by that old English spirit, which has so often heretofore braved (and, I trust, will now again) the fury of an impending tempest, that threatens the nation with no less an evil than annihilation. The liberality of your Merchants was becoming the first City, the *emporium* of the world! It was manifested in every degree; and the only strife was, who should precede his neighbour in subscribing.
>
> Hence, from this illustrious example of patriotism, I anticipate the best effects; like an electric shock, it will run through every link of the national chain, and rouse the most inert matter into energy.[69]

The meeting ended with a call for 'the cheer for Old England'. The more formal use of 'Great-Britain and Ireland' and colloquial use of 'Old England' and 'old English spirit' in this description is evidence of the process of forging a national identity in the face of possible disaster. Support for the Navy, 'the wooden walls of Old England', provided a unifying theme and merchants are able to aspire to international status on the back of their patriotic support for the country's chief means of defence.

During the Napoleonic Wars, the East India Company erected another statue in Westminster Abbey to acknowledge the debt it owed the Navy. This time the statue was in honour of Captain Edward Cooke, commander of the *Sybille*, who in 1799 protected British trade in India by capturing a French frigate in the Bay of Bengal. (He later died of wounds.) After the death of Nelson in 1805, merchants were among the civic luminaries who acted as the driving force behind public sculptures in his honour. Public patronage of this kind was new; it had been extremely rare in the eighteenth century. Monuments to Nelson were erected by public subscription in Birmingham, Dublin, Edinburgh, Glasgow, Yarmouth and Liverpool.[70] In these instances, naval achievement was honoured as a stimulus to civic pride and as part of a conscious effort to enhance the appearance of local cities and towns. The local elite had much to gain from appearing to preside over a loyal populace, as this both increased their own opportunities for employment and helped them exert pressure on dissident forces in the community. The choice of statue was in the hands of local committees and the resulting works became symbols of civic achievement. For instance, the Liverpool monument to Nelson honoured the freemen of the city as well as the hero himself and merchants were key donors with The West Indies Association giving £500 to the project.[71] Contemporary prints of the monument are accompanied by full details of its dimensions, total cost, symbolic significance and the estimated weight of the bronze needed to make the whole (22 tons). While the design of such monuments generally conformed to popular patterns, occasionally local groups could influence the finished product. The wealthy Birmingham Quakers, who rejected all military triumphalism, initially refused to contribute to the cost and obtained a portrait statue of Nelson that was much simpler than the usual idealistic monument (see Figure 4). The Birmingham tribute by Sir Richard Westmacott was one of the first Nelson memorials to be erected, on 25 October 1809, and (in less elevated mode) spawned many brass doorstops of the same design as further local tributes to patriotic heroism.

In London, the City monument to Nelson in the Guildhall was raised entirely at the instigation of the Corporation of London. The process by which the design was chosen was influenced by economic considerations and political intrigue, which damaged the principle of open competition. An unknown sculptor, James Smith (1755–1815) was chosen on a technicality, although the more eminent J.C.F. Rossi had seemed assured of the commission. Afterwards, artists were reluctant to submit to a form of competition that could so publicly damage their reputation.[72] The monument in the Guildhall, when unveiled in 1810, proved to be disappointingly derivative in many of its features. The design, which had been approved by committee, naturally emphasized the City of London's role in honouring the hero and placed at the centre of the composition a figure representing the City recording the name of the hero on an obelisk. By extension, the reputation of the Corporation was enhanced by other symbols crowded into the design, including Britannia sitting on a lion and Neptune (see Figure 5).

It might be argued that wealthy merchants were the keener to be involved with monumental tributes to naval heroes because this allowed them to enjoy a measure of reflected glory while also deflecting potential criticism of the ostentatious tributes to members of their own class. For example, when it was proposed to raise a monument to Nelson in St Paul's, it was also suggested that in future the vaults should be a depository for illustrious men or men of artistic merit, not wealthy merchants 'overgrown Contractors, luxurious Nabobs, and pampered Creoles'.[73] It was a commonplace that the ostentation of funerary monuments was often in inverse proportion to the real merit of the deceased, and elaborate monuments often attracted ridicule or resentment.[74]

IV

The middle classes were at the forefront of some of the manifestations of rekindled patriotism from the 1750s that to some extent cut across political divisions.[75] Much of this patriotism was focused on the Navy and merchants were typical of their class in this respect. Patriotic display was good for business and not only reinforced existing social status but also signalled an individual's ambition to attain the higher social heights reserved for an elite. In their own homes, the merchant class displayed art as a means of demonstrating and even enhancing their social status. The possession of art works was a badge of gentility if these objects also conformed to standards of good taste. Successful merchants were important patrons of English artists and often included in their collections marine paintings that reminded them of their commercial interests.[76] They also bought paintings of naval scenes. East India Company Director, John Boyd, had a large art collection that included seascapes by French, Dutch and English artists. There were two paintings by Charles Brooking, for example, and others by Julius Caesar Ibbetson, George Morland, Dominic Serres (a French artist who had settled in London), Samuel Scott and Turner. John Boydell, a print publisher with an enormous foreign trade who became Lord Mayor of London in 1790, presented several of the paintings in his collection to the Corporation of the City of London for display in their Common Council Chamber. These included four views of the siege of Gibraltar by Richard Paton, a portrait of Lord Rodney and two views of Rodney's victory against the French at the Battle of the Saints in 1782. A pamphlet was printed 'for the benefit of the servants who show the pictures', which also gave Boydell the opportunity to expatiate on his expensive gift. He explained that he wished to encourage contemporary British artists by displaying their pictures to advantage, to demonstrate the respect he had for his colleagues and finally to give pleasure to himself and to the public. He hoped that people in the inferior stations of life would benefit from the moral subjects in some of the paintings. Wealthier viewers were able to buy engravings of some of the pictures. Engravings of Paton's siege of Gibraltar cost 10s 6d each. John Singleton Copley's depiction of the same siege, also described in the pamphlet and on display in the council chamber, was about to be engraved by subscription. It showed a detachment of British seamen risking their own lives to rescue defeated enemies from destruction and was advertised as providing a 'display of humanity that highly exalts the British character'. Flanking this picture on either side were portraits of Earl Howe and Admiral Barrington.[77] The author of the pamphlet concludes by hoping that this example will encourage similar works to be displayed in other public buildings. Patriotism is evidenced in two ways: the pictures themselves represent nationalistic themes and the display of such works was a conscious attempt to encourage British artists. Happily at this juncture such aims coincided with the wish to improve public buildings and provide some means to enlighten the poor.

Naval subjects were also popular in the British print market. Prints had come down in price since the early eighteenth century when only the privileged aristocracy had been able to afford them. Mezzotints achieved predominance in the years 1750–80 and mezzotint was considered the perfect medium for reproducing portrait paintings because of its wide tonal range.[78] The portrait mezzotint was a major product of this market and, emulating the aristocracy, the merchant class bought printed portraits of prominent individuals. But whereas aristocratic collectors had pasted prints into portfolios for the entertainment of friends, the merchant class predominantly regarded them as decorative objects and hung them on their walls. Military figures were engraved, as were politicians, actresses and famous beauties. The aspiring classes bought portrait prints out of curiosity to see what famous people looked like, but also to associate themselves with these prominent individuals by using the prints to decorate their home. Displaying martial prints was regarded as a form of patriotism and the nationalism and social ambition of the middle classes came to influence the British print market. Mezzotints of contemporary admirals including Keppel and Rodney were popular, but earlier commanders such as Anson and Blake were also produced, contributing to a sense of pride in Britain as a maritime nation. When, during the Napoleonic Wars, the British print market suffered from an embargo on exports to France, the sale of military prints at home remained buoyant and contributed to the contemporary glorification of naval and military heroes. Dozens of different mezzotints of Nelson were produced after 1798 when he won his great victory at the Nile, and other naval officers, for example Collingwood, were also popularized in this way. Mezzotint was comparatively expensive to reproduce (the plate was so delicate it could only be used for about 100 prints), so by the 1760s its demand had driven prices up until only the upper bourgeoisie could afford to be collectors. Around this time, however, the technique of stipple engraving began to make other prints more affordable – a stipple-engraved plate could produce more than 500 prints – and by the 1780s there was a rage for stipple-engraved 'fancy pictures'. The medium was perhaps more suited to decorative subjects than the male portrait but many stipple engravings of naval figures both past and present were produced. Cameo or medallion portraits of admirals and captains were also popular. For example, the victory of the First of June in 1794 was commemorated by a Bartolozzi print showing 34 such portraits.[79]

Many other key objects that took pride of place in the homes and offices of the aspiring middle classes recorded naval achievements either directly or indirectly. They are an indication of the market for goods with a naval connection and the consequent impact on the manufacturing trades. Globes, for example, which might serve to indicate international business interests, or at least the owner's breadth of mind, often showed the track of famous voyages such as the circumnavigations of Captain Cook. Also available for purchase were room screens, embellished with the work of Britain's foremost cartographers. These items of furniture kept out draughts yet also displayed global geography and emphasized the contemporary political and economic importance of Britain's overseas colonies.[80] Today, as museums vie with each other to complete ambitious digital-access projects, it is interesting to note that there is a demand for digitally-imaged charts printed out as wallpaper for the decoration of corporate rooms and board rooms. In the eighteenth century, charts and globes were of particular importance to international merchants and these objects were both the tool and public reflection of exploration, trade, colonization and sea power.

Other items that show the extent of manufacturing interest associated with naval success include longcase clocks, which were produced to commemorate specific heroes or just to indicate general support for the Navy. Their production dates from the 1770s when manufacturers in Birmingham began to produce dials made of sheet iron painted white. White dials became popular because they were cheaper to produce than brass dials and offered superior legibility in poorly lit rooms. The dials were decorated after the ground coating had been baked and afterwards the decoration was varnished. Manufacturers produced commemorative dials on a speculative basis and their agents toured the country selling them to clockmakers who incorporated them into cases. Thousands of commemorative clocks were produced in this way, although never by the most eminent clockmakers since those who served the highest levels of society adhered to traditional designs. But since the more elaborate commemorative clocks were not cheap, it can be assumed that they were popular with the *nouveaux riches* or middle classes who wished to proclaim their loyalty. One such clock bears the motto 'Success to Brave Rodney' over a rocking ship in the arch of the dial. It was made in *c*. 1782 and commemorates Rodney's victory against the French at the Battle of the Saints that year (see Plate 5b). Other surviving clocks celebrate Nelson's victory at Trafalgar. From the 1770s, clockmakers also produced pocket watches with dials that were decorated with warships and patriotic mottos such as 'Success to the British Navy'.

Other manufacturers were quick to exploit the patriotic support for the Navy. For example, Messers Morgan and Sanders, who specialized in portable military furniture as well as the domestic kind, produced a 'Trafalgar sideboard' that they advertised in a manner calculated to appeal to social climbers. The sideboards were 'as well calculated for small rooms as for the first nobleman's mansion, as they can be made from the smallest dimensions to the very largest size'. Purchasers were led to believe that it was not only patriotic to purchase the sideboard but that by doing so they were also emulating the aristocracy. Morgan and Sanders had enjoyed Nelson's patronage – indeed they were executing a considerable order for Nelson's home, Merton Place, when news of his death arrived. Since they had little hope of payment afterwards, they made the best of a bad job by using Nelson's name to drum up business posthumously, and as a mark of respect they gave their factory the name of Trafalgar House. An engraving of their premises in the Strand indicates that they also sold beds with a naval theme – these were draped with blue curtains decorated with a yellow anchor.[81] Manufacturers also produced window draperies commemorating Nelson (see Plate 6).

The long period of war from 1793 to 1815 subdued open faction in the Navy and presented less opportunity for merchants and the City to add their weight to popular interest in naval quarrels. By the early nineteenth century, a series of celebrated naval victories and the pressures of prolonged war had brought business interests and government even closer. Great naval victories were always celebrated by illuminations in the larger cities and on such occasions merchant interests could be highly visible as they demonstrated their support for the Navy. After the Battle of the Nile, for example, the celebrations at the house of the Hudson's Bay Company in Fenchurch Street were well reported. The patriotic fervour at this period encouraged wealthy 'foreigners' to claim British identity by ostentatious acts of patriotism. Benjamin Goldsmid, the Jewish financier, threw a 24-hour party with fireworks at his house in Goodman's Fields to celebrate Nelson's victory at the Nile. He also donated large sums to an orphanage for the children of sailors who had died in battle. A key indicator towards the end of our period is Ackermann's magazine, published in serial form from 1809. Its full title, the *Repository of Arts, Literature, Commerce, Manufactures, Fashions and Politics*, indicates its range, and it regularly included 20-page inserts of 'interesting intelligence' from the *London Gazette*. The letters and reports reprinted from this government paper gave even more publicity to naval successes and individual acts of bravery, often mentioning officers by name and subscribing to the strongly loyalist view of the war at sea. Ackermann owned large premises in the Strand, also called the 'Repository of Arts', where he offered his middle-class clientele works of art, ornamental objects, illustrated books and art materials. In key areas of commercial life, the Navy was good for business and, in notable cases, helped individual merchants to make personal fortunes. No wonder, then, that merchants and manufacturers took a keen interest in the activities of the Navy and proudly associated themselves with its successes.

Notes

1   See P.G.M. Dickson, *The Financial Revolution in England*, (London and New York, 1993), p. 495; A. Redford, *Manchester Merchants and Foreign Trade, 1794–1858* (Manchester, 1934), p. 17.
2   See J.M. Price, *Overseas Trade and Traders. Essays of Some Commercial, Financial and Political Challenges Facing British Atlantic Merchants, 1660–1775* (Aldershot, 1996), Essay I, p. 107; K. Morgan, *Bristol and the Atlantic Trade in the Eighteenth Century* (Cambridge, 1993), p. 2. D. Hancock, *Citizens of the World. London Merchants and the Integration of the British Atlantic Community, 1735–1785* (Cambridge, 1995), p. 28.
3   J. Hanway, *An Historical Account of the British Trade over the Caspian Sea*, 2 vols (London, 1754), vol. II, p. iv.
4   G.F.A. Wendeborn, *A View of England Towards the Close of the Eighteenth Century,* 2 vols (London, 1791), vol. I, p. 138.
5   W. Beawes, *Mercartoria Rediva: Or the Merchant's Directory. Being a Complete Guide to Men in Business* (London, 1761), p. 573.
6   A. Smith, *An Inquiry into the Nature and Causes of the wealth of* Nations, ed. R.H. Campbell and A.S. Skinner, 2 vols (Oxford, 1976), vol. I, pp. 266–7. Cf. Soame Jenyns, *Thoughts on the Causes and Consequences of the Present High Price of Provisions* (London, 1767), p. 19.
7   For example [George Heathcote], *A Letter to the Right Honourable The Lord Mayor; the Worshipful Aldermen, and Common-council; the Merchants, Citizens, and Inhabitants of the City of London* (London, 1762), pp. 27–8; the petition of merchants engaged in the Greenland Whale Fishery (BL, Add Ms, 38, 340), ff.189–91; representations regarding the Newfoundland Fishery (BL Add Ms 38, 396).
8   See *GM*, 22 (1752), 89, for an account of the General Court of British Fishery.
9   *Mr. Reeve's Evidence before a Committee of the House of Commons on the Trade of Newfoundland* (London, 1793), p. 85.
10 *The Legal Claim of the British Sugar-Colonies to enjoy an Exclusive right of supplying this Kingdom with sugars …* (London, 1792), p. 1.
11 Ibid., p. 3.
12 D. MacPherson, *Annals of Commerce*, 4 vols (London, 1805), vol. IV, p. 381.
13 *Considerations on the Present Peace, as far as it is relative to the Colonies and the African Trade* (London, 1763), p. 56.
14 N. McKendrick, 'Josiah Wedgewood and the Commercialization of the Potteries', in N. McKendrick, J. Brewer and J.H. Plumb, *The Birth of a Consumer Society: The Commercialization of Eighteenth-Century England* (London, 1982), p. 122.
15 *GM*, 50 (1780), 351.
16 [John Nickolls], *Remarks on the Advantages and Disadvantages of France and Great-Britain with Respect to Commerce and to other means of encreasing the Wealth and Power of the State* (London, 1754), pp. 104–5.
17 Price, *Overseas Trade and Traders*, vol. II, p. 282.
18 Beawes, *Mercatoria Rediva*, p. 567; Hancock, *Citizens of the World*, p. 238.
19 *The Voice of the People: A Collection of Addresses to His Majesty and Instructions to Members of Parliament by their Constituents upon the Unsuccessful Management of the Present War both at Land and Sea* (London, 1756), p. 5.

20 *GM* 49 (1779), 100, 156.
21 *GM*, 50 (1780), 149.
22 See Smith, *Wealth of Nations*, vol. I, pp. 132, 470.
23 *Short Strictures on a Brief Examination into the Increase of the Revenue, Commerce, &*
    Manufactures, of Great Britain, from 1792 to 1799. By a Merchant (London, 1800),
    p. 21.
24 Redford, *Manchester Merchants and Foreign Trade*, p. 27.
25 For example, *GM* 44 (1771), 43.
26 T. Trotter, *A Practicable Plan for Manning the Royal Navy and Preserving our Maritime*
    Ascendency without Impressment (Newcastle, 1819), p. 17.
27 See *GM*, 57 (1787), 930.
28 C. Fletcher, *The Naval Guardian*, 2nd edn, 2 vols (London, 1805), vol. II, p. 60.
29 See *The Times*, 22 January 1795, p. 3; 31 January 1795, p. 3; 12 February 1795, p. 2.
30 *Edinburgh Evening Courant*, 26 July 1777 (copy): Phillip Stephens, Secretary to the
    Admiralty, to the Magistrates and Council of Glasgow.
31 See T.M. Devine, *The Tobacco Lords. A Study of the Tobacco Merchants of Glasgow and*
    their Trading Activities c.1740–90 (Edinburgh, 1975), pp. 139–40.
32 Ibid., p. 142.
33 A. Cameron and R. Farndon, *Scenes from Sea and City. Lloyd's List 1734–1984*
    (Colchester, 1984), p. 36.
34 D.J. Starkey, 'War and the Market for Seafarers in Britain', in *Shipping and Trade,*
    1750–1950: Essays in International Maritime Economic History, ed. L.R. Fischer and
    H.W. Nordvik (Pontefract, 1990), p. 32.
35 N.R. Stout, *The Royal Navy in America, 1760–1775* (Annapolis, MD, 1973), p. 23.
36 Morgan, *Bristol and the Atlantic Trade*, pp. 21, 22.
37 *GM*, 78 (1808), 27–8.
38 *A List of the Society for the Encouragement of Arts, Manufactures and Commerce*
    (London, 1763), pp. 16, 24, 57, 60. Cf. Hancock, *Citizens of the World*, p. 35.
    Merchants petitioned successfully for a bounty on American hemp in November
    1763.
39 For example, *GM*, 27 (1757), 208; and 62 (1792), 338.
40 *Museum Rusticum et Commerciale: or Select Papers on Agriculture, Commerce, Arts*
    and Manufactures, 6 vols (London, 1764), vol. I, p. 67.
41 R. Stevens, *The Complete Guide to the East-India Trade, addressed to all commanders,*
    officers, factors, etc in the Honourable East-India Company's Service (London, 1766).
42 Two 74s, *Bombay Castle* and *Carnatic*, were ordered in 1780. See D. Lyon, *The Sailing*
    Navy List (London, 1993), pp. 70–71.
43 Price, *Overseas Trade and Traders*, vol. I, p. 109.
44 J. Robson, *The British Mars* (London, 1763), p. 71. Cf. J. Wilson, *Letter, Commercial*
    and Political, addressed to … William Pitt (London, 1793), p. 41.
45 Smith, *Wealth of Nations*, vol. II, book IV, chapter vi. See also, for example, *A Letter*
    from a Merchant in London to his Nephew in North America (London, 1766), p. 46.
46 J.E Bradley, *Religion, Revolution and English Radicalism. Nonconformity in Eighteenth-*
    Century Politics and Society (Cambridge, 1990), pp. 17, 372.
47 S. Conway, *The British Isles and the War of American Independence* (Oxford, 2000), p.
    138.
48 S. Estwick, *Considerations on the Present Decline of the Sugar-Trade* (London, 1782),
    p. 22.
49 For example, J. Grainger, *The Sugar Cane* (London, 1764), book IV, ll. 653ff.
50 For example, *The Substance of the Evidence on the Petition presented by the West-*
    India Planters and Merchants to the Hon. House of Commons (London, 1775), p. 12.
51 *A Speech, which was spoken in the House of the Assembly of St. Christopher … for*
    presenting an Address to His Majesty, relative to the Proceedings of Admiral Rodney

and General Vaughan at St. Eustatius (London, 1782), p. 43.

52 *An Appeal to the Candour and Justice of the People of England, in behalf of the West India Merchants and Planters* (London, 1792), pp. 27, 43, 79. Others argued that the trade was the graveyard of seamen: J. Ramsey, *Objections to the Abolition of the Slave Trade* (London, 1788), p. 60.

53 J. Lowe, *An Inquiry into the State of the British West Indies* (London, 1807), pp. xvi, 7–11; 132–4.

54 J. Hanway, *The Seaman's Faithful Companion: Containing Moral and Religious Advice to Seamen* (London, 1763), pp. xxvi, 1.

55 J. Hanway, *The Seaman's Christian Friend* (London, 1779), p. 183.

56 I.S.L. Louden, 'The Origins and Growth of the Dispensary Movement in England', *Bulletin of the History of Medicine*, 55 (1981), pp. 322–42. M.E. Fissell, *Patients, Power, and the Poor in Eighteenth-Century Bristol* (Cambridge, 1991), p. 118.

57 *Considerations on the Present Peace, as far as it is relative to the Colonies and the African Trade* (London, 1763), p. 7.

58 J. Broadley, *Pandora's Box, and the Evils of Britain* (London, 1801), p. 27.

59 *The Times*, 26 July 1803, p. 1, col. c. Cf. ibid., 28 July 1803, p. 2, col. c.

60 *The Times*, 23 August 1803, p. 2, col. a. Cf. ibid., 20 August 1803, p.2, col. b; and 3 October p. 2.

61 *The Morning Chronicle*, 27 March 1804, p. 3; *CWPR*, 7 April 1804, cols 489–94.

62 L. Verity, *Naval Weapons*, Maritime Collections Series (London, 1992), p. 22.

63 R. Ackermann, ed. *The Repository of Arts, Literature, Commerce, Manufactures, Fashions and Politics*, 14 vols (London, 1809–15), vol. III (1810), p. 154.

64 *GM*, 51 (1781), 549.

65 *GM*, 75 (1805), 946.

66 See *London Chronicle or Universal Evening Post*, No. 1012 (Sat. 1 June–Tues. 21 June 1763), p. 586; *GM*, 33 (1763), 312.

67 *GM*, 68 (1798), 27.

68 Ibid., 27.

69 Ibid., 100.

70 A monument to Nelson at Portsmouth was partly financed by subscriptions from the sailors of the Trafalgar fleet.

71 A. Yarrington, *The Commemoration of the Hero 1800–1864: Monuments to the British Victors of the Napoleonic Wars* (New York and London, 1988), p. 116.

72 Ibid., pp. 96 ff.

73 *GM*, 77 (1806), 1119–20.

74 D. Bindman and M. Baker, *Roubiliac and the Eighteenth-Century Monument: Sculpture as Theatre* (New Haven, CT, and London, 1995), p. 3.

75 L. Colley, *Britons: Forging the Nation, 1707–1837* (New Haven, CT, 1992), esp. pp. 86–7; K. Wilson, '"Empire of Virtue": The Imperial Project and Hanoverian Culture, c.1720–1785', in L. Stone, ed., *An Imperial State at War: Britain from 1689 to 1815* (London, 1993), pp. 128–64.

76 Hancock, *Citizens of the World*, pp. 354, 357.

77 *A Description of Several Pictures presented to the Corporation of the City of London, by John Boydell, Alderman …* (London, 1794), p. viii.

78 See J.A. Clarke, 'Collectors and Consumerism: The British Print Market 1750–1860', in *The Martial Face. The Military Portrait in Britain, 1760–1900* (Providence, RI, 1991).

79 NMM PAH5661.

80 See D. Reinhartz, 'Interior Geographies. Map Screens from the Age of Exploration, Expansion, and Trade', *Mercator's World*, 5 (Sept/Oct 2000), pp. 32–5.

81 See Ackermann, *The Repository of Arts*, vol. II (1809), pp. 122–3 and vol. III (1810), p. 244.

Chapter 5

The Navy and Religious Opinion

Clergymen of various denominations contributed to public debate on social, political and military issues, and so helped to shape public views of the Navy. Throughout this period, the clergy was one of the most numerous and important professions in Britain, and a major force in forming popular opinion. It was the only profession giving weekly oral communication to people at large. Many clergymen published their sermons to reach a wider audience, and, as far as can be judged, the printed sermon was the single most important literary form in this period.[1] The output of the clergy was huge – as well as sermons, they published innumerable catechisms, hymnals and homilies. Sermons in church could be fashionable social events – if a preacher with a reputation for oratory was scheduled to speak, no person of taste would care to miss his performance. This was an age, too, in which religion and politics were inseparable. The Church retained the notion of a 'just war' as a means by which God punished the wicked, and it generally supported the Navy and the use of military force in the cause of national security. Even in the American colonies, until the beginning of the War of American Independence, clergymen supported the Navy as Britain's prime defence and chief means of securing overseas dominions. Afterwards they changed their tune and spoke out against what had become an enemy fleet.[2] Anglicans and Nonconformists at home could differ subtly in their allusions to the Navy: at the beginning of the conflict with America, Protestant Dissenters were largely opposed to the use of force. The outbreak of fighting served to accentuate religious divisions in the country and fired the growing resentment of Dissenters at the Anglican Church's special relationship with the state. Similarly, during the French Revolutionary Wars, Dissenters found some sympathy with the radicals in France.

I

The public image of the Navy was influenced also by religious societies of the period that reflected a close relationship between Christian philanthropy and patriotism. These societies actively supported the Navy in ways that were both pragmatic and pious. For example, the Marine Society, set up by London merchants during the Seven Years War, recruited and equipped poor boys for the sea. As a charity, the Society appealed both to humanity and to self-interest. The Navy needed men, and clearly there were boys on the streets whose misery would otherwise expose them to the gallows or another untimely death. Through the agency of the Marine Society, between 1756 and 1815 nearly 31 000 boys were clothed and sent to sea. The Society for Promoting Christian Knowledge (SPCK), an Anglican mission agency founded in 1698, set up charity schools for poor children and many of the schoolboys were also sent to sea. Unlike the Marine Society, these charity schools were not intended specifically to help the Navy but the numbers they sent to sea were significant. For example, an appendix to the Society's annual sermon for 1794 records that, in the parishes of London and Westminster, 45 charity schools had sent 1370 boys to sea. The fact that this annual statistic was recorded as a separate item indicates the importance the charity attached to this aspect of their work, and suggests it was likely to win support from the alms-giving public. The Hanoverian kings all showed support for this Society and its work.

In the eighteenth century, the Anglican Church had a pervasive influence throughout politics, law and society. Yet after 1740 the Church became so blatantly partisan and reactionary that people turned towards Nonconformism in increasing numbers, although Dissenters were not necessarily radical in politics. The unreformed parliamentary system depended on the bishops in the House of Lords to support the aristocratic oligarchy that governed the property-based social and political order. Consequently, parsons who aimed to prosper in their careers were likely to court the prevailing political party. Once such clergymen acquired positions of influence, their allegiance to their patron was usually firm – especially if they looked for further preferment. 'No man can now be made a bishop for his learning and piety,' observed Dr Johnson in his discourse on the state of the nation on Good Friday, 1775, 'his only chance for promotion is his being connected with somebody who has parliamentary interest.'[3] In the House of Lords, the bishops sat together and voted together; in 1795, for example, every bishop but one voted for a continuance of the war against France. The House was a meeting place where bishops could discuss and determine concerted courses of action. If appropriate, their fixed opinion could then be disseminated to the rest of the clergy through established routes of communication.

Though Evangelicals were increasingly active after the 1740s, it should not be assumed that the more orthodox part of the Established Church was wholly lacking in pastoral zeal. Revisionists have countered the Victorian view of the eighteenth-century Church of England as worldly and lethargic.[4] In fact it responded energetically to calls for spiritual and moral renewal in the 1780s when the loss of the American colonies took its toll on national confidence. Then in the 1790s when a revolutionary spirit seemed to threaten the establishment, the Church fostered a surge of voluntary activity. It may have been an agent of social control but in an age when popular folk beliefs and Christian beliefs existed side by side, it continued to attract powerful loyalties even if these could not be explained in purely theological terms. Though by the early nineteenth century rapid industrialization meant that in some areas the old parochial system was at breaking point, for most of the eighteenth century the lives of the majority were informed by a religious world-view. The middle classes, for example, included in their domestic routines bible reading and household prayers. As in the previous century, to some extent 'the practice of piety was a play of power relationships, a theater for social drama, and a cultural mechanism for change and continuity'.[5] Yet people were sensitive to the religious interpretation that could be placed on many everyday events and were attuned to receive sermons from a variety of spiritual teachers who adopted this strategy.

Whereas field preaching by revivalists was intended chiefly to lead the unconverted to repentance and salvation, sermons within walls had more varied purposes. They might be commemorative or seasonal, intended to raise funds or to educate. Political education was imparted mainly through the pulpit, and the ecclesiastical organization of the Anglican Church, headed by the bishops and strengthened by the influence they held over the clergy, was the most effective means of party organization then available in the country.[6] The established church preached a prudent, practical religion, assuring congregations of the wisdom of moderation and piety in this world, and holding out the promise of rewards in the next to those who steadfastly adhered to its teaching in this one. It was a doctrine peculiarly suited to a period of commercial prosperity and the acquisition of wealth. Any attempt at church reform, a movement slowly gathering momentum in the second half of the century, was effectively quashed by the French Revolution. The Terror in France led to a period of repression in Britain out of fear that the lower classes might rashly imitate their French counterparts. Traditionalists viewed the Anglican Church as a bulwark against dangerous enthusiasm and levelling tendencies that seemed about to sweep the country.

The deep implication of the Church in both the politics and social life of the nation meant that clergymen were expected to direct public opinion about such national events as war, rebellion and epidemics. The prayer to be read at Sunday service would sometimes even be circulated by Government.[7] The importance of religion to foreign policy in particular can be seen from the continued use of religious symbolism surrounding military and naval victory and defeat. Public fasting and prayer was necessary to implore the blessing of God on his Majesty's arms. War was regarded as one of the ways in which God punished a wicked country, and if war threatened it was necessary for people in all walks of life to repent and live as Christians – otherwise God might refuse to go forth with the nation's armed forces.

National days of fasting and humiliation were announced in times of crisis, and days of public thanksgiving were held to celebrate victories. The sentiment expressed in *A Prayer for the Safety of Our Fleets*, issued in 1796 was true to this tradition. The prayer was 'for obtaining pardon of our sins and for averting those heavy judgements which our manifold provocations have most justly deserved', and it was used in a service of thanksgiving held in December 1797 for the naval victories of the war.[8] Though radicals in the 1790s ridiculed the idea of the rich fasting as a religious observance when the poor regularly did so out of necessity, this religious view was still widely accepted at the end of the period. Jane Austen, for example, writing during the war with America of 1812–14, revealed that her naval brother Henry thought that America would win, whereas she thought that Britain had a better claim to God's protection. 'I place my hope of better things on a claim to the protection of Heaven, as a Religious Nation, a Nation inspite of much Evil improving in Religion, which I cannot beleive [*sic*] the Americans possess.'[9]

In war it was understood that, if the cause were just, God's support could redress any inferiority in numbers or strength of arms. So when the American colonies rebelled in 1775, a Philadelphian minister reassured his congregation that their war with Britain was hardly sinful since the colonies were fighting in self-defence: God would support them. He recalled that during the Seven Years War the British had invoked the aid of heaven by fasting and prayer – but circumstances had changed:

> But now – when they are going to murder and butcher their own children in America, that have been so obedient, useful and affectionate – we do not hear that they ask counsel of God – but if they do not let us ask counsel and assistance from the God of heaven – he is on our side, we hope, and if God is on our side we need not fear what man can do unto us.[10]

Similarly, in 1783, on a day of public thanksgiving in America for newly-won independence, a New York chaplain celebrated America's 'marvellous deliverance', comparing Britain's forces to the heathen Egyptians and the Americans to God's people, the Israelites. He tacitly acknowledged the reputation of Britain's Navy by setting great store by its recent defeat. When the conflict started, he explained, the colonies found themselves opposed to Britain's '*one hundred* ships of war, and the force and discipline of *fifty-five thousand* veterans'. Then the colonists had no more reason to expect victory than the Israelites had, 'whose only weapons of defence were the instruments of their labour' but their final triumph was proof that '*the battle is not always to the strong*'.[11] The loss of the American colonies was a severe blow to British pride and for a time diminished the reputation of the Navy and the quality of its leadership.

Most clergymen were careful to point out that going to battle against enemies was not anti-Christian if the war was necessary to preserve liberty, property and life. In 1793, the Vicar of Wellsbourne in Warwickshire, J.H. Williams, did object to having to defend the war in a fast-day sermon but this was the view of the minority of Christians. More generally, after war had broken out, clergymen actively spurred men on to fight in what they would present as a defensive war entered into only after all other means of redress had failed. Many fast-day sermons in England, especially in 1797 and 1798, insisted that patriotism should determine the Christian to fight for his country. At this later date, some of the Church of England clergy not only urged men to join the militia but actually joined themselves and had to be reminded by their bishops about the nature of their priestly office which disqualified them from bearing arms.[12]

The threat of invasion made war at sea and the state of the Navy matters of central concern to successive British governments, and therefore to clergymen. The latter were quick to react to successive invasion scares, seeking both to calm fears and encourage volunteers into the forces. At such times of widespread anxiety, Britain's earlier success against the Spanish Armada, scattered by a 'providential wind', was often used as an example of how God would support the fleet of a virtuous people. For example, when invasion threatened in 1756, the Evangelist George Whitefield added his rhetorical powers to the weight of this argument as he celebrated Britain's army and Navy:

> Invincible as the *Spanish* Armada was supposed to be, and all-powerful as the Pope, under whose broad seal they acted, might boast he was in heaven or Hell, it is plain he had no Power over the Water. *For thou didst blow, O Lord, with thy wind, and the enemy was scattered.* – And is this God the same now as he was Yesterday? And will he not continue the same for ever? Of whom should the Inhabitants of *Great Britain* be afraid? – Blessed by God, if we look to second Causes, we have a glorious Fleet, brave Admirals, a well-disciplin'd Army, experienced Officers, and, if Occasion should require, Thousands and Thousands of hearty Volunteers.[13]

The hand of Providence was seen at work in the smallest detail of all such victories: in the winds that favoured one side over another, in the fine judgement of commanders who surely owed their sagacity to God, and in the very timing of successful manoeuvres. So in 1745, the subjugation of Cape Breton by New England forces covered by a squadron of British ships was attributed to divine intervention, and God was given the credit of securing to the English the cod-fishery in those parts.[14] In this way, preachers aimed to use the vagaries of war to strengthen faith in the workings of Providence. In some measure this conventional acknowledgement of God's power also seems to have been associated with the perceived need to maintain constitutional liberty in Britain, where there was widespread antipathy towards the idea of any resident military force, and the Establishment feared giving excess power to military men. After the Seven Years War, Jonas Hanway, founder of the Marine Society, thought that the mercies God had shown to the nation in the course of the war ought to be transmitted with pious care to children. He continued:

> Sailors and soldiers are the more interested, as having been actors in those scenes of blood, in which their own lives, as well as the freedom, laws and religion of their country, were exposed to the rage of enemies. It therefore seems as *politic* [my italics] as it is pious, to keep these men in mind of that providence which superintends all human affairs.[15]

With their distaste for superstition, the clergy also considered that, if seamen could be brought to depend on Providence, they would be less likely to believe in evil omens and other superstitions.

Clergymen seem to have become increasingly anxious to gain a proper respect for the workings of Providence. In a thanksgiving sermon for peace after the War of American Independence, the Archbishop of Canterbury complained that Providence was never mentioned in general conversation about public affairs, nor referred to in the hugely popular account of Anson's voyage round the world.[16] After Trafalgar, several clergymen while giving thanks for Nelson's great victory also warned people against arrogantly assuming this was owing to the superior knowledge and management of British naval officers. The Revd James Rouquet in Bristol made the point that 'the battle is the Lord's' and that prayer was the nation's armour. Perhaps to reassure a public that had placed such enormous faith in Nelson, he also stated that though the loss of Nelson was great, people were not to think that his death left the Navy incapable.[17] The sermon was priced at 6d a copy or 5s a box, and was clearly expected to attract a wide readership through distribution. The former naval chaplain and aggressive evangelical, Richard Marks, was more critical in his reflections on the battle of Trafalgar. Speaking from his own experience of the British Navy, he declared confidently that 'there are no men who more completely look to themselves for victory, and shut out the superintending providence of God from the event of a battle'. He believed that the nation itself had sunk into this kind of irreligion: 'So long as Lord Nelson was at sea, the fear of ten thousands was quelled, and England was supposed to be in safety under *his* protection.'[18] While Marks gave Nelson credit for his humanity, he criticised the Admiral's insatiable thirst for martial fame. He acknowledged that some men went to war primarily in defence of their country, but condemned others who delighted in war for its own sake and who welcomed it as a convenient road to wealth, preferment, and honour. In similar vein, the Quaker community in

The Naval Nurse, or Modern Commander.

From Mid: to Lieutenant, | By Brave Warren & such
Bluff quickly doth rise;— | Our Foes were Opprest,—
Then next gets Command | And not by Boy Captains
By the Aid of a Prize.— | Just wean'd from the Breast.

Invented & Engrav'd by R. Attwold.

Printed for Carington Bowles, Map & Printseller in St Pauls Church yard London.

43

Plate 1 *The Naval Nurse, or Modern Commander*, by R. Attwold (artist and engraver).

Plate 2 *Captain John Bentinck (1737–1775) and his son, William Bentinck (1764–1813)*, oil painting by Mason Chamberlin. Signed and dated 1775.

Plate 3 *How a Great Admiral with a Great fleet went a Great way, was lost a Great while, saw a Great sight – & then came home for a little water.* Published by S.W. Forres, 10 December 1793.

Plate 4 *A Correct View of the French Flat-Bottom Boats, intended to convey their Troops, for the Invasion of England, as seen afloat in Charante Bay in August 1803.* Published by J. Fairburn, 17 August 1803.

Plate 5a Lloyd's £50 Patriotic Fund Sword awarded to Lt Samuel Mallock, RM, for gallantry in 1805. Mallock led a boarding party that captured a fort and battery in Muros Bay, Spain, and on the same voyage his ship captured two French privateers.

Plate 5b   Longcase clock by John Chance of Chepstow *c.* 1782, commemorating Rodney's victory at the Battle of the Saints in the American War of Independence.

Plate 6 *To the Memory of Lord Nelson*. Plate 9 of *Window Draperies*. Produced by T. Shoalon (artist) and J. Badon (engraver), 6 Oct. 1806.

Plate 7 *The Sailor, and the Field Preacher*, by Thomas Rowlandson, 25 July 1805, Rudolph Ackermann (publisher).

Plate 8 *A Sailor at a Quakers Funeral*. George M. Woodward (artist), Isaac Cruikshank (engraver), Thomas Tegg (publisher).

Plate 9a Leeds earthenware bowl and teapot, *c.* 1780, featuring portraits of Admiral Augustus Keppel.

Plate 9b   Chelsea-Derby porcelain jug commemorating the Battle of the Saints, dated 1782.
The lip is modelled as the head of Admiral George Rodney.

Plate 10 *Visit of George III to Howe's Flagship, the Queen Charlotte, on 26 June 1794*, oil painting by Henry Perronet Briggs (1792–1844). Greenwich Hospital Collection.

Plate 11a Earthenware mugs and jugs commemorating Rodney and the Battle of the
Saints, *c.* 1782.

Plate 11b Painted ivory lockets, celebrating Nelson's victory at the Battle of the Nile
in 1798.

Plate 12 'Dresses à La Nile respectfully dedicated to the Fashion Mongers of the day', October 1798. Published by W. Holland.

Plate 13   *Midshipman Blockhead. The Progress of a Midshipman exemplified in the career of Master Blockhead in seven plates & Frontispiece. Plate 1: Fitting out.* Produced on 1 August 1835 by George Cruikshank (engraver), Thomas McLean (publisher).

Plate 14   *Jack Hove Down – With a Grog Blossom Fever*. Published 12 August 1811 by X.Y. and Thomas Tegg (publisher).

Plate 15 *Things as they have been. Things as they now are. Dedicated without permission to all whom it may concern or please by their obedt servt R. Bothsides.* Published by C. Dyer, 8 May 1815.

Plate 16   *The Battle of the Nile*, by George Cruikshank (engraver), 1 July 1825.

Birmingham was at first opposed to erecting a monument to Nelson in 1805. Quakers, a small but rich and influential group, opposed all glorification of war and their beliefs allowed them to support only humanitarian projects connected to the war. Ironically, in this instance their principles led them to put forward a scheme that, if carried out, would only have contributed to the image of Nelson as hero and martyr. Believing that a practical monument would be a more suitable tribute to Nelson 'the Christian and the man', they proposed a sailors' asylum with a portico forming a triumphal arch over a statue of Nelson. Inside there would be a dispensary for sick sailors and a room containing a wax figure of the hero where sailors could pay tribute and gain courage from his example. The hope was that Nelson would act as an inspiration for others and impress them with a sense of patriotic self-sacrifice and moral duty.[19]

While, of course, God was always to be viewed as the prime cause of victory, and mortal commanders mere agents, clergymen had nevertheless earlier helped to reinforce the reputation of victorious officers and had increased public adulation of them even while they warned against such excesses. In a thanksgiving sermon for the taking of Quebec in 1759, the pastor of the church in Hartford, New London, drew the attention of his congregation to the welcome destruction of French shipping by the British fleet, and continued:

> We are not to overlook [the success of] the *resolved* and *courageous* Admiral *Boscawen*, against their *Fleet*, commanded by Monsieur *de la Clue*, off Cape *Lagos*; nor that of the enterprising, the bold and determined Sir *Edward Hawke*, over the *Brest Squadron*.[20]

When the French threatened to invade Britain in 1798, the Revd T. Maurice published a patriotic poem addressed to the Prime Minister celebrating past naval victories and providing an exhaustive list of naval heroes from Drake onwards.[21] In 1803 he republished the poem to stir the war effort and raise public morale.

In contrast, it is worth noting that some clergy helped to set standards for behaviour expected of naval officers by helping to voice the widespread indignation following Admiral Byng's failure to relieve Minorca in 1756, viewing it as a disgrace to the English flag.[22] In the years after Byng's disgrace, both clergymen and religious societies helped to publicize the Navy as an institution with a long and honourable tradition that was intimately bound up with national identity. The frontispiece to Hanway's *The Seaman's Faithful Companion*, published in 1763, crystallizes various aspects of this theme, which are fully explained to the reader (see Figure 6). The image represents the glory of Britain and shows how this is due to the bravery of its military men. It depicts Britannia, crowned with laurels after the successes of the

Figure 6 Frontispiece to *The Seaman's Faithful Companion* by Jonas Hanway (London, 1763).

Seven Years War and sitting by the shore to indicate Britain's command at sea. She points to a triumphal arch on which the initials or names of great admirals and generals are carved. Her shield and spear rest against an oak to indicate that warships, made of oak, are the country's chief strength. The women and children in the image are there to make the point that those who forsake matrimony risk cutting off the supply of manpower to armies and navies. In the background are a poor ragged girl and boy, orphans whom the Marine Society has helped to earn their own living. Hanway appended to this volume of moral instruction 'An Historical Detail of the many glorious victories obtained by his Majesty's arms in the late war; and a list of the enemies ships taken'. In this, British victories during the Seven Years War are arranged chronologically, suggesting a culmination of glory, measured chiefly in naval terms since this is followed by a list of captured enemy ships.

II

The Anglican Church explained rationally that the Navy, under God, was the chief strength and defence of the nation, and the means of its wealth and commerce. It was, therefore, reasonable to try to improve the conduct of seamen as God might not choose to fight on the side of a fleet that was irreligious. Also the Navy's behaviour abroad could be a credit or a reproach to the nation and its Christian religion. This obvious point was made by Dr Josiah Woodward in *The Seaman's Monitor, or Advice to Sea-faring Men*, an influential work first published in 1700, distributed freely to the Navy, and reaching its twentieth edition by 1812. Jonas Hanway made the same point in his introduction to *The Seaman's Faithful Companion*.[23]

Clergymen helped to shape the public image of the ordinary seaman. In their sermons on maritime themes, they invariably noted that a seaman's life was in danger at almost every moment and that such men had more opportunity and indeed more cause to come to an early appreciation of the power of God. It was a common saying that 'they that will learn to Pray, let them go to Sea'.[24] Ironically, as Josiah Woodward and Jonas Hanway remarked, while a seaman's environment ought to impress him continually with the workings of God, those who followed the sea were notorious for cursing and swearing. They were even known to utter oaths at the height of a storm, when they might be sent to meet their Maker in the next minute. Naval officers were no exception. One preacher wondered how commanders could be '*precisely exact* in all the punctilloes of respectful Carriage and *Complaisance* to those of their *own Species*, and be so horribly *un-complaisant and un-polite* in their rude Treatment of *their Maker*' by swearing themselves and allowing their men to do the same.[25]

Of course, such sentiments take no account of the reality of life on board a warship of the period. The Revd Edward Mangin, who was briefly a naval chaplain on board the *Gloucester* in 1812, found his position totally untenable. He may well have been constitutionally unsuited to a naval life, but in any case soon pronounced that 'nothing can possibly be more unsuitably or more awkwardly situated that a clergyman in a ship of war'.[26] He explained how he was forced to witness and connive at acts that it was licentious of him to condone. He quickly realized that it was futile to caution seamen against swearing when the watch was slow to report for duty or the crew were struggling to control the ship in a storm. In port, he had to turn a blind eye to the prostitutes between decks, and at all times close his ears to foul language. A naval chaplain had no real power, he concluded; only the captain had the power to check vice on board. Yet clergymen at large, by urging commanders to hold regular prayers, strongly reinforced a message also coming from the medical profession, encouraging naval officers to take more care of their men's welfare. The clergy suggested that regular worship was a means of helping to enforce discipline onboard. Jonas Hanway endorsed this view in his dedication to *The Seaman's Faithful Companion*:

> How thoughtless or irreligious soever the conduct of our common Seamen may generally be, it is obvious to the candid and discerning world, that vigilance and zeal in their superiors, may reduce them to a state of obedience to God, as it certainly does, in a greater measure, to men.[27]

In the mid-eighteenth century, public worship was neglected at sea. A Commodore wrote to a young naval aspirant in 1752, 'You will see some little outward appearance of religion, and Sunday prayers; but the congregation is generally drove together by the boatswain, like sheep by the shepherd, who neither spares oaths or blows.'[28] Between the end of the War of the Spanish Succession and the beginning of the War of American Independence only about ten chaplains entered the Navy each year. Chaplains were appointed only to the larger ships and the Eucharist was not celebrated at sea because so few chaplains were in priests' orders. *Regulations and Instructions Relating to His Majesty's Service at Sea*, first published in 1731, required public prayers to be offered twice daily at sea according to the liturgy of the Church of England, and a sermon was to form part of divine service on Sundays. In the absence of a chaplain, it was the captain's duty to hold regular public prayers, at least on the Sabbath, and to encourage his men to attend. This seems to have been a rare occurrence until the revival of religious concern in the Navy from the 1780s, largely as a result of the work of Evangelicals. Much of what when on at sea was shielded from the public eye; yet the reputation of officers at home, including their moral reputation, was indirectly affected by the perceived loyalty of their crews and the ease with which they could attract volunteers. Hanway wrote: 'It were happy if more piety, and, I will add, humanity too, were exercised by some commanders at sea. We see how easily one officer collects a crew, and how difficult it is to another.'[29]

A curious work called *A Voyage Through Hell, by the Invincible Man of War, Capt. Single-Eye, Commander* (1770) satirizes both the superficiality of the religious observance on board some ships, and the susceptibility of crews to religious enthusiasm. Almost the first act of the captain on taking command is to nail a sheet to the mast setting out the principal beliefs in God's omnipotence, yet in fulsome and confusing terms. He orders the text to be read out to the crew twice daily, weather permitting, and insists that the men are to have ten minutes to reflect on its meaning afterwards. This exercise causes consternation amongst the crew and, as they begin to puzzle over religious issues, their close-knit community fractures. The teachings of the chaplain, Mr Truth-and-Daylight, seem to disturb the men not offer spiritual comfort. In the course of a disastrous voyage, peppered by storms and hurricanes, some crewmen noisily seek salvation as they face death. Ironically, just as land is in sight, the ship sinks with its dead while those who appear to be saved rise to heaven. The author declares in his preface that his aim is to reveal the hypocrisy and deceit that passes in the world for true religion. His particular target is far from clear, but the choice of a ship for his satire suggests both an awareness of its use as a symbol of the Church and an understanding that religious instruction at sea left much to be desired.

Hanway, a deeply religious man, tried to rectify the situation. Boys from the Marine Society were given a Bible as well as a set of clothes when they were sent to sea, and the Society was a means of drawing attention to the lack of moral teaching in the Navy. When the King's Chaplain in Ordinary, Dr Samuel Glass, preached to the Marine Society at their anniversary meeting in 1774 he unsettled his listeners on this point. He stated that by the time some of the boys had been placed in the Navy, he believed that their morals had improved, but then lamented that since the Admiralty did not always provide a schoolmaster on warships, the boys received no regular religious instruction afterwards.[30] In 1779, Hanway himself wrote: 'We are accustomed to think lightly of the piety of *seamen*, as if a less portion of *christianity* were required of them than of other subjects.'[31] Until 1812 neither the Admiralty nor the Church of England attempted to recruit clergymen for naval service. If a chaplain were appointed at all, it was on the initiative of a captain. Hanway complained that in some ships 400 or 500 men were left without any chaplain since either the office was considered unimportant by the captain or it was being held as a sinecure – and from 1697 a naval chaplaincy could be held without surrendering preferment ashore. Chaplains were recruited in larger numbers during the French Revolutionary and Napoleonic Wars but there were still too few to provide even the larger ships with a clergyman each.

Hanway's message was deeply pragmatic, especially in those sections of his works addressed to potential sponsors or commanders. Britain's political and naval interests were the same, he argued: the country was dependent on commerce, and religion was interwoven with temporal interests. Just as religion was viewed as one means of disciplining the poor on land, so Hanway viewed religious teaching as one way of improving discipline at sea. If seamen could be persuaded to live a more sober life, they would live longer and be more numerous in time of war. When peace was restored, they would be more inclined to find steady employment ashore. Since it was well known that the numbers of seamen engaged in trade were nowhere near enough to support the Navy in wartime, it was highly expedient to create a more advantageous impression of seamanship to reduce the need for impressment. Hanway recommended setting up schools for boys destined for the sea so that seamanship would become a respectable calling for the common people as well as others.[32] This view of the Navy from the established Church and its supporters became increasingly important with the growth of empire – and, strikingly, it placed no direct emphasis on the need to save seamen's souls.

Hanway did at least believe that those destined for a seafaring life should be given religious instruction of a kind they could understand. He also believed that custom as well as nature was responsible for the way in which seamen behaved, and implied that the clergy had neglected the religious needs of seamen. Interestingly, the sons and nephews of various founding fathers of the Marine Society were strongly connected to the Evangelical Movement and dissenting clergy seem to have made a clear effort to understand seafaring congregations and preach to them in a way they would understand.[33] Hanway himself was adamant that men of strong passions would only be brought to religion if the clergy used direct, powerful language and tailored the message to the understanding of listeners:

> If our *shepherds* were in general, more practised in the habit and force of elocution, the natural thirst of persons of very tender or very strong affections, would be more gratified .... This seems to be the true and genuine cause, why the flock often strays into strange fields for spiritual nourishment.[34]

By 1779 Hanway was able to write that profane swearing, 'the grand moral charge against seamen' was less in use than formerly, but ironically the contents of this later work, *The Seaman's Christian Friend*, did little to dispel the popular image of the seaman.[35] Seamen are warned against duelling, drunkenness, swearing, quarrelling, gaming, whoring and even gluttony. When James Ramsay published the sermons that he had delivered aboard the *Prince of Wales* as Admiral Barrington's chaplain in 1779, he gave a similar impression. The sermons focus mostly on morality and the duty to fight in the nation's cause. The final discourses do touch on spiritual topics specifically and contain Evangelical exhortations to repentance and conversion, but these come only after a number of sermons on the sinfulness of mutiny, desertion and drunkenness, and no less than three sermons on swearing.[36] One dissenting minister at the end of the century understood how the popular image of seamen made it harder for them to reform:

> Unfortunately, however, in spite of sense and reason, the spirit of prodigality and wastefulness has long been regarded as one of the distinguishing characteristics of the seafaring life; and from the number and the arts of those who are interested in encouraging it, and from the generosity of nature from which it is of purpose supposed to spring, it has been sanctioned by custom, and is now almost converted into a professional habit.[37]

Just as they preached moderation in other walks of life, so they urged mariners to be temperate and sober and to provide for the time when they could no longer work. In this they were supported by the Marine Society.

Hanway strongly advised men not to squander money thoughtlessly and preached self-help and making provision for the future, including planning a means of earning a living ashore at the end of a war. His writings also indicate how seamen and their wives were regarded ashore. Hanway urged seamen to provide for their families, as good landmen did, and at least to ensure that their wives are able to find employment while husbands were absent at sea. Their failure to do this, and presumably the need for seamen's families to seek poor relief seems to have been one reason why sailors' wives were 'generally held in low esteem'.[38]

III

During the time of the French Revolution, new taxes and vast loans needed for the massive expansion of the military and naval establishment caused great resentment. The clergy played a vital role in helping to counteract this by persuading people that religion and loyalty to the government were essential for national security at this time, and reconciling them to greater expenditure on military force. The revolution in France frightened the propertied classes in Britain and strengthened their belief that the society under their control must be defended as a divinely ordered hierarchy. Religious arguments could be used to validate the social order and to teach people of every class the duties necessary to maintain it. To some extent Anglican clergymen may have welcomed the opportunity to promote this message as, particularly in the South-East, the clergy had become increasingly unpopular since the 1780s. The price of food had risen substantially and those clergymen who took tithes in kind saw their incomes increase so that they became more closely aligned with the gentry than before. There was a growing gulf between priests and parishioners and the wealth of many clergymen contrasted with the poverty of working people during the French Revolutionary and Napoleonic Wars. Many of the clergy therefore had a vested interest in opposing reform.

The poor harvest in 1795 resulted in food shortages in the autumn and winter of 1795–96 and in October the king's coach was attacked as he was being driven through Hyde Park. The Government responded with two acts against treasonable practices and seditious meetings; restraint, loyalty and steadfastness in religion were urged from the pulpit. Conservatives in particular looked to religion to buttress the existing order. Hannah More began issuing her cheap repository tracts. They continued at the rate of about three a month from 1795 to 1798 and were intended to encourage the lower orders to adhere to the Christian faith and turn away from the temptations of revolution. More claimed, in 1799, that more than two million had either been sold for one halfpenny or given away.[39]

The Loyal Sailor: or No Mutineering (1797) was perhaps the tract which responded most directly to a political incident, being principally targeted at those men in the Navy who mutinied at Spithead and the Nore in 1797. The disaffection in Britain's first line of defence against France caused the Government more concern than any other radical threat during the war years. Low wages and bad conditions precipitated the events, but there was also a degree of political motivation. Some 15 000 out of the 114 000 seamen were Irish quota men, of which many were former United Irishmen pressed into service as a means of repression.[40] Cells of United Irishmen in the Channel Fleet sent delegates to incite Irish seamen in the Nore, believing that mutiny would increase the chances of a French invasion of Ireland. More's tract was written as a song 'fit to be sung on board of all his majesty's ships' and the chorus enthusiastically condemns mutineering. She depicts the loyal sailor as really not intelligent enough to understand exactly what was happening in the mutiny. When a mutineer tries to win his support, he is paralysed by torn loyalties:

> But next of pay,
> He talked away,
> And hoped we'd be united!
> I hung my head,
> And merely said,
> I wish'd the thing was righted[41]

Loyal Jack is a good family man and a patriot at heart, eager to defend the nation in an emergency. To underline the warning, More adds a footnote explaining that the merchants and shipowners of London had resolved that no sailor would be employed in their service after the peace unless he could provide a certificate from his captain stating that he had taken no part in the mutiny. In this crisis, clergymen also rallied to give the Government support. The Revd T. Finch, chaplain of the warship *Caesar*, who was prevented from preaching on board due to the circumstances of the mutiny, afterwards published his *Discourse to Sailors*, distributing copies to ships in the fleet. His effort was supported by *The Gentleman's Magazine* in September 1797 with the wish that 'this plain word of exhortation' might meet with a wide circulation.[42] Catholics took little part in this initiative. The great tradition of the Catholic Apostolate among sailors almost disappeared during the eighteenth and early nineteenth centuries and was not revived until the 1890s.

Another cheap repository tract of 1795 shows how, for political and ideological motives, the adventures of a naval officer could be taken out of context and used to give religious instruction to the potentially disaffected poor. The tract concerns the wreck of Captain Inglefield's ship *Centaur*; a story that was fairly well known because Inglefield published his account on his return to England in 1783. When his ship went down, Inglefield jumped into a pinnace and left the majority of his crew to their fate. In his account he describes his 'painful struggle' – whether to save his life or perish with his ship. Love of life prevailed and he escaped with a few officers. Contemporary standards did not apparently require commanders to make the ultimate sacrifice: at his court martial, Inglefield was acquitted with honour, awarded a pension of £300 per annum in recognition of his ordeal and given the command of a man-of-war. Inglefield's account did not ascribe his escape to the workings of a divine power, but during this period of national hardship his narrative was rewritten in the third person and published as a tract to illustrate the workings of Providence. It concludes:

> In this miraculous and wonderful manner was Providence pleased to preserve Captain Inglefield and his few worthy sailors, that they might at the end of all their extraordinary perils be enabled to say, 'O that men would praise the LORD for his goodness, and declare his wonderful works to the children of men.[43]

This tract possibly performs several functions. It may be intended to show that God has the power to preserve the Navy, that some men do survive shipwreck or that in times of national crisis, a religious spirit is best. Tales of seamen preserved from shipwreck seem to have been popular. Such stories were often sensational but their titles suggested that they were 'improving'. *God's Wonders in the Great Deep*, for example, compiled by a Gravesend Printer in 1803, reprinted Inglefield's story amongst other tales of sailors' survival and also included prayers for seamen. James Stanier Clarke, former chaplain on board the *Impetueux* published *Naufragia; or Historical Memoirs of Shipwrecks and of the Providential Deliverance of Vessels* in 1805. A key aim was to offer all the excitement of a novel to the female mind 'without poisoning its principles or tainting its purity'. But he also aimed to inculcate lessons of resignation and providence, and to remind readers of the feats of endurance and skill some naval officers had performed in the service of their country. The effect of such publications was to make the Navy seem less irreligious than formerly.

We have seen that, by 1779, Hanway was already encouraging seamen to be more devout by assuring them that they already possessed all other excellent qualities. 'British seamen are always distinguished for gratitude, generosity, and other *manly* virtues', he wrote.[44] Increasingly, during the French Revolutionary and Napoleonic Wars, the authors of some thanksgiving sermons extended their praise to the lower ranks and celebrated Britain's intrepid seamen.[45] The sermons of James Stanier Clarke, also show a sympathy for the lower deck. He praised the noble character of the British seaman and his daring but humane spirit, which made him the terror and admiration of Britain's enemies. Clarke's publications helped to link the Navy with national identity. For example, he wrote that 'the noble exploits of the British navy may be said to glow in the brightest pages of our country's annals, and to obscure those of its enemies'.[46] He thought it a matter of astonishment that those who travelled the oceans and were privileged to view the most sublime aspects of God's creation could be anything other than religious and devout. He concluded that those who were not religious had been influenced by error at an early age and that the vices of a few had drawn aspersions on the profession as a whole.

The 1797 mutinies brought religious education in the Navy to the fore. Clarke hoped to influence the image of the Navy and put pressure on seamen to reform their behaviour. In 1798 he published the sermons he had composed and preached on board the *Impetueux* during operations off Brest. Three years later he reprinted them in a more elaborate form, changing the title from *Naval Sermons* to *Sermons on the Character and Professional Duties of Seamen*. The sermons include one on obedience to discipline in which he linked the hierarchical society on board a warship with political government ashore. The ship, in which everyone had his appointed station and co-operated to navigate safely through the waves, was commonly interpreted as an emblem of the social state. Clarke praised the martial court of the British Navy as 'an institution fraught with wisdom whose decrees are marked with clemency and impartiality' and explained that the social state was similarly preserved by strict adherence to essential laws. Proper discipline prepared the seaman for the mental submission that Christianity required. Clarke therefore stated, as Hanway had before him, that, because they were subject to such discipline, naval crews would be receptive to the Christian message, if it were properly presented. Clarke was able to depict seamen as capable of being touched by religion since Admiral Duncan famously held a thanksgiving service on his flagship after his victory at the Battle of Camperdown, 1797. This example was cited by other clergymen, including the evangelical Richard Marks.[47] Successive naval victories earned greater public respect for the Navy especially as mariners were represented as a tool of the state, fighting in a just war and increasingly influenced by a spirit of religion.

From the outbreak of the French Revolutionary war, the SPCK had received a steady stream of requests from captains and chaplains asking for bibles and prayer books for ships' companies. The Society granted these to promote congregational worship rather than private study. After the Spithead and Nore mutinies, captains and naval chaplains made record applications to the SPCK, requesting religious literature for their crews including bibles, tracts, prayer books, testaments and psalters. Since the SPCK made no charge to the ships it supplied, the financial burden to be met by its subscribing members proved considerable. The additional effort needed to raise funds helped to increase public consciousness of the need to encourage religion in the Navy. During the early nineteenth century, this effort became increasingly evangelical in tone and concerned with the winning of souls, but it was still generally accepted that religion was an aid to discipline and that the better Christian would prove a more valuable seaman. By the end of the Napoleonic War, one ex-naval chaplain could even cite the Navy as a means of acquiring religious knowledge. Richard Marks, trying to present a positive side to the use of press-gangs, wrote:

> Many a poor boy has been taken out of a merchant ship, filthy, and so ignorant of God and the Bible, as not to be able to distinguish his letters, or to tell who created and preserved him; and not a few of these have found all the advantages of schools, and cleanliness, and order, and discipline, in the ships of war on board of which they were conveyed: nay some of the brightest ornaments of the British navy once moved in the humble sphere of coasting sea-boys, and by the very events, so forbidding in their first appearance, were led on to rank, and wealth, and honour.[48]

Marks reassures wives and mothers that life on board a warship was not all wretchedness, swearing and tyranny. Most naval officers, he thought, were more attentive to the health and comfort of those under their command than masters and mistresses ashore were in respect of their labourers and domestics. In a footnote he noted the increasing regard for religion in the Navy and concurred with Admiral Sir James Saumarez that the best and bravest sailors were those who habitually read their bible.

Evangelists had shown themselves anxious to convert crews to Christ and their missionary zeal had a prime outlet in the Navy. As early as 1740, George Whitefield persuaded one merchant captain to let him preach to the crew during his passage home from America. In British waters, when a warship stopped them and pressed members of their crew, Whitefield took the opportunity to give the naval lieutenant a copy of a sermon and other religious works. We know that seamen could be susceptible to evangelical rhetoric. When George Whitefield was preaching to the seamen of New York, he adopted a favourite oratorical technique of choosing a metaphor and sustaining it to a climax. Making the most of his dramatic skills, he suddenly assumed a nautical tone and manner and broke in with:

> Well, my boys, we have a clear sky, and are making fine head-way over a smooth sea, before a light breeze, and we shall soon lose sight of land. But what means this sudden lowering of the heavens, and that dark cloud arising from beneath the western horizon? Hark! Don't you hear distant thunder? Don't you see those flashes of lightning? There is a storm gathering! Every man to his duty!

He then described the oncoming storm with such convincing horror that the sailors started to their feet and shouted, 'The long boat! Take to the long boat!'[49] In 1812, after only a few months as naval chaplain, Edward Mangin declared cynically that it was possible to leave a crew unreproved and vicious, and equally possible to have 'transformed them all into Methodists, or madmen and hypocrites of some other kind', but to convert them into Christians was an impossible task.[50]

A mere decade or so after the Nore and Spithead mutinies, there was bound to be some suspicion of any movement that encouraged seamen to meet in small groups for prayer, even though certain officers were known to be zealous evangelists. Possibly because seamen were thought to be susceptible to Methodism, they were used as a foil to expose preachers whom the Establishment regarded as dangerously 'enthusiastic'. The ranting Methodist was a stock figure of ridicule and in *The Sailor, and the Field Preacher* (see Plate 7) it is a seaman representing sturdy British common sense who has the last word. The itinerant preacher cries to the gullible crowd, 'I hear a voice from Heaven'. The sailor is less impressed, 'Come – Come – none of your fore castle gammon with me, you Swab – have not I been *aloft* this half hour, and if so be any orders of that kind came down – don't you think I should have heard them first?' Seamen were reputed to be contemptuous of cant and were notably shy of attending formal worship amongst predominantly land-dwelling congregations.[51] Yet the print may also have been produced in response to Methodist interest in converting ships' crews, as a print of this nature would have been aimed at a market more affluent than that of many radical groups.

Since sailors were commonly depicted as naive and honest, they were also used to expose the supposed hypocrisy of Quakers. In wartime, Quakers were out of tune with the country's military aspirations and caricaturists were able to use seamen to mock their nonconformist beliefs. In Isaac Cruikshank's engraving *A Sailor at a Quaker's Funeral* (see Plate 8), the Quaker laments, 'Alas there is no happiness this side of the grave'. Jack takes him literally and questions why he doesn't simply step to the other side then – although the implication is that the Quaker might be more comfortable if he changed his religious outlook.

IV

Clergymen, when addressing their congregations on naval subjects, were naturally able to use the well-worn trope of the sea voyage as a metaphor for life. Charitable religious foundations like the Marine Society published sermons that drew extended parallels between the journey of the Christian soul on earth and a ship at sea.[52] Whether this trope was enunciated explicitly, or not, it was so well understood that it added power to all references to the dangers experienced at sea, and heightened people's sense of obligation to the Navy. Ships and the sea had a specific religious frame of reference that was often used in sermons and religious writing. The ship was one of the earliest symbols of the Christian Church – and the Ark of Noah is also sometimes taken as an emblem. As far back as the *Apostolic Constitutions*, which were drawn up in the fourth century, a bishop surrounded by the clergy and faithful is compared to the helmsman of a ship. The sea had made possible the journeys of St Paul and (despite his shipwreck) had facilitated the spread of the Christian faith, so embarking on any voyage was potentially an act of symbolic significance. Yet the sea was also regarded with fear and suspicion. Since the notion of a sea voyage as a trope for life on earth was well known, the unstable sea came to represent the fragility of life and served to remind people why faith in God was necessary. In this context, the Church itself could be readily symbolized as a ship.

Some clergymen, striving to be topical, also seized upon popular naval events and used them to convey a spiritual message. A ship launch, an exciting event capable of bringing all social classes together, was excellent material for a sermon. And because of the latent religious symbolism inherent in the event, a ship launch also offered possibilities for clergy who specifically aimed to proselytize. From the closing decades of the eighteenth century, ship launches were given more publicity as shipbuilders gained experience in launching warships down slipways and the likelihood of accidents was reduced. The launch of a large warship would have been a talking point for weeks beforehand, and attracted thousands.[53] Often, attended by royalty, and used to promote a patriotic view of a united Britain enjoying the benefits of stable government, naval launches certainly carried a political message about the power of the nation. This is a key theme is expressed in visual representations of such events.[54] For example, in 1784, when Francis Holman painted a view of Blackwall Yard for exhibition at the Royal Academy, he showed seven ships on the stocks: three seventy-fours, two forty-fours, an East Indiaman and a West Indiaman. Blackwall was then the largest private yard in the world, and this image of naval strength was presumably intended to console viewers after the loss of the colonies as well as help to publicize Blackwall's, which had profited by the demand for ships in wartime. These ships were in fact nearly all on the stocks at the same time in 1784, and the painting represents a fair showing of the actual capacity of the yard.[55] Significantly, the official position taken by the Archbishop of Canterbury on the loss of America was that, provided British trade was revived and secured, the possession of remote colonies was actually unimportant.[56]

Here it will be useful to examine the religious interpretation of ship launches by looking in detail at a sermon of 1810 by John Theodore Barker, a congregationalist minister in Deptford. Congregationalists occupied a position somewhere between Presbyterianism and the more radical Protestants such as Quakers. They emphasized freedom of conscience and the right of each congregation to make decisions about its own affairs without having to submit to the judgement of a higher human authority. Barker's sermon marked the launching of the warship *Queen Charlotte* in Deptford (see Figure 1, p. 18) and offered a complex analysis of the spiritual meaning that could be invested in such an event. His sermon is the more interesting because it was addressed to an audience that included seamen and shipwrights, and delivered in an area that had enjoyed a long connection with the Navy. This case study reveals the potential power of non-Anglican preaching on a naval theme. It will permit us to see how a sermon functioned in its own time, and to understand how clergymen could exploit the popular feeling surrounding a ship launch. Barker found that the response to his sermon justified its publication, at a shilling a copy. His son was in the Navy, which gave his comments on shipboard life greater authority, and his congregation, skilled in ships and the sea, warmed to his theme. Barker took the ship launch – a public, noisy event – and used it to prompt his listeners to consider something very private: the soul. The exchange in his religious symbolism between the material and spiritual could not have been more marked. Yet in a sense, since most of his audience would have attended the launch, they had already enacted the message he was about to enunciate. His sermon was powerful precisely because the congregation already had ownership of the message: their actions had helped to bring it about.

Barker finds several fascinating religious lessons in the spectacle of the launch, Taking James 3.4, 'Behold the ships', as his text, he begins with a comparison between life itself and the conflicting emotions evoked at the launch of a ship (hope of success and fear of failure). The ship, he told his congregation, was to be considered as 'a resemblance' of themselves and all their interests, temporal and eternal. The ship's helm was an emblem of the tongue: just as the helm could determine the safety of the ship, so in distress the tongue could call on the Lord for help. The amazing spectacle of the ship itself, a tribute to human endeavour, ought to make onlookers consider the amazing powers of the soul and its immortality. At this point Barker assured his listeners that even 'a labouring shipwright or common sailor, though reviled and injured by his superiors or his comrades', could enjoy peace with God.[57] This statement may well have had a political resonance for his audience. The report of the launch in *The Naval Chronicle* criticized the way in which seating was segregated by class: elaborate viewing facilities were provided for those with influential friends which others were barred from using. 'Never were the narrow-minded contracted ideas of power more fully displayed than on this occasion', wrote the journalist. Those who were excluded from suitable accommodation included 'thousands of well-dressed respectable women', as well as the better class of shipyard workers. Some of these men had been turned away in such an aggressive manner that they were contemplating legal action. Finally, the journalist had quipped dangerously that 'they manage those things better in France'.[58] If this circumstance warranted such extensive reporting in the *Chronicle*, it would have been a talking point in the local community as well.

Barker continued to secure his audience by reminding them next of the Ark, the apparent origin of shipbuilding and, of course, emblem of the Christian Church. The *Queen Charlotte* would play a part of Britain's national defence and should prompt general thanks for the Lord's help and protection. Here, Barker, while conventionally ascribing all glory to God, also prompted the congregation to give thanks both for the skill of our ship-builders, and 'the spirit of enterprise and courage which distinguishes our seamen' (p. 23). In wartime, it was common for the clergy to support defensive military action and Barker typically praises the warship as a means of defending the country against invasion. Yet he abhors the thought that her decks should ever be the scene of bloodshed and carnage. He paints a vivid picture, describing how the decks of the ship, 'so lately pressed by delicate feet, should soon be strowed with mangled limbs, floating about in their own gore' (p. 23). As this scene of horror might well conjure up images of hell, it seems fitting that he ascribed this circumstance to 'the sad effects of sin' that make life far from perfect. Here the metaphor of ship launch becomes almost cinematic as Barker takes a proleptic glance at what the future holds for the ship, and by extension for the metaphorical voyager. Barker explained that a ship launch with its excitement and danger offered the public an emblem of human life, full of vicissitudes, while the ship is like the virtuous man launched into this life, an ocean of troubles and dangers. Individuals present could often feel their hopes and fears alternate with each stroke of the axe severing the props and shores securing the ship on land. The experience should remind viewers of the gradual loss of all supports in life. On the day when all worldly props are finally severed, the soul will be launched into eternity and the pious man should pray that at that final moment God finds him ready.

Next Barker repeated a common warning from the clergy on the need for good discipline on board warships. He compared the ship's officers to human reason or the superior faculty of the soul, and the crew to human passions, which should be subordinate. When both officers and crew knew their place and did their duty, then all was well. In this sense shipboard life was often held to be a microcosm of society and congregations on sea and land were advised that that much celebrated British liberty, which all Britons enjoyed, did not mean individuals were liberated from the need to obey just laws. Barker thought that there was often cause to complain of mutinies and insubordination on board ships. In the fight against irreligion and insubordination, Barker showed that accepted symbols are often best. The oratorical trick seems to be to render these symbols exceptionally vivid to the audience and to paint a mental picture that enables them to empathize with individual characters and appropriate the message to their own circumstances.

The sight of the *Queen Charlotte* might impress observers with the advancement of science in their age, but Barker was adamant that Britain had made far less progress in religion and morals. Both shipwrights and sailors should put a Christian life above worldly ambition; the labour and expense of building the *Queen Charlotte* alone were almost incalculable, he assented, but what was a ship compared to a soul? As items of exchange, there was no comparison. Here Barker has a different emphasis to that of Anglican preachers such as Clarke who intimated that technological advance justified territorial expansion. The Church at this time unreservedly praised the improvements in technical and mathematical understanding that had raised shipbuilding and navigation to new levels. Ships had become complicated machines that ensured western mastery of the seas. Naval chaplains wrote on the progress of hydrography and even indulged in cartography, as when the Revd Cooper Willyams mapped Martinique after its capture by the British in 1794.[59] This view was taken on both sides of the Atlantic before the War of American Independence. It was wholly consistent with the contemporary view that Britain's intellectual achievements justified imperial expansion, and it focused on the Navy's imperial role. During the French Revolutionary and Napoleonic Wars, clergymen like James Stanier Clarke also represented the war against tyrannical France as a fight in defence of a civilized world to preserve liberty, security and public happiness. Besides normalizing shipboard society, this argument had the effect of suggesting that Britain's despotic enemies were best opposed by sea and thus further heightened the status of the Navy. By extension, Clarke was able to argue that, by promoting trade and 'enlarging the boundaries of commercial intercourse', seamen promoted the happiness and comfort of mankind. In a thanksgiving sermon for naval victories preached in 1797, he similarly explained that, while the Navy defended Britain's shores, it secured British settlements in other parts of the world and dispensed happiness to those who 'enjoy in distant climes the blessings of British Freedom'.[60] Some viewed the war against Napoleon as religious war against atheists – their hopes of the spiritual objectives that naval power might realize seem to have been absorbed later into the missionary aspects of empire. Instead of following this route, Barker used the warship and the technological achievement it represented to remind his listeners about divine providence. The sight of such a ship ought to make land dwellers contemplate the many striking and well-known illustrations of divine Providence to those at sea. Barker was sure that many in the congregation had been brought up on stories of such naval heroes as Anson and Cook. And indeed Cook and other naval worthies were often mentioned in sermons to show the workings of Providence.[61] The spectacle of the ship, Barker suggested, should readily lead any onlookers to contemplate divine grace.

At this point Barker drew a comparison between the outward show of the naval vessel and the quality of life on board. Though he had been careful to praise the bravery of British seamen earlier, he now painted an unflattering picture of life between the decks of a man-of-war. Deftly playing on the emotions, he led his audience from laughter to condemnation in the space of a few seconds. He began by alluding to the popular saying, 'all the world loves a sailor',

> I *do* love a sailor, not merely because I have a son in the navy … . Yet, oh to think of the iniquities, the enormities, committed by them; and how few their opportunities of religious instruction … . I utter no libel: I reveal no secret. The abominations of a man of war are become proverbial. (p. 35).

Not for nothing were warships referred to as 'a floating hell', Barker continued, and building on the image of a bloody naval battle he had used earlier, he suggested that in the heat of action far too many souls slipped from one hell to another with little time for reflection. Yet Barker went on to intimate that by this time, the early nineteenth century, increased religious activity was beginning to have a beneficial effect on crews. He hoped that the seamen on the *Queen Charlotte* would make an effort to pray and sketched out how the habit of prayer might take hold among the crew, if officers encouraged their efforts. A beginning could be made with small groups meeting for prayer and bible reading when they were off duty. 'This is no fiction', he insisted. 'The substance of it was communicated by a late worthy Captain in the Navy, who was once a very serious hearer with us, and whose obituary is given in the Evangelical Magazine for last month' (p. 37). And indeed other sources confirm that this was one way in which crews were made more aware of religion.[62]

Barker also cited the case of James Covey who had both legs amputated after a battle fought under Lord Duncan. He famously blessed the day his legs were shot off, 'Well, never mind … I've lost my legs, to be sure, and mayhap may lose my life; but we beat the Dutch; d—m me, we have beat the Dutch'.[63] This part of his story was known, as recorded by a chaplain assisting as surgeon's mate, because it had been published as a typical 'amputation narrative' in Mr Pratt's *Gleanings in England*, a work that set out to illustrate the true British character. On the first day of Covey's discharge from Haslar, the naval hospital at Portsmouth, he was directed to hear a preacher at Portsea whose text that day perfectly matched his own situation. Covey was amazed that any preacher could make a sermon out of a wooden-legged sailor and immediately converted to Christ. He published his story as a halfpenny tract, which Barker duly recommended to the congregation, showing how a more religious view of the lower decks could be disseminated through the activities of the clergy. Since Barker also cited Pratt's work, he further sanctioned the view that the bravery of seamen was somehow typical of the British character.

In conclusion, Barker looked forward to the day when warships and navigation would cease to be used for destruction but be employed instead for trade or discovery. Significantly, he felt such activities would be perverted if the aim were imperial gain by 'extending territory, robbing fellow men of their property, their country or their liberty' (p. 39). Picking up on the use of a ship to symbolize the Church, he reiterated that all ships should be as churches of the living God, more numerous, pure and peaceful than any at present.

Barker's sermon was essentially opportunistic (though a good clergyman would probably always seek out a subject with contemporary resonance), and he had a vested interest in publishing the sermon afterwards since this could improve his standing in an age when preferment often depended on patronage. In the course of elaborating his central metaphor, he was careful to criticize ordinary seamen rather than officers or the Navy as an institution. As we have seen, during the French wars from 1793 to 1815, British seamen were generally praised for their courage and generosity, but there was a parallel movement to educate ships' crews in moral and spiritual values which seemed so conducive to discipline. In total, Barker's sermon vividly suggests the ways in which the launching of a ship might assume symbolic significance in the minds of ordinary people and how indeed such thoughts could be reinforced in church by a skilled orator. In the process, Barker gives several insights into the popular image of the Navy in the early nineteenth century and shows how it could be manipulated by a mixture of government and religious propaganda.

Increasingly, in the wake of the 1797 mutinies, the Navy had been represented as more and more receptive to positive religious influence. James Stanier Clarke pictured the seaman calmly reading his Bible in the midst of a rolling ocean that continually reminded him of the power of God. He praised this 'religious disposition' and attention to propriety that had appeared lately among seamen, encouraged by their commanders, and thought it would in time remove the only slur that could be made on 'the noble character of a British Seaman'.[64] By 1814, evangelicals reported that ships' crews were often to be found reading religious literature and actually their willingness to buy such titles made the Religious Tract Society consider breaking with its custom of only giving away Bibles. The Navy's global reach and its role in the protection of commerce and extension of empire allowed the service to be presented as an agent of benevolence, helping to spread the benefits of a civilized society. Whether or not this was deliberate policy, it prompted a change in public opinion so marked that, by 1814, the pulpit was more inclined to view the disbanding of the army in peacetime as more of a threat to civilized society than any release of surplus seamen.[65]

Notes

1   J. Brewer, *The Pleasures of the Imagination: English Culture in the Eighteenth Century* (London, 1997), p. 172; P.J. Corfield, *Power and the Professions in Britain 1700–1850* (London and New York, 1995), p. 104; A. Lincoln, 'What Was Published in 1798', *European Romantic Review*, 10 (1999), pp. 137–51.
2   See *A Practical Discourse to Sea-Faring Men* (Boston, 1771), pp. 7–8. *A Sermon, on the Present Situation of the Affairs of America and Great-Britain. Written by a Black* (Philadelphia, 1782), p. 11.
3   James Boswell's, *Life of Johnson*, 14 April 1775. Quoted by Norman Sykes, *Church and State in England in the XVIIIth Century* (Cambridge, 1934), p. 41.
4   J. Walsh, C. Haydon and S. Taylor, eds, *The Church of England c.1689–c.1833: From Toleration to Tractarianism* (Cambridge, 1993), p. 16.
5   B.R. Dailey, 'The Visitation of Sarah Wight: Holy Carnival and the Revolution of the Saints in Civil War London', *Church History*, 55 (1986), p. 455.
6   Sykes, *Church and State in England*, p. 77.
7   See *A Form of Prayer and Thanksgiving to Almighty God to be used at Morning and Evening Service …* (London, 1762) for the taking of Martinique. Also *A Form of Prayer to be used … upon … the Day appointed by Proclamation for a General Fast and Humiliation* (London, 1782) for success in the war against America.
8   *A Prayer for the Safety of Our Fleets, by His Majesty's Special Command, March 9th, 1796.* Printed on card. MOD (N)L–P(NS) 184.
9   J. Austen, *Jane Austen's Letters*, ed. D. Le Faye, 3rd edn (Oxford, 1995), p. 274.
10 Revd J. Carmichael , *A Self-Defensive War Lawful* (Philadelphia, 1775), p. 32.
11 Revd I. Evans, *A Discourse, delivered in New-York … on 11th December 1783* (New York, 1783), p. 11.
12 *GM*, 68, Pt I (1798), 385–6.
13 G. Whitefield, *A Short Address to Persons of all Denominations, Occasioned by the Alarm of an intended Invasion*, 3rd edn (London, 1756), p. 18.
14 C. Chauncy, *A Sermon preached the 18th of July, 1745. Being a day set apart for Solemn Thanksgiving to Almighty God, for the Reduction of Cape-Breton …* (Boston, 1745), p. 24. Cf. J. Mayhew, *Two Discourses Delivered October 9th, 1760* (Boston, 1760), p. 50.
15 J. Hanway, 'An Introduction to Archbishop Synge's Essay on Christianity made Easy', in *The Seaman's Faithful Companion* (London, 1763), p. 77.
16 W. Blackhouse, *God the Author of Peace and Lover of Concord. A Sermon preached at the Parish Council of Deal, on Thursday, July 29, 1784* (Canterbury, 1784), p. 11.
17 Revd J. Rouquet, *Thanksgiving Sermon, on account of the Victory … 21st October 1805* (Bristol, 1805), pp. 11–12.
18 [R. Marks], *Nautical Essays: or, a spiritual view of the ocean and maritime affairs: with reflections on the battle of Trafalgar and other events* (London, 1818), pp. 158, 168. Some of the shorter essays had been published earlier for free circulation to the fleet.
19 A. Yarrington, *The Commemoration of the Hero 1800–1864: Monuments to the British Victors of the Napoleonic Wars* (New York and London, 1988), pp. 104–5; 108–9.
20 E. Williams, *Mr Williams's Thanksgiving Sermon* (New London, 1760), pp. 15–16. Cf. 'Honor not *Man* in Opposition to *God*', Chauncy, *A Sermon preached the 18th of July*, p. 9.
21 T. Maurice, *The Crisis of Britain: a poem* (London, 1803), p. 26.
22 For example, S. Haven, *A Sermon … Occasioned by the Remarkable Success of His Majesty's Arms in the Late War* (Portsmouth, NH, 1763), p. 31.
23 J. Woodward, *The Seaman's Monitor; or, Advice to Sea-Faring Men*, 15th edn (London, 1801), p. 1. Cf. Hanway, *The Seaman's Faithful Companion*, pp. 1, 3.
24 T. Smith, *A Practical Discourse to Sea-Faring Men* (Boston, 1771), p. 20.

25 Ibid., p. 36.
26 H.G. Thursfield, ed., *Five Naval Journals, 1789–1817*, Navy Records Society (London, 1951), p. 8.
27 Hanway, *The Seaman's Faithful Companion*, pp. i–ii.
28 C. Aspinall-Oglander, ed., *Admiral's Wife. Being the Life and Letters of the Hon. Mrs Edward Boscawen from 1719 to 1761* (London, 1940), p. 9.
29 Hanway, *The Seaman's Faithful Companion*, p. xii.
30 S. Glasse, *A Sermon Preached before the President, Vice-Presidents, and Governors, of the Marine Society* (London, 1774), p. 24.
31 J. Hanway, *The Seaman's Christian Friend; Containing Moral and Religious Advice to Seamen* (London, 1779), p. xvi.
32 Ibid., pp. xxvii, xxxii.
33 See A. Brown, *Dr Brown's Sermon on the Dangers and Duties of the Seafaring Life; preached before the Protestant Dissenting Congregation, at Halifax* (Boston, 1793), p. 8.
34 Hanway, *The Seaman's Faithful Companion*, p. 80 (misnumbered as 70).
35 Hanway, *The Seaman's Christian Friend*, p. xviii.
36 Revd J. Ramsay, *Sea Sermons, or a Series of Discourses for the use of the Royal Navy* (London, 1781).
37 Brown, *Dr Brown's Sermon* (Boston, 1793), p. 39.
38 Hanway, *The Seaman's Christian Friend*, pp. 128ff; 155–6.
39 H. More, *Cheap Repository Shorter Tracts*, new edn (London, 1799), p. iv.
40 The Quota Acts, passed in the British Parliament in 1795, compelled each county and borough to provide a quota of men for service in the Navy.
41 H. More, *The Loyal Sailor; or No Mutineering* (1800?), p. 4.
42 *GM*, 67 (1797), 771.
43 *Wonderful escape from shipwreck. An account of the loss of His Majesty's Ship* CENTAUR, Cheap Repository Tract (Bath and London [1795?]), p. 12
44 Hanway, *The Seaman's Christian Friend*, p. 40.
45 For example, S. Horsley, *The Watchers and the Holy Ones. A Sermon on Thursday December 5, 1805* (London, 1806), p. 26.
46 J.S. Clarke, *Sermons on the Character and Professional Duties of Seamen*, p. 20.
47 [Marks], *Nautical Essays*, p. 160.
48 Ibid., p. 26.
49 Quoted in G. Whitefield, *Sketches of the Life and Labours of the Rev. George Whitefield, with two discourses preached in the year 1739* (Edinburgh, [1849]), p. 266.
50 Thursfield, *Five Naval Journals*, p. 14.
51 R.C. Blake, 'Aspects of Religion in the Royal Navy *c.*1770–*c.*1870' (MPhil thesis, University of Southampton), 1980, p. 47.
52 For example, J. Murray, *The Happy Voyage Compleated, and the Sure Anchor Cast* (Newbury-Port, Mass., 1785), p. 10.
53 *The Times* estimated that the launch of the *Queen Charlotte* on 17 July 1810 attracted 20 000; The *Naval Chronicle* 100 000 (XXIV, 1810. pp. 35–7).
54 M. Lincoln, 'Naval Ship Launches as Public Spectacle 1773–1854', *The Mariner's Mirror*, 83 (November, 1997), pp. 466–72.
55 The painting is at The National Maritime Museum (BHC1866).
56 Blackhouse, *God the Author of Peace*, p. 20.
57 J.T. Barker, *The Ship Launch. The Substance of a Sermon, preached at Deptford, on Occasion of the Launching of the Queen Charlotte. July 17th 1810* (London, 1810), p. 13.
58 *The Naval Chronicle*, XXIV (1810), pp. 35–7.
59 See J.S. Clarke, *The Progress of Maritime Discovery, from the Earliest Period to the Close of the Eighteenth Century, Forming an Extensive System of Hydrography* (London,

1803) and Revd C. Willyams, *An Account of the Campaign in the West Indies in the Year 1794* (London, 1796).

60 Clarke, *Sermons on … Seamen*, pp. 79ff, 103, 270.

61 Ibid., pp. 116–17.

62 See Blake, *Aspects of Religion in the Royal Navy*, p. 78.

63 S.J. Pratt, *Gleanings in England; descriptive of the Countenance, Mind and Character of the Country*, 2 vols, 2nd edn (London, 1801), vol. II, p. 542.

64 Clarke, *Sermons … Seamen*, pp. 43, 46.

65 F. Brown, *The Evils of War. A Fast Sermon, delivered at North Yarmouth, April 7, 1814* (Portland, 1814), p. 15.

Chapter 6

Waiting on the Shore

Women contributed significantly to the public image of the Navy although only a limited number actually went to sea. This chapter has three parts. The first looks at women who served in the Navy and knew it at first hand. The second considers how women represented the Navy in their writing, and as consumers by what they chose to wear or display. The third concerns representations of naval wives and mothers, and argues that even in their traditional, supportive role, women contributed to perceptions of the social importance of the Navy.

I

Women did go to sea with the fleet and so featured in representations of the Navy. For example, although there were no female officers in the Navy, there were a few female warriors, celebrated in ballads and chapbook literature. These were heroines who disguised themselves as sailors, or soldiers, and went to war in search of loved ones, or just to be near them. Such heroines are depicted as patriotic, adventurous and true to their love. That a woman might spend months on a ship without her sex being discovered seems far-fetched today, but there are well-attested cases of women who served in the Navy dressed in men's clothes. As represented, these women played their part in the running of the ship. They could go aloft, reef and steer, and fight in battle. A folk version of *The Constant Lovers of Worcester* even depicts a woman as surgeon's mate:

> In man's apparel then ...
> [Resolved] to try her fate;
> And in the good ship where [her love] rid
> She went as surgeon's mate.[1]

Such ballads were enormously popular for a long period, most circulating in print as commercial songs from 1650 to about 1850. Women participated in all stages of production – as printers, as ballad sellers, and probably also as ballad writers. The educated classes knew these popular ballads but they were mostly aimed at the common people and throw light on the experience of lower-class women. Survival in this disruptive period demanded assertiveness, stamina and ingenuity from women as well as men, particularly among the lower classes.

The ballads applaud rebellious behaviour in the face of parental or other social constraint. The heroines' feats were perhaps not beyond belief in an age when some women rode in male breeches, when masquerading was a popular entertainment and when adopting a disguise seemed a real option in a crisis. Ballads about women pretending to be men help to explore the question of gender and the extent to which gender differences are a matter of costume, and of course a seaman's dress was particularly distinctive. Typically, such ideas are not pursued beyond the penultimate verse – by the end of the song, the heroine usually marries her sailor and returns to a domestic environment. But in an age when the familiar methods of public communication were commonly directed towards celebrating male heroes, female warrior ballads constitute a remarkable counterpoint. The popularity of these ballads is the more intriguing because it obscures a process of slippage whereby the more mundane achievements of women at sea went largely unrecognized. Numbers of women at this time were far from being passive onlookers in wartime. They went to sea in their own capacity without any need to disguise themselves as men. The wives of warrant officers traditionally accompanied their husbands on board ship and other women were taken aboard, depending on the tolerance of commanding officers. But if ships were not exclusively a male space, once at sea they would have been strictly gender-segregated. In battle, women had specific roles: they served as nurses or powder monkeys, helping to bring gunpowder from the magazines to the guns. We know that one woman actually took the place of her wounded husband as part of a gun crew, but such behaviour was exceptional.[2] At the Battle of the Nile a woman died of her wounds; another gave birth to a son. The lives of these women were not celebrated publicly, and although by the early nineteenth century their bravery might have been recorded, the old stories of females who served at sea in disguise seem to have had a broader appeal.[3]

This is evident in Hannah Snell's account of her time at sea, which, gives a working-class woman's view of the Navy in the mid-eighteenth century. She writes that she disguised herself as a man and joined the marines to find her lover, but was drafted to serve in Admiral Boscawen's fleet, bound for the East Indies. Her story is the more interesting because it gives a rare account of life on the lower deck. Snell complains bitterly about naval food. On the way to the Cape of Good Hope the fleet met with bad weather and the crews were reduced to short allowance for 17 weeks. The food was 'very salt and very bad', and to make things worse the men were given only a pint of water a day each. Snell also reveals the hardships that could result in the confined space of a ship when arbitrary power was given to unsatisfactory officers. In the absence of the captain, the lieutenant was put in command. He bore a grudge against Snell and punished her severely for alleged theft: she was put in irons for five days, given twelve lashes at the gangway and tied for four hours to the foretop-mast head. The crew helped her to take revenge on the lieutenant and dropped a block on his head. But Snell has no illusions about seamen. Given shore leave, she recounts how they immediately set off to look for women and 'her Ears were every Moment pierced through with the most execrable Oaths that could be invented'.

Eventually Snell escaped from the marines and made her way back to London where she published her story. An outline of her adventures in *The Ladies Magazine* happens to be followed by notice of the execution of one Katharine Conway, an Irishwoman of 45, sentenced to death for forging a seaman's will. The notice gives an insight into the snares that awaited seamen ashore and how the publicized actions of criminal females could make seamen appear victims.[4] Snell afterwards made her living on the stage, playing a 'jovial tar' and singing such patriotic songs as 'Britannia's Gold Mine; or, the Herring Fishery for Ever'.[5] One of her songs was printed in *The Ladies Magazine* in June 1750. It condenses the appeal of female warriors into a few verses exemplifying patriotism, passion, courage and sensationalism. Snell describes herself:

> In the midst of Blood and Slaughter,
> > Bravely fighting for my King;
> Facing Death from e'ery Quarter,
> > Fame and Conquest Home to bring.[6]

Her performances, both literary and theatrical, were clearly targeted to her audiences: readers of chapbook literature wanted sensationalism; theatre audiences wanted jolly musical entertainment. Snell is interesting because her career combines two modes of representing the Navy: textual representation and, on stage, a form of personal display. Her published account, ostensibly gained from inside knowledge, presented a much harsher view of naval life than that depicted in works by women later in the century. An early feminist of the 1780s, Anne Frances Randall, failed to emphasize this point when using Snell as an example of disinterested female bravery:

> When a man exposes his person in the front of battle, he is actuated either by interest or ambition: woman, with neither to impel her, has braved the cannons thunder; stood firmly glorious amidst the din of desolation ... and yet she is, by the undiscriminating or prejudiced part of mankind denominated the *weaker* creature.[7]

In this way, those seeking more freedom for women were able to use Snell's account subtly to undermine the Navy's achievement. Naturally they were in a minority.

II

It has been argued that in the eighteenth century men and women increasingly came to inhabit separate spheres. The separate spheres model posited that, due to increasing prosperity which gave women more leisure time, and the growth of a restrictive concept of femininity, middle- and upper-class women were steadily enclosed within the private, domestic sphere and enjoyed little or no part in the masculine, public sphere. More recently, this model has been revised. The realities of life for men and women were more complex and, depending on individual circumstances, personalities and relationships within marriage, women might participate significantly in an active public sphere. While eighteenth-century writing may have propagated idealized concepts of femininity, we should not mistake such rhetoric for reality. Distinctions between private and public spheres were often blurred.[8] Indeed, in an age of servants and little real privacy, what was understood by the terms 'private' and 'public' was different from what we understand by them today. Aristocratic women were active in politics, especially during elections, and genteel women took on a set of responsibilities and pursued a range of activities outside the home.[9] War may have accentuated the perceived functional differences between men and women but it also served to enlarge the field of women's activities, as they helped to fundraise and performed other tasks to support the war effort.[10] Tradesmen may well have tried to assert their credit worthiness by demonstrating that they could afford to relieve their wives of any part in business, but of course among the labouring classes, women still worked to supplement the family income, playing a vital role as wage earners.

Ostensibly, women had few means of public communication at their disposal – the writing of novels, perhaps songs and poetry. But, as consumers, they exerted influence on the production of a range of goods conveying opinion about public matters. This consumer demand was shaped and stimulated by print and entrepreneurial initiatives that commodified culture and capitalized on the opportunities to create goods for a burgeoning consumer society. The range of objects commemorating individuals and battles, often aimed at a female market, meant that women could assert clear patriotism in their own social environment. Their choice of jewellery might affirm loyalty to loved ones, or their support for common causes. Commemorative fans, ribbons and patch boxes had the same effect. Aspects of interior decoration over which women had influence – family portraits, decorative picture frames, figurines, plaques featuring profiles of naval heroes, candlesticks – could all be used to convey opinions about national affairs. Many of these items were produced in quantity, for both the top and bottom ends of the market. In this way, the naval successes of the French wars put the names of Admirals Howe, Jervis, Duncan and others into households at practically all social levels.

Many of these items would have been used on a daily basis and would have formed part of the social context in which naval events would have been 'read'. For example, tea drinking was arguably an essential part of the social life of genteel women.[11] At the tea table a woman could show off both her person and her taste in china. Since manufacturers were eager to exploit the market for commemorative ware, even the choice of a teapot allowed women to demonstrate popular and political allegiances. The vogue for commemorative china gained momentum from the mid-eighteenth century. Admiral Vernon's capture of the Spanish stronghold Porto Bello in 1739 first offered Britain's developing pottery industry the opportunity to meet a significant demand for souvenirs from a patriotic public and teapots and bowls were manufactured to celebrate the event. Tea sets were later produced to show support for popular causes, as in 1778 when the reputation of Admiral Keppel, commander-in-chief of the Channel Fleet, came under severe attack (see Plate 9a). Keppel had encountered the French fleet off Ushant and after an inconclusive skirmish, the enemy escaped under cover of darkness. Subsequently, his second-in-command, Sir Hugh Palliser, brought charges against him of neglect of duty and misconduct. The court martial attracted much publicity and popular feeling was on Keppel's side. When he was acquitted with honour, celebrations followed. A surviving teapot of this period has Keppel's portrait on one side and 'Captain Cook being directed by Britannia' on the other. It indicates how commemorative items permitted women to endorse complementary aspects of naval endeavour – conquest and exploration – just as the two were linked in women's poetry of the period.[12] In 1782, the objects produced to celebrate Admiral Rodney's victory over the French at the Battle of the Saints included teapots and other china in a range of materials from fine porcelain to cheap earthenware (see Plates 9b and 11a). Many admirals were commemorated in this way, and ownership of such pieces might testify to patriotic support for the wars against the French or more particular support during elections for the political ambition of naval officers.

There were well-publicized instances of aristocratic women adopting naval motifs as ornament. The ladies in the royal party in Henry Brigg's oil painting of King George III's visit to Admiral Howe's flagship on 26 June 1794 are wearing small gold anchors on chains round their necks (see Plate 10). Such women often set a trend, and after important victories, commemorative jewellery rapidly became fashion items. Certainly, women wore gold anchors to mark Nelson's victory at the Battle of the Nile in 1798, which were engraved with the name and date of the battle. Painted ivory lockets were also produced to celebrate the victory (see Plate 11b). These trinkets, on public display in some sort wherever they were worn, did much to promote Nelson's personal popularity. Some examples of lockets celebrating Nelson's victory indicate the loyalty of seamen to their commander (important since the mutiny of the Fleet had taken place in the previous year). Illustrations on other examples convey the message that victory in such naval engagements will earn lasting fame for those who take part. The wearing of these lockets was actually part of the process whereby popular heroes did secure fame. The same is true of commemorative ribbons and fans. Haberdashers and fan makers were particularly swift to cash in on the celebrations surrounding Nelson's victory at the Battle of the Nile, reflecting the growing commodification of the Navy. A print of 1798 shows that, in dress at least, men as well as women were in the grip of Nelsonmania (see Plate 12). The wearing of commemorative jewellery worked to enhance the public standing of women as well as the reputation of the Navy, and in this way the souvenir industry helped to give women a public voice. The verses inscribed on fans, for instance, were clearly not the wearer's own, but women endorsed their meaning by purchasing the fans in the first place and then using them in public. Some trinkets, including fans and vinaigrettes, permitted women a range of gestures that might serve to endorse or complement the significance of the message displayed on the item. Vinaigrettes were tiny hinged cases that held a sponge soaked in aromatic vinegar behind a pierced grille, and women sniffed them at critical moments either to ward off odours or to prevent fainting fits. Many silver-gilt vinaigrettes were produced engraved with portraits of Nelson and his flagship, *Victory*. Women were perceived to be the softer sex but chose to wear tokens of battle, including the depiction of violent scenes such as the sinking warships. The effect of such ornaments on feminine ideology can perhaps only be a matter of speculation.

Some of the more popular commemorative items featuring the Navy may have been acquired merely as souvenirs. Others may have been treasured chiefly for their personal significance. For example, in the early nineteenth century, lockets incorporating a painting made on ivory were popular. Some surviving examples show Hope leaning against a large anchor on the shore while a warship departs in the background and they have a compartment at the back to take a curl of hair. But other items representing the Navy or naval events seem to have been commissioned by women with a wider, more public purpose in mind. Ten years after the Battle of Copenhagen, the wife of Rear Admiral Thomas Graves, Nelson's second-in-command in that battle, decided to order some Irish table linen to commemorate the victory. She asked her daughter to write to her Aunt Catherine to explain the commission:

Her Ladyship has a great wish to have the Battle of Copenhagen wove in a Table Cloth of the manufacture of my father's native Country [Ireland] and he assured her that you would readily assist in the accomplishment of her wishes. Would you therefore have the goodness to inquire in your Neighbourhood, what kind of design would be required for the purpose. We could send you a print of the Battle of Copenhagen or an enlarged drawing of it, as also a drawing of the [family] Crest to put round the border.[13]

Britain was still at war with Napoleon in 1811. The linen would bring real social advantage to the family, allowing it to signal publicly its involvement with the victory at Copenhagen at important family dinners. Since Graves was Irish, the linen might also be a useful method of reminding guests of his service to king and country and enhancing his social standing.

Sometimes such tactics could produce an adverse effect. When Emma Hamilton furnished Nelson's house at Merton (where she and her husband, Sir William, also lived in a notorious *ménage à trois*), she placed a fragment of the mainmast of *L'Orient* and a bust of Nelson as Victor of the Nile in prominent positions in a hall. The main staircase in the north wing was liberally decorated with engravings of naval actions and heroes, and portraits of herself. Even their china reflected Nelson's achievements. Of course, it was usual for families to decorate silver and other items with their coat of arms; Nelson's household simply differed in the degree to which this was realized. When Emma, Nelson and Sir William visited the Royal Porcelain Factory at Worcester in August 1802, they ordered a large dinner and breakfast service (although only the breakfast service was completed before Nelson's death). They chose the standard Worcester pattern in a Japan style but Nelson's coat of arms had to appear on some of the major pieces and all other pieces had the original design adapted to incorporate references to Nelson's various campaigns. Lord Minto, diplomat and friend, stayed at Merton in 1802 and disapproved of both the décor and Emma's relationship with Nelson:

The love she makes to him is not only ridiculous, but disgusting: not only the rooms, but the whole house, staircase and all, are covered with nothing but pictures of her and him, of all sizes and sorts, and representations of his naval actions, coats of arms, pieces of plate in his honour, the flagstaff of *L'Orient*, etc. – an excess of vanity which counteracts its own purpose. If it was Lady H's house there might be a pretence for it; to make his own a mere looking-glass to view himself all day is bad taste.[14]

Nelson was able literally to use Emma to reflect his own image. She wore a bloodstone brooch showing him in profile (his gift to her). He also gave commemorative trinkets to other female friends and acquaintance. Charlotte Nelson, for example, received an ivory toothpick case inscribed 'Nile'. But, as Minto indicates, it was accepted that some women might use the Navy and naval heroes as a means to define and promulgate their own identity, as did Emma Hamilton.

Kathleen Wilson's examination of gender and eighteenth-century imperialism demonstrates the involvement of women – actresses in this case – in disseminating an imperialist vision that both defined, and was defined by, constructions of masculinity[15] The same is broadly true of a much wider segment of female society. In addition to shaping the representation of the Navy by their patterns of consumption, women helped to promote an image of the Navy and its role on a daily basis through their musical performances in family drawing rooms or at local gatherings. Until about 1770 musical performances would have been mostly accompanied on the harpsichord or clavicord; later the piano surpassed these rivals. Britain's large and expanding middle class was eager to gain prestige and ready to spend on activities that offered opportunities for both enjoyment and improvement. Leisure and refined entertainment achieved high priority, and in the 1770s the prosperous middle classes started to make the piano a more popular instrument in England. By the 1780s, it had also become popular in Scotland, and several piano manufacturers set up business in Dublin before 1790. Ownership of a piano became a badge of gentility; the ability to play it a necessary feminine 'accomplishment'. The *Piano-Forte Magazine*, published each week between 1797 and 1802 at 2s 6d a copy, was conceived as part of a scheme to enable readers to buy a piano by weekly payments. London became a centre of piano manufacture, exporting many instruments to France because of the ease of transport. It became fashionable to identify the instrument as quintessentially English – given the proximity of France and war with the French.[16]

One of the attractions of contemporary magazines for women although edited and mostly written by men, was that they included pull-out sheet music and songs, some of which had a nautical theme. For example, *The Lady's Magazine* of June 1760, included 'By the Force of our Ships. A Loyal Song'.[17] Such songs became more popular during the long period of war from 1793 to 1815. Anna Seward, for instance, wrote an ode on hearing of Nelson's victory at the battle of the Nile in 1798. After the original stanzas had been sung at a music meeting in Birmingham, news of Admiral Warren's victory reached England and Seward rapidly appended four more verses to her ode.[18] Nautical songs were often performed in London theatres and subsequently published in cheap collections priced one penny. A typical volume of 1812 is *Braham's Whim; Or songster's Delight: comprising all the modern fashionable and sea songs now singing at the theatres of London and convivial clubs*. While actresses helped to perform some of these songs in the theatre, the wider social and cultural role of women is reflected in their performance of these songs in domestic and semi-domestic settings. Characteristically the songs feature fun-loving, devil-may-care seamen. Though some mention a girl in every port, by this later date they are more likely to feature Jolly Jack Tars who are faithful to one girl whom they often think of at sea. The seamen are brave, honest, loyal and fatalistic about their chances of survival. The songs rehearse various scenarios: the sailor's joyful return, often three or four years after leaving, during which his family or loved one has had to struggle to survive; his shipwreck and death; or the loss of a limb followed by beggary and want. These options, repeated with slight variations in many songs, possibly helped to normalize disruptive occurrences that were being acted out in homes all over the country. To some extent, the situations depicted in the songs are reflected in other cultural items of the period. Scenes of parting were popular with pottery manufacturers, and it was usual for such images to be accompanied by a matching one of the sailor's happy return. The happy, fatalistic, seamen reflected in Charles Dibdin's songs were reproduced in porcelain sailor figures. These proved so popular that earthenware ones were produced for a wider market.

Women, in singing nautical songs, had a role in disseminating government propaganda. Charles Dibdin or his sons wrote many of them, and Dibdin was awarded a pension of £200 a year for keeping his London theatre open nightly one hot July when he was '*instructed* to write, sing, publish, and give away what were termed War Songs'.[19] We know that women had nautical and patriotic songs in their repertoire. Emma Hamilton's songbook, for example, included songs celebrating Nelson's victory at the Nile. These depicted a Navy composed of men who were both brave and compassionate: 'As British Tars were ever brave, | So soft humanity we have'. They also represented the Navy as safeguarding British freedom: 'Mars guards for use, | What freedom did by Charter gain.' Not all the patriotic songs were so upbeat. 'The Sailor's Life', inscribed in Emma Hamilton's own hand, ends 'Soon a wreck his vessel lies, o'er him billows roar | Home, and all its Social Joys, he shall see no more.'[20]

The sea songs replicate themes found in women's poetry of the period, notably shipwreck, and may have provided an outlet for female anxieties. One poem begins:

> Twas at night, when the bell
>   had told twelve,
> And poor Susan laid on her pillow,
> In her ear whisper'd some flitting elve
>   Your love is now toss'd on a billow
>   Far, far at sea![21]

Other songs prompt the listeners to be charitable to maimed seamen and to those made widows and orphans by the war:

Poor Nancy with her infants screaming
Wander'd on the rocky shore;
She ask'd of all, if he were coming,
But her Ben was now no more.
Convulsive sobs each word suppressing
Fix'd her in a wild despair;
A form so piteous and distressing,
Crav'd a Briton's fost'ring care.[22]

Collections of sea songs probably owed much of their popularity to their human content. Women are also urged to be faithful in their husband's absence. For example, one song, entitled 'Steady as She Goes', relates how faithful Polly sat reading the papers one day, saw that her sailor's ship had docked at Plymouth and rushed to the port. The moral is clear: 'Prove faithful to your sailor brave, | While he is on the foaming main'.[23]

Naturally, female 'public' displays involving personal adornment or musical performance were generally patriotic and conventional. Women were often brought into the rhetoric of war as potential victims needing to be secured from rape and seduction, so this uncritical response to the military is not surprising. One naval recruiting poster from the French Revolutionary War calls upon Englishmen to protect and defend king and country against 'all *Republicans* and *Levellers*, and against the Designs of our NATURAL ENEMIES [the French] who intend … to make WHORES of our *Wives* and *Daughters*'.[24] But in their published works, women had scope to present a more complex picture of the Navy.

Some women seem to have considered detailed aspects of the Navy. A letter to *The Gentleman's Magazine* in 1758, ostensibly by a female hand, made the shrewd point that commanding officers presented a clear target in battle, long before Nelson's fate confirmed it. The correspondent explained that, although guns were more effective at short range, a close engagement exposed commanders to danger. A captain was distinguished by his uniform and more likely to be shot at than any other single person on board.

> I take the liberty of proposing that there should be an express order, that in the time of an engagement all the officers should be dressed like the common sailors, having some little distinction known to the ships crew … but so small as to be invisible to the enemy.[25]

The author commented mysteriously that many readers may think the letter is written by someone in the Navy but 'the writer is a lady, and one who now has no connection with, or is anxious for the safety of any particular person in the navy'. This suggests that if the writer is indeed a woman, she has suffered a loss from just such a consequence as she described. Alternatively, if the correspondent has merely adopted a female persona, it is an interesting reflection on contemporary concepts of masculinity that suggested improvements to the safety of officers were felt to be more appropriately voiced by a woman.

Just as women were expected to help celebrate naval victories and individual acts of heroism, so it was assumed that they would play a role in charitable initiatives aimed at relieving those maimed in battle. After the Seven Years War, *The Gentleman's Magazine* carried 'An Address to the Public in favour of disbanded Soldiers' (prefaced by the explicit statement that whatever was said of soldiers applied to seamen too). The Address was clearly aimed at female readers:

> The Fair Sex have ever distinguished themselves by their approbation of the brave. In *their* hands I will leave the cause. Let them promote and encourage subscriptions for employing disbanded soldiers and it will be a mark of cowardice not to follow their example. Whatever lady has lost or saved a husband, son, a brother, a lover, will remember their own terrors, their own returning felicity; and will pity and reward the companions of those dear objects of their affection.[26]

After the end of the Napoleonic Wars there were many ex-seamen begging in the streets. The same plea for charity was conveyed in prints of the period and one example shows a young girl being shown the proper charitable response to disabled seamen (see Figure 7).

At the height of the conflict with Napoleon, Britain had 1000 ships and a navy of over 140 000 men. Nicholas Rodger has estimated that in the Seven Years War only about 20–25 per cent of seamen in the Navy were permanently married and that the service was mostly composed of young, single men.[27] Many of the men in the later period may not have been in stable relationships but they had mothers and sisters. It is easy now to forget the effect that Britain's large navy had on the domestic lives of thousands of women, not least because it seems to have been taken for granted at the time. The death of sailors at sea was a common theme in women's poetry of the period. Given the contemporary popularity of detailed shipwreck narratives, it was perhaps easier for women to imagine tempests affecting individual seamen than scenes of battle. In their poetry, they were more than six times more likely to allude to sailors than to the Navy. In their drama and prose, maritime references occur less frequently but the same trend continues – though with a lower ratio. Poems relating to sailors become increasingly popular in the Napoleonic War period. Women frequently wrote about the agony of waiting at home and show a heightened sensitivity to weather patterns. In doing so they both increased support for peace and excited sympathy for bereaved families in need of charity.[28] By helping to relieve the burden of the poor in this way, they contributed to the war effort. But any domestic note in their

THE BLIND SAILOR.

Figure 7 *The Blind Sailor.*

celebratory poetry has the effect of undermining the hero-creation effect. Anna Seward's earlier poem on the death of Cook demonstrates this clearly. Having praised the explorer's achievements, she addressed Mrs Cook:

> Ill-fated Matron! – far, alas! In vain
> Thy eager glances wander o'er the main! –
> 'Tis the vex'd billows, that insurgent rave,
> Their white foam silvers yonder distant wave,
> 'Tis not his sails! – thy Husband comes no more!
> His bones now whiten an accursed shore! –

By way of consolation, having conjured up this grim picture, Seward averred that Cook's fame would increase as Britain continued to celebrate his voyages. She pictured the explorer on 'immortal plains', choired by angels 'while he waits for *Thee*'. Mrs Cook doubtless spent months and years of her marriage waiting for her husband to return; now the tables seemed to be turned.[29]

Seward's lavish praise of Cook's achievement, also led her to question the more familiar, martial role of the Navy. Cook, she claimed, was exceptional in that he was motivated by benevolence:

> While half the warring world, in senseless strife,
> Dire thirst of power, and lavish waste of life,
> Sent their hoarse thunders o'er the seas to roar,
> And dye the distant waves in human gore.

Mary Robinson's poem 'Lines Written on a Day of Public Rejoicing' similarly bursts the bubble of celebration by recalling the many men sacrificed to win victories at sea:

> *While* shouts and acclamations rend the skies,
>   From the deep ocean, bleeding, cold, and wan,
> See groaning *spectres* in a phalanx rise,
>   To mourn the mis'ries of ambitious *man!*[30]

Robinson defined each corpse by their relation to women or their families: as a parent, husband or son, and asks readers to remember 'the wretched suff'rers who in anguish pine – | The soldier's, sailor's kindred – left behind!' Such poems struck a subversive note, though their sentiments can be interpreted as resulting chiefly from female sympathy and emotion. Poetry with a nautical theme focusing on loss, fear and sadness offered women a publicly acceptable vehicle for describing deep emotion. No wonder that, through a process of slippage, women came to compare their own traumas to that of the shipwrecked sailor. A sonnet by Charlotte Smith has a lone speaker musing by a rocky shore:

> Already shipwreck'd by the storms of Fate,
>   Like the poor mariner methinks I stand,
>   Cast on a rock; who sees the distant land
> From whence no succour comes – or comes too late.[31]

In contrast, female novelists of the early nineteenth century were more concerned to represent the Navy in society. This is better understood if their own works are culturally located. In an age much concerned with *politeness* and proper behaviour in company, the conduct of the Navy ashore was intimately related to female concerns. Middle- and upper-class women were taught to think of seamen in a particular way. In the 1770s, books written 'for the amusement and instruction of the fair sex' confirmed a view that had been gaining ground from the early decades of the century: that the society of virtuous women had an improving effect on men.[32] Sailors, deprived of this influence for long periods of time, lacked social graces. In 1779, Dr William Alexander set out this argument with 'the utmost plainness and simplicity of language' so that female readers might grasp it:

> We have just now observed, that men secluded from the company of women, become slovenly in their persons, and rough and untractable in their manners; but this is not all, even their gait assumes a more uncouth appearance, and their voice a hoarser and less musical tone; their sensations become less delicate, their sentiments less religious, and their passions seem to have more of the brutal, than those of the rest of their sex; circumstances which appear but too conspicuous in sailors, miners, and other people who either spend the greatest part of their time altogether without women, or in the company of such as have lost every female excellence. Should it be alleged, that these alterations are owing to the horrid trade of war, in which these sailors are so often engaged, the same thing should then be observed in soldiers. Should we have recourse to the surliness of the winds and waves, against which they maintain a perpetual combat, though these may in some measure account for their behaviour, yet it will appear to an accurate observer, that the ultimate cause is to be found only in the want of that social intercourse with the other sex, which of all things has the most powerful tendency to soften and humanize the mind.[33]

Alexander apparently uses his medical skills of close observation to present a factual, if unflattering image of the seaman. Women are given an explicit moral role that seems to have gained acceptance because the idea that the society of women had a civilizing influence was inculcated in officers too. This is reflected in Dr Fletcher's, *The Naval Guardian*, a work published over twenty years later to inculcate 'prudence, fortitude, and paternal care in the breast of the officer'. Fletcher's book consists of a series of letters supposedly written by a captain, a naval surgeon and a chaplain, interspersed with poetical allusions and some dramatic pieces. There is a certain Lady B whose second son is destined for the Navy, but her scruples have to be overcome by the surgeon and the chaplain before she will let her son enter the service. She is uneasy because in her experience officers are blunt to the point of rudeness and seem to think that politeness was unsuited to men of true courage. The reply is reassuring: such behaviour is understandable. At sea officers are cut off from the means of improving in politeness but they are 'sensible that this is to be found in conversation with virtuous women'.[34]

Yet women needed to exercise caution when embarking on any social intercourse designed to improve seamen. Alexander warned of the dangers presented by men newly released on shore:

Man, secluded from the company of women, is not only a rough and uncultivated, but a dangerous, animal to society; for, in such a situation, the animal appetite is daily gathering strength, till at last it becomes almost quite ungovernable; a fact well known to the inhabitants of sea-ports, who have too frequent opportunities of seeing the force of that ungovernable passion, with which sailors returned from a long voyage, commonly dedicate themselves to the worthless women who attend on account of their money. (p. 325)

Yet he concluded that the benefits of mixed society were not confined to men alone. Women would find that it was in their interest to mix in conversation with men. This would check attacks of male insolence and so make men less dangerous to either their virtue or their happiness. Such arguments accept that the moral authority of a virtuous woman gave her a beneficial public role, even though at this time occupational opportunities for some women were being restricted.

Mrs Parsons, who published *The Convict, or Navy Lieutenant. A Novel* in 1807,[35] omits all direct reference in this work to the supposed improving effect of female society. The hero, Thompson, is the third son of a country curate, placed in the Navy at 11 years old and left to make his way in the service without the smallest hope of any assistance from interest or fortune. We are asked to believe that he has been uncorrupted by his surroundings. His father's last admonitions were to avoid drunkenness and swearing, and this he has done although it has often made him an object of ridicule. Thompson is the frank, honest seaman of earlier authors, firmly in the mould of Smollet's Tom Bowling, but with more sentiment. He lacks a polished education, 'The reading of Thompson had been very confined; – of ancient history he knew little, and still less of the manners and customs of the present age', but Parsons implies that Thompson's integrity more than compensates for this narrow understanding: 'of fashionable vices, seduction and adultery, he knew nothing' (vol. II, p. 68). Yet though Parsons idealizes her sailor hero, through him she criticizes aspects of the Navy, including unfair procedures for promotion. Thompson complains to his friend:

Many great lords sons are put on board admirals ships to be posted up as fast as possible … . Boys tread upon the heads of men, and many youths, to my knowledge, are put in command, that between you and I, know no more how to steer a ship, or box the compass, than little Jack the cabin boy. – But what then, they have interest! they must be hoisted aloft, while many a honest lieutenant, who knows his duty, has fought for king and country, seen much in hard service, and is fit to command a seventy-four, may grow grey. (vol. II, p. 76–7)

The issue of promotion was of great interest to women because it related to the marriage market. Parsons is alert to the difficulties of officers who tried to support a wife and family on their modest pay and her hero states that no man should marry under the rank of captain (vol. II, p. 73). She emphasizes that a seaman's family necessarily shared the uncertainties of his fate, 'the boast of Britain and their country's bulwark, how inadequate to their services is the pittance of the wages they receive! How shamefully disproportioned the prize-money so dearly obtained at the risk of life – and certain misery to their families if they fall.' (vol. II, p. 230).

In some respects, Jane Austen's depiction of the Navy in *Mansfield Park* and *Persuasion* is less idealized and more radical. The novels were written between 1811 and 1816, when public gratitude towards the Navy was at its height but, unusually for female writers of this period, she offers an extended examination of the Navy as it related to society and relations between the sexes. She considers the issue of women being carried on board warships, and her representation of naval officers engages with the contemporary debate about the nature of femininity and a woman's role. She also explores the class tension caused during wartime and its aftermath by the rapid social rise of successful captains from non-aristocratic backgrounds.

Mrs Croft, the admiral's wife in *Persuasion*, has been 'almost as much at sea as her husband' and insists, rather unconvincingly, that 'women may be as comfortable on board, as in the best house in England'.[36] Accompanying one's husband on a man-of-war hardly constitutes full participation in the public sphere, or even (given Mrs Croft's privileged position as the wife of the ship's commander) participation in the world of work. Yet in contending, however ironically, that naval life can be quite civilized, Austen also manages to represent women as resilient and resourceful partners who do not need to be safely confined in the home. Captain Wentworth, on the other hand, apparently believes that women are too sensitive and frail to be looked after properly on a warship. He has just been explaining to the Musgrove sisters that the officers' accommodation at least can be arranged to give a degree of comfort. Nevertheless he tells Mrs Croft that he would never willingly admit any ladies on a ship of his, except for a ball or a visit. This, he claims, is not owing to a lack of gallantry on his part, but 'rather from feeling how impossible it is, with all one's efforts, and all one's sacrifices, to make the accommodations on board such as women ought to have' (p. 93).

Captain Harville, a disabled officer living on half-pay, adds a further dimension to the debate in *Persuasion* by showing that seamen can play a central part in the home. His lameness prevents him from taking much exercise and he is thoroughly domesticated. His work revolves around household chores and he spends much of his time improving his family's small house at Lyme. 'He drew, he varnished, he carpentered, he glued; he made toys for the children, he fashioned new netting-needles and pins with improvements; and if everything else was done, sat down to his large fishing-net at one corner of the room' (p. 120). Harville allows Jane Austen to depict sailors as sensitive, family men. He eloquently describes the seaman's pain at separation from his family and his joy at seeing them again after a long voyage (p. 238). Though Austen had never been to sea and may have simply found it easier to write about naval officers in a domestic setting, she concludes this novel by blurring still further the notion of separate spheres and emphasizing the domestic qualities of naval personnel. Anne, the heroine, marries Wentworth and we are told that the only shadow over her happiness is the fear that Britain might once again go to war. She 'gloried in being a sailor's wife, but she must pay the tax of quick alarm for belonging to that profession which is, if possible, more distinguished in its domestic virtues than in its national importance' (p. 254). Since naval officers predominately feature in this book, Austen may not be including men of the lower deck in this encomium. Nor are the officers in her earlier novels all entirely faithful – Admiral Crawford in *Mansfield Park*, published in 1814, was 'a man of vicious conduct' who brought his mistress under his own roof as soon as his wife died.[37] The niece who had been living with them was forced to seek another home in order to preserve her reputation.

In *Persuasion* Jane Austen gently makes fun of the received wisdom that conversation with the female sex had a civilizing influence and that seamen, deprived of female society, became brutal and uncouth. Captain Wentworth, home at the end of the war, remarks (none too seriously) that anybody between 15 and 30 could have him for the asking. 'A little beauty and a few smiles, and a few compliments to the navy, and I am a lost man. Should not this be enough for a sailor who has had no society among women to make him nice?' (p. 86). But Wentworth had already shown that, in his choice of a wife, he was likely to be extremely particular. Austen also suggests in this novel that the Navy was an accepted destination for troublesome, disappointing sons who presumably failed to respond to the influence of female conversation. Richard Musgrove was sent to sea because he was stupid and unmanageable on shore, and afterwards his family heard little from him. He was scarcely regretted when news of his death finally reached the family home, though subsequently he became a more pathetic figure in his mother's memory (p. 76).

Austen's representation of the Navy also needs to be read in the context of contemporary debate about how politeness or desirable behaviour in social spaces relate to masculinity, and the degree that masculine display might safely reach before it might be rated foppishness. In *Persuasion* Jane Austen depicts naval officers as frank, hospitable and trustworthy. They have an easy manner, contrasted with the 'formality and display' of those who cut a figure in society yet exhibit an inflated idea of what is proper to their rank. The openness of naval officers distinguishes them from personable but dishonest characters such as Mr Elliot, Anne's cousin. Austen's naval characters have commonsense and lack personal vanity. In this respect,

Admiral Croft is contrasted with Anne's father, Sir Walter Elliot, a minor aristocrat with a cash flow problem who rents out the family home to the Admiral. The indolent Sir Walter expends his small stock of energy in strenuously trying to push back the years to maintain his handsome appearance. The only feature of Sir Walter's home that gives the Admiral any discomfort is the number of mirrors adorning the walls of the dressing room.

As Dr Fletcher's *The Naval Guardian* indicates, by 1805 the social standing of the Navy, in a more polite age, had already improved. Fletcher suggests that it is the opinion of women who have helped to bring this about, confirming the contemporary importance of women's representation of the Navy. The high character of the Navy might not be appreciated in inland towns, he writes, yet in different courts of Europe and in sea-port towns, 'its rank is *defin'd*; and in most assemblies the officers are held in a superior point of view by both sexes; but particularly by the female, who all must allow to be the best qualified judges to take distinctions in such cases' (p. 111). One might suspect that the advances of preventative medicine had also helped to make naval officers more attractive partners on shore. Earlier in the century, poor diet at sea meant that officers contracted scurvy as their crews did, and even in the early stages this meant bad breath and rotting teeth. Lady Anson described a visit her husband had received from Captain Rodney and several other captains returned from Louisbourg, 'whose company was so offensive from the state of their health, as to make it but just possible to bear the cabin with them, not even almost after they were gone'.[38]

Austen's representation of naval officers throws additional light on their social status at the end of the Napoleonic War. In *Mansfield Park*, Mary Crawford explains that for the Navy, as for the army, the profession was its own justification: 'It has everything in its favour, heroism, danger, bustle, fashion. Soldiers and sailors are always acceptable in society. Nobody can wonder that men are soldiers and sailors' (p.136). This reflects a current attitude that the army or Navy was self-evidently an appropriate male career. For example, in 1799 Mary Anne Radcliffe, an early advocate of female rights, contended that men should stay well clear of all occupations that might be undertaken by widowed or destitute women trying to avoid prostitution. 'For in times like the present, is not the aid and assistance of men required in the military and naval departments?' Since men could be much better employed in military service than in filling occupations better suited to women, Radcliffe implied that only effeminate men would, for example, be content to work in a haberdasher's shop.[39]

A man's rank in the Navy had long been all-important to his womenfolk since, by association, it affected their own status. In the 1750s at the Plymouth weekly assemblies, only the daughters of higher-ranking officers could be elected to lead the proceedings.[40] In *Mansfield Park*, Mary Crawford states grandly, 'Post captains may be very good sort of men, but they do not belong to *us*.' Fanny's midshipman brother, William, complains that at the Portsmouth Assembly no girl will dance with any seaman unless he has a commission, and when his aunt suggests that William meet his cousins in Brighton, he cannot imagine that a 'poor, scrubby midshipman' will be welcome in such a smart place. Austen offers a convincing picture of lesser officers ashore when Fanny visits her parents in Portsmouth. She is embarrassed by her father, Lieutenant Price, disabled for active service but still equal to drinking good liquor with his friends. In this episode, Austen emphasizes, like Parsons before her, the narrow interests common to many career officers resulting from their limited education. Lieutenant Price had 'no information beyond his profession; he read only the newspaper and the navy-list; he talked only of the dock-yard, the harbour, Spithead, and the Motherbank; he swore and he drank, he was dirty and gross'. He had no real work to do ashore and every day wandered to the dockyard expecting to meet a 'brother lounger' with whom to while the hours away. There is a parallel here with the aristocratic male characters in the novel who for long periods have only to fill their time and survey affairs which their employees manage in detail. Yet Austen's contemporaries may have been uncomfortable at the thought that men from Lieutenant Price's class might, through the fortunes of war, enter the ranks of the landed gentry. A naval officer's training at least ensures that Fanny's father can improve his manners in genteel company, as when he meets Henry Crawford in Portsmouth, but he neglected to escort his daughters properly in public. Yet though Price might lack social graces, events prove that he has a stronger sense of parental discipline than many of his betters. On hearing of his niece's adultery he exclaims, 'But by G— if she belonged to me, I'd give her the rope's end as long as I could stand over her. A little flogging for man and woman too, would be the best way of preventing such things.'[41]

In *Persuasion*, Sir Walter objects to the Navy 'as being the means of bringing persons of obscure birth into undue distinction'. Since he is a vain man, obsessed by appearance, he also finds the Navy distasteful on the superficial grounds that life at sea causes premature ageing. The tone of the novel makes it clear that snobbery such as this was becoming untenable. A naval officer, especially in a provincial town like Bath, could be an asset at social gatherings. Anne's sister Elizabeth, as vain and formal as their father, discovered that, in Bath at least, a man of such an air and appearance as Wentworth was a coveted guest. 'The past was nothing. The present was that Captain Wentworth would move about well in her drawing room.' The 1801 census revealed that in the resort town of Bath men accounted for only 39 per cent of the population, and at social gatherings they must have been in great demand. There could be no objection to Wentworth marrying Anne now that he had won promotion, for 'Captain Wentworth, with five-and-twenty thousand pounds, and as high in his profession as merit and activity could place him was no longer nobody'.[42] He was quite worthy to address the daughter of a baronet who had not the sense either to manage his own fortune or make the best of his privileged situation in life. And yet, had Anne disobeyed her family and married Wentworth at an earlier stage in his career, there could have been no guarantee that she would not end up in straitened circumstances similar to those of Mrs Price in *Mansfield Park*. With good reason, conduct books warned women about the glamour attached to military service just as popular songs warned women not to trust sailors.[43]

III

Women rarely refer to domestic arrangements when they mention the Navy in their published works. Jane Austen is an exception and private letters confirm the accuracy of references in her novels. Women were part of the support mechanism that kept men at sea, and they could perform that task well or ill. They could help their loved ones pack, for example, and ensure they were provided as well as they might be for the months at sea ahead. In *Mansfield Park*, when Fanny Price returned to her chaotic family in Portsmouth, she helped sew shirts for her brother Sam who was just about to join the Navy and 'did so much, that the boy was shipped off at last, with more than half his linen ready' (p. 383). In 1798, Nelson, on his way to the Mediterranean was trapped for ten days at St Helen's by adverse winds. Unfortunately he spent some of the time going through his linen and found it very different from his wife's list. Letters began to fly between them as more and more items were discovered to be missing. Lady Nelson could only reply feebly, 'I wish very much it had been in my power to send your things more comfortably'.[44]

After the Napoleonic Wars ended, it was possible for commentators to be more consistently humorous about a naval officer's career and George Cruikshank produced, from sketches by Captain Frederick Marryat, a series of prints called 'The Progress of a Midshipman Exemplified in the Career of Master Blockhead'. The first print depicts the fitting out of young Blockhead before he goes to sea (see Plate 13). It shows his mother weeping – not surprisingly since her son seems destined for the sickly West India Station. Her grief probably renders her own efforts ineffectual but packing is clearly the responsibility of the female side of the family; her husband seems more concerned with the expense of sending his son to sea. Many of the items destined for Blockhead's sea-chest are concerned with preserving health or supplementing rations: medical handbooks, Epsom salts, rags for wounds, James's Powders (reputed to be efficacious against fevers in hot climates), pickles and tablets of portable soup (the eighteenth-century equivalent of stock cubes). This image offers a rare representation the Navy in the domestic sphere. It hints at some of the pressures that resulted in sons being sent to sea (paintings on the wall signal that that Blockhead comes from a naval family), and indicates the basic knowledge that families needed about medicine and food preservation in order to equip their sons for life overseas. Use of such gendered images was a means of shaping public opinion about the Navy and about female roles.

There were various opportunities for women attached to seamen to use the connection in order to display female worth. Catherine Jemmat, daughter of an admiral, published her memoirs in 1762. She included a poem to her young brother on his first going to sea, in which she earnestly encouraged him to be 'mindful of heav'n' and to trust to providence.[45] Mothers might translate their fears for young sons into morally uplifting letters such as those written by Jane Davis who published in 1801 *Letters from a Mother to her son: written upon his return from his first voyage at sea*. She warned her young offspring, 'As sailors are more exposed to danger than any other class of men, I hope that you are more particularly attentive to the concerns of your soul.' Believing that 'thoughtless profusion and unsuspecting credulity' were characteristic of sailors, she feared the snares that awaited her son on shore as much as the perils at sea, and warned him bluntly against spending his money on prostitutes.[46]

As indicated, Jane Austen's representation of the Navy in her novels also throws light on the particular situation of seamen's wives. They had to be prepared to travel to see their husbands on leave, and their fears might affect their ability to act even if they were ready to take on extra responsibility in their husbands' absence. In *Persuasion*, even the formidable Mrs Croft reveals, 'The only time I ever really suffered in body or mind, the only time I ever fancied myself unwell, or had any ideas of danger, was the winter that I passed by myself at Deal, when the Admiral (*Captain* Croft then) was in the North Seas. I lived in perpetual fright at that time, and had all manner of imaginary complaints from not knowing what to do with myself, or when I should hear from him next' (p. 95). Since two of Austen's brothers were in the Navy, personal experience might have helped her to reproduce convincingly the phrases women used to represent the Navy and its effect on their lives. In the same novel, Anne Elliot explains to Captain Harville that women, left to their own devices, are apt to brood. 'We live at home, quiet, confined, and our feelings prey upon us. You are forced on exertion' (p. 236).

Not unnaturally, long periods of apprehension seem to have been common to many naval wives. Frances Boscawen preferred to live in the country but moved to London once she was married because she wanted to be close to the seat of news and because London was a direct journey for her husband whenever his ship was in port. She wrote to her husband, then Captain Edward Boscawen:

I was a great beast for not writing to you yesterday. I ask your pardon, my dear Ned, and I don't intend to serve you so any more. But indeed, I had nothing agreeable to tell you, for the high wind at S. W. on Thursday night made me so excessively uneasy that I got no sleep (for I fancied you sailed on Tuesday). I thought you in danger, and I was so thoroughly disturbed that I jumped up in the morning before anybody came near me, 'tired of my restless couch'.[47]

Yet wives of seamen could seek to define their identity partly through the specific duties of that role. Depending on their station and disposition, they could write cheering letters to their husband as Frances Boscawen did, or fretful ones as Frances Nelson did. The periodic household upheavals and journeys to whatever home port in which their husband's ship had docked could add excitement to otherwise mundane lives, but no doubt were also often a source of vexation and worry. In 1801, Jane Austen wrote somewhat ambivalently to her sister of her family's impending move to Bath, 'there is something interesting in the bustle of going away, & the prospect of spending future summers by the Sea or in Wales is very delightful. – For a time we shall now possess many of the advantages which I have often thought of with Envy in the wives of Sailors or Soldiers'.[48] Women's representations of the Navy enabled them to represent their own sex as loyal and faithful while also providing an outlet for female anxiety as they waited at home.

Women certainly helped raise the status of the Navy as a popular institution, intimately bound up with British identity and, by the end of the Napoleonic Wars, with a strong claim on public gratitude. Their works celebrated individual heroes or naval types; their musical performances and patterns of consumption reinforced contemporary propaganda and helped to bolster public morale in wartime. In this respect, ship launches at which elite women featured prominently (not only in the naming ceremony but also as spectators) added to the social standing of the Navy and further boosted morale. Once the state had furnished St Paul's with monuments to naval heroes and opened them to public inspection, women's writing helped to publicize them.[49] Women's more subtle literary productions questioned the human cost of war and explored the tensions of a militarized society, but in the main their activities kept the Navy in the public eye and increasingly sentimentalized the service, helping to consolidate a standard public response to the Navy as an institution.

Notes

1   I am indebted to Dianne Dugaw for this discussion of contemporary balladry.;
    see, 'Balladry's Female Warriors: Women, Warfare, and Disguise in the Eighteenth
    Century', *Eighteenth-Century Life*, 9 (2) (1985), 1–20 (p. 3).
2   W. Ireland, *The Sailor Boy. A Poem in Four Cantos; illustrative of the Navy of Great
    Britain*, 2nd edn (London, 1822), p. 141.
3   The bravery of women at sea is recorded in S.J. Pratt, *Gleanings in England;
    descriptive of the Countenance, Mind and Character of the British Country*, 2 vols, 2nd
    edn (London, 1801), vol. II, p. 542.
4   *The Ladies Magazine*, ed. J. Goodwill, I (1750), p. 269.
5   *The Female Soldier; Or, The Surprising Life and Adventures of Hannah Snell* (London,
    1750), pp. 30, 65, 67, 165.
6   *Ladies Magazine*, ed. J. Goodwill, I (1750), p. 282.
7   A.F. Randall, *A Letter to the Women of England, on the Injustice of Mental Subordination.
    With Anecdotes* (London, 1788), pp. 43–4.
8   For a discussion of this issue, see H. Barker and E. Chalus, *Gender in Eighteenth-
    Century England: Roles, Representations and Responsibilities* (London and New York,
    1997), pp. 19–24.
9   For example, A. Vickery, *The Gentleman's Daughter: Women's Lives in Georgian
    England* (New Haven, CT, and London, 1998).
10 L. Colley, *Britons: Forging the Nation 1707–1837* (New Haven, CT, and London,
    1992), pp. 261–2.
11 See E. Kowaleski-Wallace, *Consuming Subjects: Women, Shopping, and Business in
    the Eighteenth Century* (New York, 1997), pp. 19–36.
12 For example, P. Wheatley, 'To a Gentleman of the Navy' (1774), *The Poems of Phillis
    Wheatley*, ed., J.D. Mason Jr (Chapel Hill, 1966), p. 83; A. Seward, 'Death of Cook'
    (1780), in *The Poetical Works of Anna Seward; With Extracts from her Literary
    Correspondence*, ed. W. Scott, 3 vols (Edinburgh, 1810), vol. II, p. 35.
13 Quoted in R. Prentice, *A Celebration of the Sea* (London, 1994), p. 37.
14 Quoted by C. Oman, *Nelson* (London, 1947), p. 498.
15 K. Wilson, 'Empire of virtue: the imperial project and Hanoverian culture, *c.* 1720–
    1785', in L. Stone, ed., *An Imperial State at War: Britain, 1689–1815* (London, 1994),
    pp. 128–64.
16 C. Ehrlich, *The Piano, A History*, revised edn (Oxford, 1990), pp. 14–20.
17 *The Lady's Magazine, or Entertaining Companion for the Fair Sex*, ed. Oliver
    Goldsmith, II (London, 1760), 225. Cf. 'A Song, in The Fair', ibid., I (1760), p. 225
    which celebrates British naval and military victories.
18 Seward, *The Poetical Works*, vol. III, pp. 115–18.
19 T. Dibdin, *Songs by Charles Dibdin*, 2nd edn (London, 1881), p. xxviii.
20 *Emma, Lady Hamilton's Songs*, 2 vols (*c.* 1810; NMM Library ref. PBE6757), I, nos
    1, 10. Cf. J. Dale, *Nelson and the Navy. A Sonata for the Piano Forte – in commemoration
    of the Glorious 1st August, 1798, etc.* (London, 1798).
21 'Far, far at Sea!', in *Cupid Wounded: or, the Mischievous Bee: Being a Collection of
    entire New Songs sung at all the Places of Public Amusement* (London, ?1815 and
    ?1820), p. 7. This entire collection is about the parting of sailors and loved ones.
22 'Poor Ben', *Cupid Wounded*, p. 8.
23 'Steady as she Goes', *The Young Men and Maids Delight, Being an entire new and
    choice collection …* (London, n.d.), p. 7.
24 A recruiting poster issued at Shoreham in *c.*1797 (NMM 659.133.1:355.216:094).
25 *GM*, XXVIII (1758), 275.
26 *GM*, XXXIII (1763), 120–21.

27 N.A.M. Rodger, *Wooden World. An Anatomy of the Georgian Navy*, (London, 1986), p. 79.

28 For example, Seward, *The Poetical Works*, vol. I, pp. 134–5; 142, 143; Mary D., 'The Billow' in *Lady's Magazine* (Supplement for 1805), 36 (1805), p. 713; M. Robinson, 'Lines Written on the Sea-Coast' , *The Poetical Works of the late Mrs Mary Robinson: including many pieces never before published*, 3 vols (London, 1806), vol. II, pp. 205–6.

29 Seward, *The Poetical Works*, vol. II, pp. 45–6.

30 Robinson, *The Poetical Works, vol. III*, pp. 253–4.

31 C. Smith, 'Sonnet XII. Written on the Sea Shore. – October, 1784', in *Elegiac Sonnets and Other Poems*, 3rd edn (London, 1786), p. 13.

32 See J. Fordyce, *The Character and Conduct of the Female Sex and The Advantages to be derived by Young Men from the Society of Virtuous Women. A Discourse in Three Parts* (London, 1776), pp. 78, 97; and J. Georgia, 'The Joys of Social Intercourse: Men, Women and Conversation in the Eighteenth Century' in K.L. Cope, ed., *Compendious Conversations: The Method of Dialogue in the Early Enlightenment* (Frankfurt, 1992), pp. 249–56.

33 William Alexander, MD, *The History of Women from the Earliest Antiquity, to the Present Time*, 2 vols (London, 1779), p. 315.

34 C. Fletcher, *The Naval Guardian*, 2nd edn, 2 vols (London, 1805), vol. I, pp. viii, 12. First published 1800.

35 Parsons, Mrs, *The Convict, or Navy Lieutenant. A Novel*, 4 vols (Brentford, 1807).

36 J. Austen, *Persuasion*, ed. D.W. Harding (Harmondsworth, 1965), p. 93.

37 J. Austen, *Mansfield Park*, ed. T. Tanner (Harmondsworth, 1966), p. 74.

38 Quoted in Rodger, *The Wooden World*, p. 102.

39 M.A. Radcliffe, *The Female Advocate; or An Attempt to Recover the Rights of Women from Male Usurpation* (London, 1799), pp. 28–9.

40 C. Jemmat, *The Memoirs of Mrs. C. Jemmat*, 2 vols (London, 1762), vol. I, pp. 50–51.

41 Austen, *Mansfield Park*, pp. 91, 253, 256–7, 381, 395, 428.

42 Austen, *Persuasion*, pp. 49, 231, 250.

43 For example, [William Kenrick], *The Whole Duty of Woman. By a Lady* (Exeter, 1794), p. 44.

44 Quoted in Oman, *Nelson*, p. 275.

45 [J. Davis], *Letters from a Mother to her son: written upon his return from his first voyage at sea* (Stockport, 1801), p. 27. C. Jemmat, 'An Acrostick on my brother's going to sea', in *The Memoirs*, vol. II, p. 137.

46 [J. Davis], *Letters from a Mother to her son: written upon his return from his first voyage at sea* (Stockport, 1801), pp. 27, 29.

47 C. Aspinall-Oglander, ed., *Admiral's Wife. Being the Life and Letters of the Hon. Mrs. Edward Boscawen from 1719 to 1761* (London, 1940), p. 55 (31 Oct. 1747).

48 J. Austen, *Jane Austen's Letters*, ed. D. Le Faye, 3rd edn (Oxford, 1995), p. 68.

49 See [Maria Hacket], *A Popular Account of St. Paul's Cathedral: with a Description of The Monuments and other interesting particulars* (London, 1816).

Chapter 7

The Navy and its Doctors

This chapter focuses on works of naval medicine and examples of public interest in the health of the Navy. Few authors writing about medicine and the sea in the eighteenth and early nineteenth centuries have considered how medical discourses construct the objects of their enquiry in social terms. Such terms play little or no part in the seminal account of the development of naval medicine provided by C. Lloyd and J.S. Coulter; or in the detailed accounts by K.J. Carpenter and others of the development of a cure for scurvy. The same might be said of discussions outlining the beginnings of institutional care during this period, although such studies do show how civilian hospitals played an important role in projecting images of civic well-being, philanthropy and medical 'progress'.[1] But it can be argued that medical discourse is always shaped by social assumptions – for example, about gender, race, or class – which it tends to naturalize. I argue here that discourses of naval medicine naturalized, and so helped to promote, particular assumptions about the Navy, which were supplementary to their immediate medical concerns.

I

In the second half of the eighteenth century, doctors and men of science increasingly influenced public opinion by publishing their work in books and essays aimed at the polite reader.[2] The Navy offered excellent opportunities for medical observation – in wartime, on voyages of discovery or in specific experiments on crews. Medical writings helped to complicate the public image of the Navy, although works by naval surgeons were generally products of their own desire for greater recognition and higher status. All warships carried surgeons.[3] These men had first-hand experience of both life at sea and the Navy as an institution, but in the eighteenth century they were often poorly trained. As one handbook for naval surgeons made clear, they were expected to acquire much of their skill on the job, and were apt to view ships' crews as a testing ground. 'For common and general Parts of Surgery,' wrote John Atkins in 1737, 'I know no better School to improve in, than the NAVY, especially in time of War. Accidents are frequent, and the Industrious illustrate Practice by their Cures.'[4] The status of naval surgeons was lower than that of their counterparts in the army. Naval surgeons were often dissatisfied with the lack of respect shown them on board ship and with the class of men with whom their assistants were forced to associate below deck. They did not obtain officer status and a uniform until January 1805, and even afterwards surgeons were still subordinate to lieutenants on the ships in which they served. Until their rank and salary improved in 1805, they were badly paid and subject to dismissal at the end of a war; some later achieved success in civilian practice, but on the whole their skills were lightly regarded ashore.[5] In this period, works concerning naval medicine often reveal signs of tension between physicians and naval surgeons. In 1798 a well-qualified doctor could still write dismissively of a surgeon's ability: 'It is a notorious truth, that at sea they amputate like the barbarians of Abyssinia; only with this difference, they use a knife instead of a hatchet.'[6] And as late as 1808, a former naval surgeon was still complaining about the practice in the army or navy of accepting raw apothecaries' boys as hospital mates or assistant surgeons, 'whose whole education has been acquired, in the course of a year or two, behind the counter of some obscure apothecary or barber-surgeon'. Worse still, he thought some naval surgeons continued to perform operations 'in a way that would disgrace a farrier of any repute'.[7]

In the first half of the eighteenth century, there were several well-known treatises and guides for ship surgeons. It was recognized that crews on long voyages generally became ill, whether or not individuals met with accidents or were wounded in battle. The various causes of sickness were not well understood – there was no conception of vitamin deficiency or of germ theory – and in the course of the century, as Britain worked to achieve and maintain naval supremacy, shipboard diseases became a more pressing problem. It was the circumstances of Anson's circumnavigation and expedition against Spain in the 1740s that drew particular attention to seamen's health.[8] Anson did finally capture a Spanish treasure ship but during the course of his arduous commission he lost over 80 per cent of his ships' company: four men from enemy action and more than 1300 from disease. After this tragedy, doctors scrutinized accounts of the voyage, searching for clues that would explain the level of sickness. For a while the Admiralty considered fitting all warships with Samuel Sutton's machine for extracting foul air out of ships, but balked at the expense. The published account of Sutton's invention included a supporting 'Discourse on the Scurvy' by the King's own physician, the suave Dr Richard Mead, who maintained that foul air contributed to the disease. He conceded that humanity alone might not prompt greater care for seamen's health but argued that considerations of policy, military success and professional honour made such care advisable.[9] Mead's intervention itself suggests an element of self-interest; here was an opportunity for a prominent clinician to increase his standing by aligning himself and his profession with wider national aims.[10] The Anson episode was followed by a steady flow of publications on naval medicine, by many doctors whose writings suggest a comparable awareness of both their own and their readers' self-interest. In their essays on specific diseases or epidemics and in general handbooks, they helped to bring the health of the Navy to the public's attention.

Of course, it is difficult to determine precisely who read these medical books, other than doctors themselves who supportively quoted each other; but clearly their works did not fall dead from the press. Of the contemporary books footnoted here, 50 per cent enjoyed a second edition and over 30 per cent three or more editions. Roy Porter and others have shown that in the eighteenth century, sufferers played an active role in managing their own state of health and turned to a variety of books, magazines and pamphlets for medical advice. Public-spirited, well-informed, responsible people were expected to have a general familiarity with medicine. For example, the surviving record of borrowings from the Bristol subscription library between 1773 and 1784, shows that works of medicine and anatomy were provided for general readers. Popular publications instructed in medical self-help and played an important role in the diffusion of medical initiatives. This was the case with the *Gentleman's Magazine*, at least until 1810 or so when it began to report on the medical profession in a way that implied that subsequently the lay public would have little involvement in its activities. At its peak the magazine had a circulation possibly of over 10 000 copies and far more readers. In its pages medical books were both listed and reviewed, and readers shared information about specific ailments or wrote in to ask for particular advice. In 1767, for example, one correspondent described a home-made bandage as 'a method to cure, or at least prevent, the increase of any naval rupture', indicating the commonplace nature of such injuries at sea and the spirit of self-help that enabled sufferers to cope with such chronic ailments.[11] Editors of the magazine certainly felt that the health of seamen was of sufficiently broad interest to carry articles on the subject and also to justify the expense of including prints of Haslar naval hospital, Portsmouth.[12]

II

A detailed examination of references to naval medicine in the *Gentleman's Magazine* during this period helps us to estimate the degree of public interest in keeping crews healthy. In the mid-1750s there was substantial curiosity in the ventilation of ships. The Revd Dr Hales, Clerk of the Closet to the Princess of Wales, suggested various means of introducing fresh air into the lower decks, which were reported with recommendations by ship's captains. Hales also published proposals for fumigating ships to rid them of infection. These proposals applied to merchant ships as well as naval vessels but such descriptions vividly communicated to readers the claustrophobic, airless conditions below deck on warships and the importance of cleanliness to reduce disease.[13] The *Gentleman's Magazine* soon became a favoured means by which naval officers disseminated to a wider public useful health tips gleaned on longer voyages. The captain of the *Tyger* sent in a letter 'containing some few Observations that may be of public Service' in 1755 because he felt that his observations could not be better communicated 'than thro' the Channel of the Gentleman's Magazine'.[14] He wrote from St Augustin's Bay, Madagasgar, and congratulated himself on keeping the ship's crew healthy. 'I have had about three fevers in the ship since I left *England*, which were occasioned by drinking great quantities of spirits at *Plymouth*, but Dr *James*'s Powder soon removed these.'[15] The letter shows how, in passing on medical advice, a particular image of hard-drinking seamen could be reinforced. It also confirms that naval officers were often aware of recent works on naval medicine. The correspondent had ordered his ship's doctor to treat a severe case of scurvy according to the recommendations of Dr Anthony Addington who wrote an essay on sea scurvy in 1753. He also expected his men to drink and bathe in sea water every day, leading by example himself, and believed that this had kept scurvy at bay. In 1760, the captain of HMS *Torbay* wrote to the *Gentleman's Magazine* from Plymouth Sound explaining that he had kept his ship healthy by enforcing cleanliness. He shamed men who were found to be dirty or to have sold their clothes for drink, fumigated the decks and treated the few scorbutic cases on board with lemon juice.[16]

Issues linked to naval medicine and the image of British seamen were actually debated in the *Gentleman's Magazine*. At the time of great controversy about the state of the Navy following Admiral Byng's court martial in 1756 for alleged cowardice and neglect of duty, one correspondent perceived a link between scurvy and idleness in the Navy. He pointed out that scurvy was more prevalent in the Navy than in the merchantmen, even though warships were better ventilated from having gunports, and suggested that it was fortunate for the crews of merchantmen that their ships were less well manned since they were obliged to keep up a healthy sweat. He continued, 'it is well known in the navy, especially on board large ships, what numbers continually sculk [*sic*] below, and there indulge themselves in sleep and inactivity', adding, 'it is a doctrine, 'tis true, that will be in no ways agreeable to unthinking tars.'[17] The Editor was moved to disagree, pointing out the extent to which sailors suffered on Anson's circumnavigation and noting that the late Dr Richard Mead who had read accounts of the voyage and talked with Anson never mentioned inactivity as the cause. The Editor also referred to Mr Pascoe Thomas's account of the Anson voyage which described how sailors suffering from scurvy were falsely accused of idleness and kicked and punched to do their duty when utterly incapable of it. This gives an insight into naval discipline of the time and the desperate situation that could result on board if the numbers of sick rose to a level that left too few seamen to work the ship.

In 1758, when British fleets were fitting out for long voyages, the *Gentleman's Magazine* printed Thomas Reynolds's proposals for the management of the sick in the Navy on the grounds that they had never been published before and might help to save lives. Reynolds, a former naval surgeon, recommended good food, warm clothes, and the paternal care of officers. In doing so he conveyed an image of a navy prone to drunkenness – seamen, he argued, must be mustered regularly and forced to display their clothes to prevent them from selling them for drink. Reynolds also throws light on the kind of men who served in the Navy at that time and what drove them to sea. He commented that when seamen were dangerously ill,

> many of them reflect with great severity on their own misdoings, which brought them first to sea, and consequently into their present calamitous condition, being now under the fullest conviction that if they had regarded the admonitions of their parents and friends, and in obedience to their advice would have submitted to get their bread by honest judicious means, they might have lived a less hazardous as well as a more easy life in the midst of peace and plenty.[18]

In the 1760s and 1770s, while Britain was engaged in no major war, the *Gentleman's Magazine* carried less information about naval medicine, although general medicine was still a popular topic and methods of smallpox inoculation attracted particular attention. By 1779, when the war with the war with the American colonies was going badly, medical correspondents to the *Gentleman's Magazine* were advising general inoculation of the poor and citing the advantage to Britain's army and navy. If inoculated, 'the soldier and sailor [would] do service to their country without fear of being cut off in prime of life to the great loss and disappointment of the public'.[19] Military medicine again featured more strongly in the magazine from the onset of the French Revolutionary Wars. In 1793, Dr Moseley's new edition of his *Treatise on Tropical Diseases* was welcomed as useful and important: 'Our distant colonies, our militia, our fleets, and armies, are under great obligation to this writer.'[20] In 1794 a correspondent warned readers against using any substitute for Dr James's Powders in the Tropics, explaining that when the Sick and Hurt Board had asked the College of Physicians in 1789 whether or not to supply warships with the less expensive *puvis antimonialis*, the College could only report that no trials had been conducted that allowed them to say it was any better.[21] While the prime purpose of this correspondent was to defend an established remedy against rival substances, he raised the public profile of naval health in the context of the cost of national defence and the progress of medicine. At this time, sea scurvy once more became a matter for debate in the Magazine. An inhabitant of Lincoln recommended the juice of goose grass while earlier letters were cited blaming scurvy on putrid air and salt provisions. A 'Friend to the Navy' proposed that the Admiralty supply the root of the garden carrot, which was easily casked and less liable to spoil than lemon juice; another recommended instead 'small spirit of vitriol'.[22] The average reader could be pardoned for being none the wiser.

Medical findings, as they related to the Navy, were also frequently reported in *The Times*. On 1 December 1796 readers were informed, 'Dr. CARMICHAEL SMITH's mode of stopping contagion, by nitrous fumigation, is now very properly adopted through the whole of the British Navy, and will certainly be productive of the most salutary consequences.' This piece referred to James Carmichael Smyth's book, published earlier that year, describing an experiment to reduce infection on board the *Union* hospital ship which had docked at Sheerness with about 200 sick on board.[23] Such notices helped to keep naval medicine firmly in the public eye – as did open disputes between doctors themselves. On 26 December 1807, for example, 'an Old Navy Surgeon' wrote to *The Times* refuting Dr Harness's claims to be responsible for the prevention of scurvy in the Navy by introducing lemon juice into men's rations. As the correspondent pointed out, it had first been necessary to discover how to preserve lemon juice – and Dr Gilbert Blane discovered this as one of the commissioners for sick and wounded seamen.

Seamen, their families, and all those who travelled by sea, naturally had a keen interest in finding out how to stay healthy on long voyages or in tropical climates. An appeal printed in five issues of *The Times* during 1794 illustrates the quality of this common interest and shows how patent medicines and the writing of naval surgeons were recommended to a wider reading public. The appeal is addressed 'particularly to the officers of the army and navy serving in the West Indies and other hot climates'. The writer explains that violent fevers in the West Indies have been fatal to many officers in the previous year and given serious alarm to the friends of those destined to serve there. He claims that doctors who have practised in that climate recommend James's Powders, and continues, 'for more positive proofs of its efficacy, reference may be had to Dr James's "Dissertation on Fevers"; in which accounts are published from Surgeons of our ships, both in the *East* and *West Indies*, where the crews had been seized with violent malignant Fevers, and cured after other means had failed, by taking this medicine'.[24] As we have seen, the first print in George Cruickshank's series 'The Progress of a Midshipman Exemplified in the Career of Master Blockhead' (see Plate 13), suggests that naval families took this advice to heart or at least that it was well known. Young Blockhead is destined for the West Indies and his parents have taken the precaution of putting James's Powders into his sea chest. Clearly, medical works were relevant to the imperial enterprise, although after the Battle of Trafalgar, there are fewer references to the health of the Navy in the *Gentleman's Magazine*, indicating that public interest in the topic slowly waned.

III

The perspective of doctors writing about naval medicine changed and developed in the course of the eighteenth century, and successive publications helped to shape public understanding of how it impacted on naval life. Earlier books on naval medicine published in the 1750s may have been partly written to counteract the damning descriptions of naval surgeons in Tobias Smollett's *Roderick Random*.[25] The novel appeared in 1748, was a great success and remained popular for decades. Smollett's account of Admiral Vernon's disastrous attack on Cartagena and the death of thousands in the British fleet from yellow fever, was based on his eye-witness experience there as a surgeon's mate. A patriotic Scot with perhaps little sympathy for Britain's imperial mission, Smollett denounced Vernon's ability to lead, to carry out combined operations, and even to take proper responsibility for his men, although in reality Vernon worked hard to improve conditions in the Navy. Smollett depicted life on board a ship of war as a stinking ordeal with little chance of survival if this depended on the ship's surgeon. It was the worst possible propaganda for the Navy and naval medicine. No wonder if doctors attempted publicly to reaffirm the primacy of medical discourse over Smollett's racy and colourful descriptions.

But in the 1750s doctors themselves displayed marked anxiety over the scale of the naval health-care problem. Whenever it manifested itself in home waters, it was frequently in excess of any resources that port towns could muster. When a fleet returned, many hundreds of men could be put ashore with scurvy. Dr John Huxham, a physician in Plymouth, was so appalled by the numbers he saw suffering from scurvy that he drew up proposals for preventing the disease and distributed copies to the captains of warships:

> I have known many a Ship's Company set out on a Cruize in high Health, and yet in two or three months return vastly sickly, and eaten out with the Scurvy, a third Part of them being half rotten, and utterly unfit for the Service. – About four or five weeks after they have been out, they begin to drop down one after another, and at length by Dozens, till at last scarce half the *Complement* can stand to their Duty.[26]

Huxham's account implies that scurvy was unavoidable on longer voyages. Certainly the sailors had no control over the sequence of events. Yet Huxham understood that scurvy was linked to poor diet and that 'Apples, Oranges, and Lemons, alone, have been often known to do surprising Things in the Cure of very deplorable scorbutic Cases'. He recommends the use of vinegar to purify water on board and the addition of 'inferior wines' to the seaman's diet. In justifying the additional cost of these rations, he alludes to Britain's dependence on the Navy for defence and imperial ambition, drawing a parallel between Rome and Britain: Rome issued its soldiers with vinegar and wine, and if Rome thought such lives worth the expense, why shouldn't Britain have as much regard for *its* sailors who were 'altogether as brave and useful to the Commonwealth?'[27] Huxham contributed to the growing public image of the Navy as an essential tool of empire. He also suggested that seamen were undervalued and, given the current medical provision, almost certain to become ill in the service.

Doctors continued to use John Huxham's patriotic arguments when lobbying the public. Others, to the very end of the period under review, emphasized the economic case for better health care at sea: Parliament expended vast sums on hospitals and medical supplies; it was expensive to replace men and support invalids; savings could be made if crews could be kept healthy; seamen, by the very nature of their calling, represented a considerable investment. Dr Thomas Trotter, a naval surgeon who became Physician to the Fleet in 1794, reiterated the accepted view:

> The soldier can be perfected in his exercise in a few days; and it little avails what kind of trade he has been employed in; but no person will have the hardihood to contend, that a seaman's duty can be learned in less than seven years, or after twenty-one years of age. He must be accustomed to it from boyhood; for no adult being can ever be brought to endure the privations, dangers, and hardships, which are inseparable from a sea-life.[28]

Doctors throughout this period reinforced a perception of the Navy as a demanding profession requiring both skill and endurance.

Manning the Navy was a persistent problem and Government had taken some steps to encourage volunteers.[29] But in the mid-eighteenth century, the need to attract men to the service and preserve them once in it did not immediately win ministers' support for improved health measures, although medical provision in the Royal Navy still exceeded that in the merchant service. In 1757, James Lind, a dedicated naval doctor, could refer to this with national pride (after all, in the French navy seamen had their pay stopped when ill). On occasion, therefore, doctors represented the Navy as honourable employment with some degree of security:

> Nor is it a small additional Pleasure, to a Seamen in the Royal Navy to reflect, that whatever Misfortunes, incident to his Way of Life, may befall him, in the Service of his country, he will be honourably rewarded, and, under many Circumstances of but small Accident, obtain a Pension for Life.[30]

Large naval hospitals (Haslar in Portsmouth, begun in 1745, and Stonehouse, near Plymouth, begun in 1758) were visible reminders that the government ostensibly took great care of the health of its seamen and, by association, that the Navy was acknowledged to be of vital importance to the nation. Dr George Pinckard, Deputy Inspector-General of Hospitals to His Majesty's Forces, described Haslar in just such terms:

> Connected with our country's greatness, it called up a similar train of ideas, and I felt it an honor [*sic*] to England that so noble an institution should offer, to our brave tars, the comforts required in sickness. Too much cannot be done for our navy, nor can the provision for our sick and wounded defenders be too liberal; they merit all their country can bestow.[31]

Pinckard was writing during the Napoleonic Wars when there was general consensus about the debt that the country owed to the Navy; nevertheless, Haslar was a remarkable building – completed in 1761, it was for many years the largest brick building in Europe. Built at great expense, naval hospitals provided valuable statistics on the frequency of diseases and helped to spread good practice formerly confined to isolated ships. Together with the hospital built at Greenwich for retired seamen, they were often reproduced in prints. Greenwich Hospital early became a tourist attraction.[32] In 1789, its two chaplains wrote a history of the hospital which invited readers to regard the building as a work of national grandeur as well as a monument to wisdom and benevolence. The history was used as a guidebook which, adapted or augmented, saw eight English and two French editions by 1820.

Doctors of the mid-eighteenth century commenting on naval health were able to position themselves as reformers. They depict the Navy as an institution bound by tradition, in which sickness was fostered by 'too strict an Attachment to Old Regulations and Customs'.[33] If the role of reformer offered opportunities to increase their status in some quarters, another role as servants of the state usefully seeking to point out economies, offered opportunities in others. Yet, their writings were probably compromised in the eyes of the authorities since surgeons, throughout the period, were also clearly writing in the hope of improving their own pay and conditions of service.[34] They were seemingly caught between two imperatives – between wanting to do good and wanting to do well. Doctors reiterated similar arguments over decades until the beginning of the nineteenth century, which suggests that their efforts to improve the treatment of sailors did not easily win support until the exigencies of the Napoleonic Wars made the conservation of seamen imperative.

IV

Important developments in medical care naturally had an impact on the way in which doctors represented the Navy. From the mid-eighteenth century, doctors placed greater emphasis on observation and on recording both the symptoms of illness and the effect of medicines in order to categorize results and produce statistics.[35] Military hospitals, and, from 1770, newly-founded dispensaries, added impetus to this trend by providing opportunities for the study of disease.[36] When Dr John Pringle, Physician-General of the British army from 1744 to 1752, found that military diseases had been neglected by earlier writers, at the forefront of developments, he began to collect factual observations about different diseases and to compile his own statistics. In this area, medical works had the potential to impress on the reader uncomfortable truths that patriotic discourse about the armed forces tended to conceal, and medical writings attested to the human cost of victories glorified in the public media. Pringle's case histories of men dying in agony, in sordid circumstances, owe their power to his clinical descriptions of horrific symptoms, and must have offered a contemporary counterpoint to campaign accounts of a more heroic nature. Pringle opened the bodies subsequently to see what he could further record. In illness and in death the body was a field for observation.

Dr James Lind, in 1757, similarly represented the Navy as an excellent subject for medical observation. Warship crews, being both disciplined and confined to a small area, lent themselves to this practice:

> All the ships, which compose a squadron, are under the same influence of diet and of climate, the circumstances of the men being likewise in other respects for the most part similar. Hence an infection may often spread itself unsuspected over a town or village, while in a fleet of ships its influence becomes more apparent, from its confinement to one or more ships.[37]

Lind was well qualified to make such an observation, having a claim to be the inventor of the controlled experiment. In 1747, on board the *Salisbury*, he chose 12 scurvy patients with spots, lassitude and putrid gums. Their cases were as similar as he could find and he began to treat them with a variety of commonly used (mostly ineffective) remedies for the scurvy; the two sailors eating citrus fruit clearly fared best. Lind's experiment had its limitations and his report on twelve patients taking no fewer than six different remedies would have no authority today. At the time, however, his findings were disregarded for a different reason: by deigning to stoop to a practical level and actually observing the effects of medicines on the body, Lind exposed himself to the scorn of physicians at the upper end of the medical profession who diagnosed on a theoretical basis, often without seeing the patient.

Medicine was ever a conservative profession, but capable naval doctors were a force for change since there was real pressure on them to find ways of keeping seamen healthy.

When Gilbert Blane was appointed Physician to the Fleet in 1780, he determined to make the best use he could of 'the advantages which this field of observation afforded'.[38] The fleet had sailed to the West Indies – a notoriously unhealthy location for British seamen where the death rate was one in seven. Blane collected and arranged into tables all the available facts concerning the causes of disease. The Commander in Chief ordered every surgeon in the fleet to send Blane a monthly return stating the prevalence of sickness, mortality figures, and other circumstances relating to the health of their ships. This allowed Blane to regulate hospital admissions, to keep the Commander in Chief informed, and also to collect a body of facts relating to the causes and course of disease.

Statistical evidence helped doctors like Gilbert Blane to promote a better image of the Navy, particularly at the end of the century when healthcare at sea had improved – mostly due to advances in preventative medicine. During the French Wars of 1793–1815, approximately 100 000 British seamen died. Of this number about 12 per cent died from enemy action, shipwreck or similar disaster; 20 per cent died from accidents; and no less than 65 per cent from disease. But, following improvements in hygiene, ventilation and diet, mortality in the Navy had decreased substantially. Lemon juice was finally included in seamen's rations in 1795, although scurvy remained a scourge to the very end of the war. Cleanliness was strictly enforced and actually mentioned in instructions to naval commanders from 1806. The sick-bay on warships was improved and better equipped. Using tables of mortality, at the end of the Napoleonic War, Blane was able to calculate that, if the Navy had been as subject to disease in 1813 as it had been in 1779, the number of deaths in 1813 would have been 6674 higher. He concluded triumphantly, 'Under such an annual waste of life, the national stock of mariners must have been exhausted'. Clearly, medicine had helped to win the war. Blane was able to depict a more caring, more effective navy but he had to admit that, though his statistics proved that mortality in the Navy had decreased, the death rate was still high compared to that of men 'of the same age, in other situations of life'.[39]

From the 1780s, the weight of numerical evidence added validity to doctors' published findings, but these works also confirmed the impression that military forces, subject to orders, could be used as the basis of experiment.[40] In general, people at this time were still apt to challenge their doctors. If they did not like the treatment, and could afford to do so, they sought second and third opinions. When Lind experimented on seamen to find a cure for scurvy, the men presumably had no choice as to whether they took vinegar, elixir of vitriol (sulphuric acid), or citrus juice for their complaint.

Voyages of exploration had also allowed various remedies to be tested on seamen and observations to be made. For example, Bark (quinine) was administered for fever on James Cook's *Resolution* voyage and proved more effective than the usual copious bleedings.[41] This result was verified by Dr William Robertson, naval surgeon on board *Juno* and *Edgar* from 4 April 1776 to 30 November 1781. The two ships served in American waters, in the Mediterranean and the Channel. During the voyage, Robertson compiled accurate tables detailing the success of different methods of treating fevers on board, and showed the great efficacy of using Peruvian bark.[42] Cook had been celebrated for keeping his crews healthy and almost free from scurvy. (Only one man died from scurvy on his *Endeavour* voyage.) Published accounts of Cook's voyages carefully recorded the medical and dietary regimes and were influential in promoting the role of paternalistic commander.[43] In fact, after Cook, scurvy was associated with bad shipboard management. Joseph Adams, physician at a London smallpox hospital, shows how records of Cook's *Endeavour* voyage were still being used in the early nineteenth century. Adams wrote a paper on the elusive 'itch insect'. He suspected that there might be a connection between such insects and stubborn eye infections. As evidence, he quoted a letter from Sir Joseph Banks describing how a Tahitian woman had used splinters of bamboo to extract minute lice from the eye when Cook's seamen were troubled with a tormenting itch around the eyelids.[44] Even if naval doctors applied what proved to be mistaken theories and administered ineffective medicines in their treatment of illness, the observations they recorded were extremely important to the investigations of later doctors attempting to define diseases. Seamen were often in the front line in more ways than one.

Historians have tried to use Michel Foucault's discussion of French Enlightenment medicine, notably his *The Birth of the Clinic* (1963), as a model for interpreting developments in British medicine at this time – with varying success. At another level, however, Foucault's analysis does afford a model by which to understand some of the ways in which medical men in Britain came to exercise greater control over their patients. Certainly, this control is evidenced in naval medicine. Sailors were institutionalized and, although doubtless they learned to work the system, their commanders had a high degree of control over their bodies and actions. Mary E. Fissell has analysed the way in which, towards the end of the eighteenth century, when doctors were trained more in hospitals, the diagnostic process altered in two ways: first, doctors took more notice of the signs of disease in the body (rather than of what patients wanted to tell them about their symptoms); second, they favoured anatomic enquiry after death. Fissell argues that the essays which doctors published helped to reconstruct the meaning of illness in ways that shifted the authority from patient to medical man. She also notes that many surgeons given this new hospital-based training subsequently made their career in the Navy but, as we can see, their influence there would have reinforced an existing trend.[45]

V

The writings of naval doctors helped to bring about a more paternalistic ethos of command operating on board the King's ships and helped to publicize the development. Gilbert Blane in particular encouraged a paternalistic relationship between officers and men. He deduced that the health of a ship depended principally on the power of officers – even more than on doctors. Different ships in the same fleet had varying numbers of sick even when they had been at sea the same length of time and the men had been fed on the same food. Evidently, the prevention of illness depended chiefly on order and discipline which officers alone could enforce.[46] Professional standards and peer group pressure had created a code of behaviour based on strong leadership. Doctors helped to modify this by publicly emphasizing the parent-like responsibilities of naval officers to their men. In 1794 Sir Roger Curtis, captain of the *Brunswick*, wrote: 'It has been wisely said, that the fatherly care of a commander is the *Seaman's best Physician.*' The crew, he thought, were 'entitled to kindness in return for obedience'.[47] It has been argued that Curtis's remark indicates that officers resented the influence that preventative medicine brought naval surgeons and wished to return to an older paternalism.[48] Now it is true that, by the end of the century, order was enforced by strict discipline in large warships that were likely to have significant quotas of landmen and pressed men.[49] Yet most key works of naval medicine from the 1780s to the end of the Napoleonic Wars continue to promote the concept of fatherly care that Curtis had internalized.[50] Curtis continued by stating that commanders should have in their libraries the works of medical men like Gilbert Blane and James Lind to enable them to carry out their duties. This persistent medical theme should be viewed in the context of increasing support in society, from the mid-eighteenth century for what had traditionally been considered softer, 'feminine' values.[51] Once again, medical works helped to promote a vivid image of an aspect of naval life, though individual commanders would have determined the degree to which it matched reality.

During the period, naval doctors increasingly complied with and helped to bolster the stereotypical view of a navy comprised of honest Jack Tars. Since impressed men were so apt to desert, this image of the British seaman may have been widely publicized in the hope that men would live up to it. Certainly, it complemented the support naval doctors generally gave to a paternalistic bond between officers and men. Thomas Trotter displayed a subtle difference in attitude when he wrote in 1797 that 'to relieve effectually the distresses of a particular class of men, as the British seamen, we must associate with the character, and keep aloof from none of their frailties'.[52] Trotter attributed the 'striking singularities' in the character of the British seaman to sea life itself and to the infrequent contact it afforded with the common manners of society. The courage of such men, partly innate, was increased by their habits of life. They associated with others who were accustomed to danger and who, 'from national prowess, consider themselves at sea, as rulers by birthright'. Trotter's balanced description of the character of a seaman, has often been quoted:

> The mind, by custom and example, is thus trained to brave the fury of the elements, in their different forms, with a degree of contempt, at danger and death, that is to be met with no where else, and which has become proverbial. Excluded, by the employment which they have chosen, from all society, but people of similar dispositions, the deficiencies of education are not felt, and information on general affairs is seldom courted. Their pride consists in being reputed a thorough bred seaman; and they look upon all landmen, as beings of inferior order … . Having little intercourse with the world, they are easily defrauded, and dupes to the deceitful, wherever they go: their money is lavished with the most thoughtless profusion; … . With minds uncultivated and uninformed, they are equally credulous and superstitious … . The true-bred seaman, is seldom a profligate character; his vices, if he had any, rarely partake of premeditated villainy, or turpitude of conduct; but rather originate from want of reflection, and a narrow understanding … . In his pleasures he is coarse, and in his person slovenly: he acquires no experience from past misfortunes, and is heedless of futurity.[53]

Trotter was writing during the Revolutionary and Napoleonic Wars when victories at sea were celebrated above all others. He recognized, for example, that newspaper accounts of sea-battles portraying the Navy as the chief means of securing the independence of a free people helped to win it great patriotic support until 'the names of our great admirals are therefore revered as so many tutelatory dieties of our island'.[54] By 1798 it was possible to complain that 'it is the fashion to extol our sailors and overlook our soldiers, as of little or no consequence'.[55] When the physician George Pinckard visited Haslar in 1795, he was moved to exclaim that, however difficult it was to describe the character of seamen, 'yet it may be given in one short sentence, for – *they are a race of heroes!*'[56]

But seamen were also notoriously intemperate and often accused of recruiting their strength for work by getting drunk. Doctors did little to efface this image despite elsewhere helping to promulgate the image of the likeable Jack Tar. Throughout the period, they sternly warned seamen against the dangers of intoxication, as was common in contemporary writings addressed to the poor.[57] Additionally, stray comments in medical publications reveal another, harsher side to life in the Navy. Gilbert Blane, for example, noted that 'nothing tends more to shorten life than excessive bodily labour and watching' and consequently seamen are in general short-lived: 'their countenance and general appearance make them appear older that they really are by several years'. Thomas Trotter alluded to the destructive effects of mercury treatment for venereal disease on seamen's constitutions already weakened by scurvy and hard labour, 'hence ... that rotten old age so early to be found among them.'[58] Dr C. Fletcher, advocated the appointment of chaplains to warships, claiming that seamen deprived of the benefits of public devotion were activated only by fear, and when discipline was relaxed once ashore they broke all bounds of restraint.[59] Caricatures of the time allude to the damage sailors inflict on their health by excessive drinking, but made both the seaman and his doctor figures of fun, perhaps reflecting a popular desire for a more transparent medical discourse that allowed ordinary people to understand their ailments and take effective action. For example, *Jack hove down with a Grog Blossom Fever* (see Plate 14) shows Jack rejecting treatment from an incompetent doctor: 'You may batter my Hull as long as you like, but I'll be d—m'd if ever you board me with your Glyster pipe.' That sailors drank excessively was nothing new, but only naval doctors claimed that such intoxication was a disease. This print is further evidence that the market for medical material was wider than the profession itself. It indicates, too, how certain details relating to the image of the Navy, being of wider public interest, might be promulgated to a less literate audience.

VI

The writings of naval doctors further confirmed what the public had long apprehended, namely that seamen were a source of contagion in ports and coastal towns, and a threat to the local population. Wharves, the chief resort of sailors for business and pleasure were understood to be desperately unhealthy places. The *Gentleman's Magazine* for June 1782 printed an extract from the Post Letter from Plymouth, which replicated the contents of almost all the letters from the sea ports then apparently suffering from an outbreak of influenza. 'The present epidemical disorder rages violently here, and at Dock; also on board the men of war lying here. The troops in town too, and in barracks, are affected with it, more or less; scarce a family, but has some person ill in it.'[60] The great outbreak of yellow fever in Philadelphia in 1797 was traced to seamen arriving from the West Indies. The American physician, Benjamin Rush, believed that every ship should be obliged by law to carry a ventilator 'calculated to prevent not only the decay of ships and cargoes, but a very frequent source of pestilential diseases of all kinds, in commercial cities'.[61] Naval hospitals took stringent measures to prevent infection escaping into neighbouring areas (and deserters escaping anywhere). British seamen might be admired, but their company was best avoided.

The reality of life at sea could hardly be appreciated by those who had never left the land. To some extent, the writings of doctors helped to create an appreciation of the space on board ship and a sense of what it was like to be in the Navy. Doctors observed that a species of distemper broke out in crowded, ill-ventilated ships similar to jail-fever on land.[62] Indeed, men at sea were confined to a species of jail, forced to breathe poisonous air and associate with carriers of disease. It was natural, then, that naval doctors came to insist on strict procedures of hygiene and cleanliness. James Lind, regarded as the founder of naval hygiene in England, strongly advocated preventative medicine, which he considered often more effective than any attempt to cure illness. His observations concerning probable sources of contagion on ships had earlier presented a baleful picture of the constitution of the Navy in wartime:

> In the Equipment of a Fleet there are two Sorts of Men from whome the Sickness may be apprehended, *viz.* Sailors imprest after a long Voyage from the *East* or *West Indies*, or the Coast of *Guinea*, and such idle Fellows as are picked from the Streets or the Prisons.[63]

As Lind's work gained acceptance (and we have seen that by the 1790s commanders were advised to buy his books for their own use), his advice came to change administrative procedures on board ship. For example, he advised that the captain who regulated impressed men should record the details of a seaman's last voyage and order him fresh provisions if that voyage had been sickly. Similarly, he was to record the last place of residence of all landmen and enquire of their state of health.

Ironically, though it might be considered a basic human right to be allowed the self-management of one's own health, preventative medicine had to be strictly enforced to be effective. In 1780, Gilbert Blane wrote that since pressing men was unavoidable, and since it was the greatest means of generating and spreading disease, it was necessary to prevent the effects of contagion on newly pressed men: 'this is done by stripping and washing their bodies; by cutting off their hair; and destroying all their clothes, before they are allowed to mix with the ship's company in which they are going to enter'.[64] This procedure amounts to an initiation ceremony, encouraging a loss of identity. Some critics, referring to the work of Foucault, consider that 'the conceptualization of the body as property owned and operated by an individual is a relatively recent phenomenon of bourgeois culture'.[65] Certainly, self-management was effectively denied the seaman – Lind considered that any man found remiss in keeping his clothes and bedding aired and dry 'should be compelled to become more cleanly'. In a short time, doctors were legitimately able to represent British warships as more disciplined and better run than those of the French, which were dirty and badly ventilated.[66]

Mutilation was common in the Navy and men were taught to bear the loss of a limb with equanimity. Amputations are portrayed as opportunities to display personal courage, and here doctors contribute to popular conceptions of heroism. For example, the surgeon Edward Ives relates how a 16-year-old boy, almost as a matter of personal honour, endured the amputation of his leg without a groan that could be heard a yard away.[67] In contrast, protracted deaths from fever or dysentery or scurvy, do not lend themselves to this treatment and are described according to their symptoms, not as individual acts of bravery that can be used to encourage others. Amputation was one instance, perhaps, when patients could be asked to exercise great self-control. In other cases, once they had placed themselves in the hands of a doctor, the severity of the treatment (vomits, purges, blisters) meant that patients had limited control over the consequences. This emphasis on amputation is reflected in popular prints. Caricatures like *Shiver my timbers, Jack* … show a pragmatic attitude to dismemberment while humourously playing on seamen's supposed naivety (see Figure 8). In military circles at this period, death from disease seems to have been considered ignoble – 'The death of cowards, and of common men'.[68] Wounds, on the other hand were a badge of bravery.

In the 1790s, doctors who were politically active diagnosed widespread ill-health in Britain as symptomatic of the rottenness of the *ancien régime* body politic[69] (Parliament, after all, had taken little interest in organizing healthcare provision). In doing so, they embraced the idiom of natural human rights, which included the right to be healthy. People, they contended, were entitled to competent advice about their health and its self-management. Opinion thereafter was divided. Should ordinary people, given basic information about healthcare, be left to treat themselves? Or should they always be encouraged to seek trained help. (The problem was that people rarely acted in their best interests, were absurdly credulous when it came to health matters, and often had to be compelled to follow doctors' orders.) Ironically, the example of the Navy indicated that oligarchy was far from inimical to the health of the people: once cleanliness was enforced, health improved. The fleet was inoculated with vaccine against smallpox long before there was widespread inoculation in Britain's cities, or even in the army – sailors had little choice. (During the War of American Independence, some militia had been inoculated in an attempt to control disease in military camps but this had provoked opposition from local residents who feared that smallpox would spread and affect local trade.) Shortly after Edward Jenner published his discovery that vaccination with cowpox matter protected humans from smallpox, the first trials on selected ships took place in

Figure 8 *Droll Doings No 29. Shiver my timbers, Jack* ... Produced by F.C. (?) (artist) and William
Spooner (publisher).

September 1800.[70] Naval doctors, by celebrating these advances and
representing the Navy as a successful experiment in controlled healthcare,
lent support to the government and helped to reduce the widespread
prejudice against smallpox inoculation. In this instance, an apparent denial
of basic rights produced better propaganda for the ruling classes, and actually
promoted better health care for society at large.

On the other hand, doctors were broadly united in their condemnation of impressment. The most sustained criticism of the Navy was focused on this one issue – it was in direct opposition to propaganda celebrating the liberty of the British people and its negative effect on the Navy's image was extremely hard to counter. Moreover, impressment clearly had a detrimental effect upon the health of crews. As John Huxham wrote:

> The usual Method of impressing Seamen on their Return from long and tedious Voyages, void of Necessaries, chagrined at not seeing their Friends and Families, and most commonly in a bad state of Health, and not allowed Time and Opportunity to recover it, hath been the Bane of thousands: And I could wish, for the Honour of the Nation, a Method of manning our fleet could be found out more consistent with common Humanity and *British* Liberty.[71]

Thomas Trotter observed that a newly impressed seaman had 'a sulkiness of disposition' which was only gradually overcome and which caused problems for both the commander and the doctor. The seaman watched 'every opportunity for effecting his escape'; he was also liable to try to deceive the doctor, assuming diseases in order to be 'an object for invaliding'.[72] After the Napoleonic Wars, when there was less pressure for all good patriots to support the Navy as an institution, Trotter wrote a vigorously argued paper against impressment. Holding up the spectre of the 1797 naval mutinies and making a case for creating a more contented body of men, he dismissed the argument that pressing was sanctioned by custom. He contended that the popular celebration of British seamen was both hollow and cynical:

> The seaman is like the victim in sacrifice, that is gilded and decked out to be consumed; for his valour is blazoned with triumphal songs and feats, while himself is dragged from his home and his endearments, and ultimately consigned to neglect.[73]

Yet, as indicated above, there is a sense in which doctors helped to create the type that the public loved to extol: 'the plain and honest, though unthinking seaman' who was nevertheless a great lover of his country.[74] The paternalistic relationship between officers and men, that doctors helped to foster, can only have encouraged a lack of responsibility in sailors. The emphasis doctors came to place on enforced cleanliness and preventative medicine helped to deprive the men of individual identity.

Unremarkably, perhaps, in these medical writings there seems to be a tension between the general and the particular. Doctors observed individual symptoms and individual cases and then tried to generalize in order to deduce common causes and cures – which would help them to advance in their careers. A similar tension in attitudes to the Navy existed in the country at large: the public had a keen sense of the debt society owed to the Navy, but a distaste for individual sailors whom they tried to efface from their conscience. The difference, of course, is that the more committed doctors also cared for the individual. This is evident in Thomas Trotter's conclusion to his paper on impressment, when he makes a sad plea for the seaman. He writes:

> I am afraid there has been too often a want of sympathy for his condition, by seeing him in his idle hours of dissipation and low pleasure. His slovenly appearance and awkward gait have to the beholder's eye, too frequently obliterated all the remembrance of his naval glory; and the honours of … the battle of the Nile, Camperdown, Trafalgar, etc, have been at once forgotten, on seeing him stagger from the bar of a tavern.[75]

This was an age of great public interest in health matters and growing medical consumerism.[76] As we have seen, by 1815 progress in preventative medicine had brought about real improvements to healthcare in the Navy with further implications for civil medicine. Doctors in many ways continued to promulgate those stereotypical views of the Navy favoured by ballad- and printmakers, the popular theatre and some government propagandists. Nevertheless, their publications also helped to convey to a wider public both improvements in conditions of naval service and associated developments in the ethos of command. Over time medical writings therefore made a significant contribution to the public image of the Navy as an institution.

Notes

1   See C. Lloyd and J.L.S. Coulter, *Medicine and the Navy 1200–1900, Vol. III* (Edinburgh and London, 1961). For scurvy in particular, see K.J. Carpenter, *The History of Scurvy and Vitamin C* (Cambridge, 1986). Useful works on institutional care of the period include: M. Ignatieff, *A Just Measure of Pain: The Penitentiary in the Industrial Revolution, 1750–1850* (London, 1978); C. Hamlin, 'Predisposing Causes and Public Health in Early-Nineteenth-Century Medical Thought', *Social History of Medicine*, 5 (1992), pp. 43–70; C. Lawrence, *Medicine and the Making of Modern Britain, 1700–1920* (London, 1994).

2   Throughout 'doctors' is used to denote all medical practitioners, including surgeons, although strictly only physicians were MDs.

3   There were few physicians in the Navy. Larger overseas squadrons carried one. See N.A.M. Rodger, *The Wooden World: An Anatomy of the Georgian Navy* (London, 1986), p. 20.

4   J. Atkins, *The Navy-Surgeon: or a Practical System of Surgery*, 2nd edn (London, 1737), p. x.

5   Even towards the end of the period, when their status had improved, since their numbers had increased they still found it difficult to gain positions ashore in peacetime. See *GM*, 73 (1803), 5.

6   J. Ring, *Reflections on the Surgeons' Bill: in answer to three pamphlets in defence of that bill* (London, 1798), p. 36. Ring (1752–1821) was trained at Winchester College and published tracts on vaccination.

7   C. Dunne, *The Chirurgical Candidate; or, Reflections on Education: indispensible to complete Naval, Military, and Other Surgeons* (London, 1801), pp. 20, 83.
8   For example, see *GM*, 28 (1758), 160.
9   S. Sutton, *An historical Account of a New Method for extracting the foul Air out of Ships etc., Second edition … To which are annexed … A Discourse on the Scurvy by Dr. Mead* (London, 1749), p. 73. Thanks to Mead's influence, Sutton's ventilators were installed in warships 10 years after their invention. See *GM*, 34 (1764), 275.
10 C. Lawrence confirms that scurvy was a key area in which doctors advanced their claims for higher social status. See his 'Disciplining disease: scurvy, the navy, and imperial expansion, 1750–1825', in D. Miller and P. Reill, *Visions of Empire: voyages, botany and representations of empire* (Cambridge, 1996), pp. 81 and 85.
11 See R. Porter, 'Lay Medical Knowledge in the Eighteenth Century: the Evidence of the *GM*', *Medical History*, 29 (1985), pp. 138–68 (p. 149). For reviews, see *GM*, 33 (1763), 602; and 39 (1769), 156.
12 See *GM*, 17 (1747), 467–69; 21 (1751), 408; 60 (1790), 493.
13 *GM*, 24 (1754), 114–15, 543–4.
14 *GM*, 25 (1755), 175. The latest medical publications were also advertised in the *GM*. See ibid., 478.
15 Ibid., 175. Cf. *GM*, 28 (1758), 160.
16 *GM*, 30 (1760), 557.
17 *GM*, 26 (1756), 418–20.
18 *GM*, 28 (1758), 105. See also ibid., 61-3.
19 *GM*, 49 (1779), 68–70, 193.
20 *GM*, 63 (1793), 291. Cf. *GM*, 73 (1803), 897.
21 *GM*, 64 (1794), 422.
22 *GM*, 62 (1792), 604; 64 (1794), 690; 68 (1798), 823, 945, 1029.
23 See J. Carmichael Smyth, *An Account of the Experiment made at the desire of the Lords Commissioners of the Admiralty, on board the Union Hospital Ship* (London, 1796).
24 *The Times*, 24 April, 16 May, 15 August, 5 September and 29 September 1794.
25 See W. Turnbull, *The Naval Surgeon*, (London, 1806), p. vii.
26 J. Huxham, *An Essay on Fevers* (London, 1750), pp. 47–8.
27 Ibid., pp. 26, 264. See also J. Lind, *An Essay on the Most Effectual Means of Preserving the Health of Seamen in the Royal Navy* (London, 1757), pp. xiv–xv.
28 T. Trotter, *A Practicable Plan for Manning the Royal Navy and Preserving our Maritime Ascendancy without Impressment* (Newcastle, 1819), pp. 37–8. Cf. G. Blane, *A Short Account of the Most Effectual Means of Preserving the Health of Seamen, particularly in the Royal Navy* (n.p., 1780), p. 2.
29 For example, the 1758 Navy Act enforced more frequent paying of ships. It also introduced a new mechanism by which men might send money home, free, by government channels.
30 Lind, *An Essay*, pp. 109–10.
31 G. Pinckard, *Notes on the West Indies written during the Expedition under the Command of the late General Sir Ralph Abercomby*, 3 vols (London, 1806), p. 42. Greenwich Hospital was supported by a tax on seamen.
32 See S. Monks, 'National Heterotopia: Greenwich as Spectacle, 1694–1869', *Rising East: The Journal of East London Studies*, 2 (1) (1998), pp. 156–66.
33 This is true of three of the four prominent doctors publishing between 1745 and 1760. See Lind, *An Essay*, p. xvi; R. Mead, 'A Discourse on Scurvy' in Sutton, *An Historical Account*, p. 75; T. Reynolds, *GM*, 28 (1758), 210.
34 For example, see T. Trotter, *Medicina Nautica*, (London, 1797), p. 18.
35 See U. Tröhler, 'Quantification in British Medicine and Surgery 1750–1830; with Special reference to its Introduction into Therapeutics' (PhD thesis, University of

London, 1978). Also, O. Keel, 'The politics of health and the institutionalisation of clinical practices in Europe in the second half of the eighteenth century', in W. F. Bynum and R. Porter, eds, *William Hunter and the Eighteenth-Century Medical World* (Cambridge, 1985), p. 231.

36   I.S.L. Loudon, 'The Origins and Growth of the Dispensary Movement in England', *Bulletin of the History of Medicine*, 55 (1981), pp. 322–42.

37   J. Lind, *An Essay*, p. 36. Army surgeons advised the same for doctors in the colonies, see G. Cleghorn, *Observations on the Epidemical Diseases in Minorca, from the year 1744–1749* (London, 1751), p. v.

38   G. Blane, *Observations on the Diseases incident to Seamen* (London, 1785), p. v.

39   G. Blane, *Select Dissertations on Several Subjects of Medical Science* (London, 1822), pp. 2–3, 22.

40   The Sick and Hurt Board conducted 17 experiments on ships' crews, 1740–82. See P.K. Crimmin, 'The Sick and Hurt Board and the Health of Seamen, *c.*1700–1806', *Journal for Maritime Research* (December, 1999), p. 10. <http://www.nmm.ac.uk/jmrmembers/articlesnow/wip10001/wip10001_sick-and-hurt-board-all.htm/>. Contemporaries understood that naval medicine could benefit the public. See *GM*, 28 (1758), 209.

41   J. Millar, *Observations on the Management of the Prevailing Diseases in Great Britain, particularly in the Army and Navy* (London, 1779), p. 204.

42   J. Millar, *Observations on the Change of Public Opinion in Religion, Politics, and Medicine on the Conduct of the War; on the Prevailing Diseases in Great Britain; and on Medical Arrangements in the Army and Navy*, 2 vols (London, 1805?), vol. II, p. 38.

43   See *GM*, 47 (1777), 179.

44   J. Adams, *On Morbid Poisons*, 2nd edn (London, 1807), p. 307.

45   M.E. Fissell, *Patients, Power, and the Poor in Eighteenth-Century Bristol* (Cambridge, 1991), pp. 145, 148–9.

46   Blane, *A Short Account*, p. 4.

47   Sir Roger Curtis, *The Means Use to Eradicate a Malignant Fever, which raged on board his Majesty's Ship Brunswick, at Spithead in the Spring of the Year 1791* (London, 1794?), p. 24.

48   See Lawrence, 'Disciplining disease'.

49   See Rodger, *The Wooden World*, p. 346.

50   See Blane, *A Short Account*, p. 4, and *Select Dissertations*, p. 71; Millar, *Observations on the Change of Public Opinion*, p. cxvi; Turnbull, *The Naval Surgeon*, p. 49; C.A., Hutchison, *Practical Observations in Surgery: more particularly as regards the naval and military service*, 2nd edn (London, 1826), pp. 192.

51   For example, see T. Eagleton, *The Rape of Clarissa* (Minneapolis, MN, 1982), pp. 15–16.

52   Trotter, *Medicina Nautica* (London, 1797), p. 4.

53   Ibid., pp. 38–9.

54   Ibid. (London, 1797), p. 37.

55   Ring, *Reflections on the Surgeons' Bill*, p. 39.

56   Pinckard, *Notes on the West Indies*, vol. I, pp. 42–3.

57   See Atkins, *The Navy-Surgeon*, p. 8. Also, T.M. Winterbottom, MD, *Medical Directions for the Navigators and Settlers in Hot Climates*, 2nd edn (London, 1803), p. 9; T. Trotter, *An Essay, Medical, Philosophical, and Chemical on Drunkenness* (London, 1804); Turnbull, *The Naval Surgeon*, p. 112.

58   Blane, *Observations on the Diseases incident to Seamen*, p. 323, and T. Trotter, *Observations on the Scurvy* (London, 1786), p. 89. Cf. Trotter, *Medicina Nautica*, p. 41.

59   C. Fletcher, *The Naval Guardian*, 2nd edn, 2 vols (London, 1805), vol. I, p. 169.

60   *GM*, 52 (1782), 306.

61   B. Rush, *Medical Inquiries and Observations: containing an account of the yellow fever, as it appeared in Philadelphia in 1797*, Vol. V (Philadelphia, 1798), p. 55.

62 For example, J. Pringle, *Observations on the Diseases of the Army in Camp and Garrison* (London, 1752), p. 291.

63 Lind, *An Essay*, p. 1.

64 Blane, *A Short Account*, pp. 8–9.

65 V. Kelly, and D.E. Von Mücke, *Body and Text in the Eighteenth Century* (Stanford, Calif., 1994), p. 6.

66 Blane, *Observations on the Diseases incident to Seamen*, p. 109.

67 E. Ives, *A voyage from England to India in the Year MDCCLIV and an Historical Narrative of the Operations of the Squadron and Army in India under the command of Vice-Admiral Watson and Colonel Clive* (London, 1773), p. 133.

68 J. Armstrong, *The Art of Preserving Health: a poem* (London, 1744), book III. ll. 630.

69 R. Porter, *Doctor of Society: Thomas Beddoes and the Sick Trade in Late-Enlightenment England* (London and New York, 1992), p. 158.

70 Jenner published his *An Inquiry into the Causes and Effects of the Variolae Vaccinae* in 1798. See *GM*, 71 (1801), 318; 73 (1803), 520. In 1822, Blane wrote that enforced inoculation against smallpox in the navy and army 'has by no means been followed among the civil population of England' (*Select dissertations*), p. 354.

71 Huxham, *An Essay on Fevers*, pp. 264–5.

72 Trotter, *Medicina Nautica*, p. 40. Cf. Hutchison, *Practical Observations*, pp. 142, 184.

73 T. Trotter, *A Practicable Plan for Manning the Royal Navy and Preserving our Maritime Ascendancy without Impressment* (Newcastle, 1819), pp. viii, 30.

74 Blane, *Observations on the Diseases incident to Seamen*, p. 97.

75 Trotter, *A Practicable Plan*, pp. 31–2.

76 D. Porter and R. Porter, *Patient's Progress: Doctors and Doctoring in Eighteenth-Century England* (Oxford, 1989), p. 214.

Chapter 8

Post-War Blues

This chapter looks at the continuity in the early nineteenth century of certain myths and attitudes surrounding the Navy, and also at changes in perception caused initially by the growing prominence of the army and then by peacetime conditions. The post-1815 period saw a subtler commodification of the Navy than the earlier, enthusiastic production of commemorative ware: images of seamen and warships were routinely used to help sell a range of goods from children's books to sheet music. Equally, the Admiralty began to see that its own products had a marketable value: in 1819, the Hydrographer was instructed take appropriate measures to enable the public to buy Admiralty charts at reasonable prices. The post-war Navy was slowly and painfully forced to adjust to a different, more commercial world and to reassess its relevance to a post-war society that had fewer pressing martial preoccupations.

I

In October 1815, the *Gentleman's Magazine* reviewed a newly published sermon intended to promote a Waterloo subscription fund. The reviewer noted the ascendance of the army in the public estimation and congratulated his countrymen on 'the Genius of Britain', which had secured so great a victory at Waterloo. He continued, 'a new field of contest is open to her valiant sons, and the laurels to be gained by land are soon to equal (surpass they cannot) … that naval wreath of glory, which so long had graced her brows'.[1] The evident anxiety of this reviewer to be even-handed in his tribute to both services may owe something to the controversy that had followed the Lord Castlereagh's proposal in Parliament (only days after Waterloo) for a national monument to the fallen dead. The Navy was by now extremely sensitive about its status and reacted badly to any suggestion, including Castlereagh's, that seemed to give pride of place to the army. A contributory factor in the waning of the Navy's popularity had been its failure to win a decisive victory in the 1812–14 war with America, even though at the outset of hostilities the American force had consisted of only eight frigates and 12 sloops. *The Times* had stated bluntly that, 'It is inconsistent with common sense to deny that our naval reputation has been blasted in this short but disastrous war.' Such outright condemnation clearly made an impression on those who were pondering the state of the Navy, and several authors openly deliberated possible causes for the disgrace.[2] In these circumstances, a retired naval officer writing songs and odes to supplement his income had no compunction about focusing on the army as well as the Navy in order to boost his sales.[3]

Byron, writing his epic satire *Don Juan* in September 1818, teased readers about the waning popularity of the Navy and the ease with which the public forgot about those who had defended Britain's shores:

> Nelson was once Britannia's god of war,
> And still should be so, but the tide is turn'd;
> There's no more to be said of Trafalgar,
> Tis with out hero quietly inturn'd;
> Because the army's grown more popular,
> At which the naval people are concern'd;
> Besides, the Prince is all for the land-service,
> Forgetting Duncan, Nelson, Howe, and Jervis.
>
> (canto I, octave iv)

Byron, who averred that the only sentiment to which he remained constant, other than a love of liberty was 'a detestation of cant', deftly noted the manipulation of public image in this instance. Jane Austen was similarly facetious when writing *Sanditon* early in 1817. Her protagonist, Mr Parker, principal resident of a new seaside town, bitterly regretted naming his house after Trafalgar because 'Waterloo is more the thing now'.[4] The Peninsular Campaign and Waterloo were fresh in the public's memory and inevitably carried more weight than earlier naval victories.

After 1815, the Navy therefore had to confront both peacetime reductions and a lessening of public support. The one category of naval employment subject to drastic cuts at the end of every war was seamen. In spite of the difficulties of recruitment at the beginning of every conflict, no government wished to be viewed as advocating long-term service. Fleets had to be paid off promptly in order to save money and also to safeguard public order – sailors were liable to become riotous if they had to wait any length of time for their wages. After more than 20 years of war, the transition to peace was not easy. Deflation and economic distress followed the end of hostilities: the shipbuilding boom contracted and demobilized soldiers and sailors flooded the labour market. Between 1814, when Napoleon was deported to Elba, and 1820 the number of ships in commission dropped from 713 to 134, and the number of seamen from 140 000 to a mere 23 000. In a significant and well publicized step which highlighted the repercussions of this massive reduction, the Court of Directors of the East India Company acted to prop up the Marine Society. The Company took six marine boys on each of its ships to be apprenticed for two voyages, 'in consequence of the limited demand of the navy'.[5] The usual fears of a crime wave after demobilization seemed to be confirmed by the rapid rise in the number of people committed for trial in England and Wales. From 1811–13 to 1825–27, for example, the numbers committed in London and Middlesex rose 53 per cent faster than the population as a whole, although better policing possibly helped to inflate the figures. The disillusionment of former servicemen was certainly conducive to social discontent: many found it hard to get work, especially the disabled; others were owed back pay, prize-money or pensions. Predictably, seamen squandered in a few days the money that had taken them months and years to earn. The *Naval Chronicle* lamented that 'these poor fellows are wandering about London and all the out-ports, without money and without employment'.[6] Such indigents were easily attracted to popular political movements which to others seemed to threaten social stability. Contemporaries also noted with disgust that 'gypsies and other imposters frequently impose on landmen in the garb and language of distressed seamen'.[7] In one much publicized case, an imposter first received a set of clothes from the Committee for the Relief of Distressed Seamen, and later four shillings because he claimed that he had found a ship and needed to equip himself more fully. He presented himself a third time, nearly naked, for more funds but was recognized and sentenced to a good flogging and a month in Bridewell.[8] Such instances did much to prejudice ordinary people against ex-seamen.

Yet the Navy was not felt to be so great a threat to civil liberties as a standing army. Its supporters argued that even in peacetime the Government should maintain the Navy at an imposing level because several nations, including the United States, would rejoice if it were allowed to decline. A naval officer of 1819, typically complaining that the comforts and salaries of officers in the army were unfairly superior to those in the Navy, argued strongly for the upkeep of the service. He pointed out that Britain could never have as powerful an army as its more populous European neighbours and therefore needed to maintain a strong navy for its defence.[9] *The Times* had complained in 1816 that a large army was being supported unnecessarily: 'An alarming and unwieldy military system has been built up and cherished, in preference to our glorious marine – the natural, the invincible, the constitutional, the economical guardian of the British empire.'[10] The army stationed in the British Isles after 1815 was actually double the size it had been before the war. As pressure for democratic reform increased, some Whigs and radicals saw an ulterior motive in the government's apparent preference for the army. The author of *The Black Book; or, Corruption Unmasked!* announced:

> The cheap, natural, and most effective defence of his country is certainly the navy; but ministers think otherwise. With them the *army*, and not the *navy*, is

a primary object. Of 16 millions, the estimated expense of the army and navy, upwards of 10 millions is for the army alone … . Now, why this lavish expenditure of the army? – why its preference to the navy? Plainly this, – ministers are not apprehensive of foreign aggression, but of domestic resistance.[11]

Whigs and radicals criticized the government for wasting large sums of money on military expenditure, and such accusations were often linked to an unfounded claim that the government was planning to establish a military despotism in England. Actually, the administration was in dire need of funds and anxious to make savings wherever possible. Since 1816, when the Commons had insisted on the abolition of the hated property or income tax introduced by Pitt as a temporary expedient in wartime, indirect taxation had fallen more heavily on the poor than on the rich. The radicals had welcomed the abolition of the property tax but, though this had the effect of restricting the government's options for raising public funds, they continued to accuse the government of extravagance. In the absence of any major crisis abroad, the Navy was highly vulnerable to cutbacks and the demands for retrenchment were insistent. Over 25 per cent of all reports about the Navy in *The Times* between 1815 and 1825 related to calls for greater economy in the service to relieve the terrible burden of tax on the nation. Increasingly, the Navy had to divert such ships that remained in active service away from home waters to cover mounting duties on foreign stations. This had the effect of slowly diminishing its presence and impact on the public consciousness at home.

In spite of the need for retrenchment, public interest was still aroused by the different pension and compensation payments operating in the Navy and army. This issue had obtained widespread press coverage following debates in the House of Commons. A subordinate army officer in receipt of a pension for some wound, would find the award increased if he were promoted up the ranks, but an officer in the Navy would have to resign his pension if he were promoted.[12] Similarly, the overall discrepancy in pay for officers in the army and Navy was roundly debated in the House. Some felt that these anomalies should be addressed in order to promote cordial relations between the two services so they would successfully cooperate in joint operations during wartime.[13] Others added that systems of ranking in the Navy and army ought to be reconciled, lest a sense of injustice affected morale among naval officers and led them to think of the Navy as a '*secondary profession*'.[14] The role of the newspaper press was becoming increasingly important for all aspects of popular politics at this period and extensive coverage of these apparent injustices increased general understanding of naval grievances. The press became even more closely associated with public opinion and some newspaper reports intimated that the British people themselves wished to see a more even-handed system in operation.

In the period following 1815, the Navy's waning popularity was reflected in the declining number of prints with a naval theme. The market for straightforward naval ephemera and commemorative ware also contracted rapidly, although Sir Edward Pellew's successful bombardment of Algiers in 1816, forcing the Dey of Algiers to abolish Christian slavery, produced several commemorative medals. Instead, contemporary prints in the aftermath of war drew attention to the change in the fortunes of the average naval officer. Often ironic, such prints could deflate egos but they also excited pity for those men who had suffered such an abrupt change in fortune and prospects. A caricature, *Things as they have been. Things as they now are*, published on 8 May 1815, shows an officer bisected, the left half of the body typical of a self-confident, victorious naval officer of the recent war and the right half reflecting the post-war service in straitened circumstances, vulnerable to government cut-backs and efficiency savings (see Plate 15). The form of the print neatly captures the schizophrenic view many officers must have had of their status when their circumstances changed after so long a period of conflict. The vogue for prints comparing the present status of the Navy with its former glory continued into the 1820s. A coloured lithograph, *Things as they were, 1783. Things as they are, 1823*, presents two contrasting images of young naval officers on deck.[15] Superficially, naval life seems to have improved: the uniform of the more modern officer is tailored and stylish, while the ship's side of 1823 is painted a tasteful green. But the modern officer lacks the spirit and enthusiasm of the earlier Tar. Both the self-conscious uniform and the green paint of 1823 suggest misplaced assiduity or simply a lack of more warlike activities to occupy the time. Another finely balanced caricature, *Things as they were, 1757. Things as they are, 1827*, invites similar nostalgia.[16] The seaman of the eighteenth century in this print is certainly a little overweight and slovenly. On the other hand, the officer of 1827 appears to be a dandy: his waist is corseted and his chest padded. And whereas imposing warships coast off-shore in the earlier image, the scene from 1827 features pleasure yachts in the background.

Other prints of the period emphasize that the post-war Navy holds limited career prospects. *A mid on half pay. Tower Hill*, published in 1825, shows a midshipman cleaning shoes to supplement his meagre salary. His sextant, the instrument that should symbolize his skill and prospects, has long since been pawned and he uses the case to hold his polish and rags.[17] Midshipmen, as non-commissioned officers, did not normally qualify for half-pay – and this is the point of the title. At the end of the war, however, those men who had passed the lieutenant's examination but were still waiting for appointment to a ship were mostly promoted to the half-pay list, even though they had never served as commissioned officers.[18] At this period, the drastic run-down of the Navy had left employment for about 15 per cent of available lieutenants only and promotion was extremely difficult to secure. Even those officers lucky enough to be employed found that in peacetime the Navy offered few opportunities to obtain distinction. The hardships of officers on half-pay and of naval widows struggling to bring up families were covered by a sympathetic press. The *Gentleman's Magazine* printed a letter expressing regret that a newspaper had recently reported 'that a Lieutenant in the Navy, on half-pay, was taken up for stealing some silver spoons'.[19] The correspondent considered that such degrading conduct could only have resulted from genuine distress and urged the government to increase the allowance for such officers – but there was little enthusiasm within the ministry for increasing the cost of the pensions list.

II

After the war, the Navy substantially ceased to be regarded as an arena of opportunity where men of worth but little wealth could make their mark. In part this was due to the perception that 'interest' or patronage was of increasing importance in the promotion stakes, although it had always been the case that neither luck nor talent alone would secure a rapid rise through the ranks. Ironically, those that complained that long service and ability without interest were insufficient to win promotion also cautioned against unthinkingly promoting men from the lower decks. Commentators warned that such men 'are more distinguished for swearing, and *chawing tobacco*, than delicacy of sentiment, or a knowledge of their duty'.[20] In the post-war Navy, the social position of commissioned officers rose considerably. There were fewer vacancies and so candidates of social standing had a better chance of obtaining them. This made the Navy more class-bound and less democratic than in wartime, although it also had the effect of raising the status of commissioned naval officers in the public estimation.

Crucially, after the end of the Napoleonic War, the lack of arrangements for the retirement of older officers and the continued acceptance of young officer-volunteers (though on a reduced scale), created a serious logjam in promotion. This problem was not resolved by natural wastage until mid-century and the issue caused much discontent. In 1822, *The Times* commented that, if reports to the House of Commons were correct, many of the newly promoted lieutenants had entered the Navy since the peace, while hundreds of midshipmen who had served ten or twelve years still had not been promoted.[21] The newspaper was primarily concerned about an apparently unnecessary addition to the pension list contributing to the number of officers on half-pay who had to be supported by the nation. In the following year, a House of Commons debate about promotion in the Navy underlined the strength of feeling on the issue. Opinion was divided between those who considered that young, unknown officers should never be promoted over the heads of older men, and those (like Sir George Cockburn in the Admiralty) who argued that there needed to be an element of youth at each rank or the Navy would be disadvantaged in any future war. To men with practical experience of the Navy, it was obvious that any warship had to have both junior and senior officers. The opposition motion contesting the Admiralty's policy with regard to promotion was defeated, but the press at once seized on certain statements made in the House which seemed to undermine meritocracy in the Navy. An editorial in *The Times* claimed that in the debate clearly absurd principles had been asserted as if they were incontrovertible:

> It was argued that young men of rank should be received with avidity in to the navy, and advanced with a certain degree of preference; because they did honour to the profession, or as if its respectability depended upon them … . The insolence of this argument is equal to its stupidity … . Admit men of virtue and talents, and promote them in proportion to their merit, and *they* will defend their profession.[22]

Correspondents to the *Gentleman's Magazine* wrote at length about the importance of a capable Navy and proposed schemes for reforming the system of promotion so that worthy men would not be neglected in peacetime.[23] But with no war to fight it was hard for such men to display fitness for promotion. At least the Navy was substantially employed in preventing smuggling on British coasts at this time owing to the heavy duties on foreign spirits. By 1824 about 1700 men were engaged against smugglers but, while this duty sometimes led to heated fighting, it did not win men honour. One MP commented that when seamen came back from a service of that kind, 'they were in general more fond of the gin-cag than of the gunpowder-cask' and believed that officers would take any other men to crew a warship before those who had been on anti-smuggling duty.[24] Ironically, once the Navy had been reduced, merchants claimed that it now provided an inadequate defence for overseas commerce and that the French employed proportionately more warships in safeguarding their trade in the West Indies, the Mediterranean and the Levant.[25]

Perhaps because the Navy had ceased to offer many the chance of a reasonable career, or maybe because there was no immediate need to persuade young men to risk their lives at sea, popular publications written in the aftermath of the war offered a dim view of the contemporary Navy. The poem, *The Adventures of Johnny Newcome*, written in 1816, offered a dismal picture of life on a warship, particularly since the enthusiastic hero of the poem is subjected to unjust punishments by a tyrannical captain.[26] What seemed to provoke most criticism and public sympathy was not the principle of flogging itself but the fact that in the Navy, unlike in the army, flogging could be awarded arbitrarily without court martial. Those who wrote specifically for children after the war addressed similar themes. The author of *Pleasant Stories; or, Histories of Ben the Sailor and Ned the Soldier* (1818), warned readers against going to sea. The uncle in the story, an old seaman, protested 'all I have gained, after six-and-twenty years of hard service, is plenty of flogging, many hard knocks, and a broken constitution'.[27] His nephews ignored the advice and Ben joined the Navy all the same, determined to do better than his uncle. After many years he returned with some praise for the humanity of sailors but just as disillusioned. He came back, 'a cripple, with a broken constitution' to be cheated out of his hard-earned wages and prize-money by 'swindling agents'.[28] Another children's book, *The Sailor Boy; or, First and Last Voyage* (1825), also warned young country boys tempted by thoughts of adventure or a desire to travel not to join the Navy. The hero found his first voyage so daunting, that he was only too glad to return to his village and look after his grandmother's garden, as before.

Such publications were hardly good advertisements for the Navy, prompting others to write in its defence. One ex-seaman with apparently 50 years' knowledge of the service, expanded on recent improvements. Though individual captains might be bad, punishments were generally less frequent and less severe. Food was better, the seaman performed less work on board than the average manual labourer and the health enjoyed by crews was little short of wonderful – thanks mostly to improvements in hygiene. This ex-seaman pointed out that many more crew members than formerly were able to read and since there were now more chaplains in the Navy, Divine Service was performed more regularly. He hoped that sailors were beginning to develop a more moral code of conduct and he offered encouragement by implying that the public still had a high regard for those who served in the Navy. Recalling how many seaman were seen in rags on the streets of London at the end of the war, cold, hungry and filthy, he blamed this on their own improvidence rather than on their country's neglect. In one day and night of 'beastly riot', they had spent, or been robbed of, sums of money that would have kept them in plenty until they could find employment. 'They had received liberal wages, and had thrown them away instead of using them!' Yet their thoughtless behaviour had not prevented the charitable public from raising subscriptions to relieve their distress.[29] Reading between the lines, it seems that improved conditions on board ship had not produced a material improvement in the behaviour of sailors themselves. It is also fair to say that, while many ordinary people still held the Navy in regard, among the maritime section of the population which had endured the operation of the press-gangs throughout 20 years of war, the Navy was deeply unpopular.

Any defence or enumeration of improvements in naval life was undermined by a pamphlet published by Admiral Hawkins in 1822 entitled *Statement of Certain Immoral Practices in HM Ships*. Hawkins described the chaotic and immoral behaviour that officers countenanced on the lower decks when warships in port. His descriptions were so graphic that the pamphlet was widely circulated and soon went into a second edition. Contrary to regulations, he explained, prostitutes were commonly ferried out to the ships, remaining there for as long as the vessels were in port even though some married men legitimately had their wives and children on board. After reading the work, British gentlemen were heard to declare that 'nothing could ever induce them to send a son into the navy'.[30] Public opinion of naval officers suffered a greater blow as the pamphlet was also reviewed in popular monthlies with a circulation in Europe and the United States. The custom of allowing prostitutes on board ship was of long standing and considered an unavoidable evil – though of course it had hardly been aired in public before. Officers reasoned that it was preferable to keep the men happy on board ship since it was difficult to persuade them to return if they were granted shore leave. But those who leapt to the Navy's defence at this juncture complained that the author of the pamphlet had presented isolated instances of gross indecency as the absolute norm. Sir C.V. Penrose, a retired admiral who advised the Government on naval affairs, contended that, given the improved state of order, discipline, instruction and morals in the Navy, the best regulated warships were 'admirable schools for youth'. In fact, he feared an 'excess of refinement' which might undermine the Navy's superiority. Penrose considered that, while many people appreciated Britain's great naval victories, they were by no means well informed 'of the great moral, social, and intellectual improvement that had been effected by the benevolent energies of naval officers, and fostered by the most liberal encouragement and support of the naval government'.[31] In view of these great improvements in the Navy, Penrose felt that it would be possible now to stop prostitutes coming on board and to allow only decent married females to be with their husbands. He also argued that while the need for impressment was accepted even by mutinous seamen, the time was approaching when naval life would be so attractive, it should be possible to recruit men without resorting to press-gangs.

A retired naval surgeon was also prompted to write in response to Hawkins's pamphlet on prostitutes and he too wished to enforce the orders that prohibited such women from coming on board. But he boldly asserted that, although the bodily needs of sailors had been taken into account when introducing better health measures on board, the men had been considered as machines to perform a given service and next to nothing had been done for to improve their minds or morals. He argued, as other naval surgeons had done, that the regime of life at sea encouraged a dependency in seamen that made them more easily duped by prostitutes and sharpers ashore. At sea, the average crew member was treated as one unable to manage himself:

> In every well-regulated ship, he is watched over as boys are watched over at school; his person is examined, and kept clean; his clothes are counted over

periodically; and the officer of the division he belongs to reports at general musters every article of his dress which is discovered to be missing.[32]

It was no wonder that on shore crews were tricked and robbed, and that so many of the stout sailors begging on the streets, when questioned, confessed that they would have had enough money to last them until they found work had they not lavished it on prostitutes. The author took the problem seriously because its social repercussions were wider than individual tragedies:

> Our Navy may justly be considered to give the tone of moral feeling and conduct to a large proportion of our population. Principles engendered in a ship of war, are disseminated by the unceasing change and distribution of officers and seamen, not only through their own body, but among their families, (for what family has not some near relative at sea?) and to all with whom they associate on shore. (p. 25)

British colonies, the surgeon thought, were also sensibly affected by the character of seamen, and foreign nations also formed their opinion of the religion and morality of Britain from the conduct of the Navy.

Pressure for reform in the Navy slowly built up. With the peace came strident calls for more humane ways of manning the Navy as alternatives to impressment. There were various suggestions: an apprenticeship system, a register of seamen listing their qualifications, or using a ballot to raise seamen in wartime. Figures of some public note, including Dr Thomas Trotter, wrote feelingly against impressment. Other commentators alleged that the combination of pressing, enforced unlimited service and strict discipline was responsible for the bad character of many seamen. The 1816 supplement to the *Gentleman's Magazine* pointed out that it was more reasonable to expect virtuous conduct from men who were closely tied to society and that the current system of pressing and then denying crews shore leave actually militated against this.[33] In 1823, *The Times* argued that the present state of the law regarding impressment was due for reform and bemoaned the lack of legislation regulating the discharge and maintenance of seamen after periods of service.[34] Punishments at sea also attracted public attention. Many deemed them necessary to counteract vice. Senior naval officers, including Vice-Admiral Sir C.V. Penrose, consistently argued for the retention of corporal punishment, claiming that on the whole it was administered justly – though Penrose had to admit that it acted only as a deterrent and rarely improved men.[35] Rather inconsistently, he also suggested that steps should be taken to make the Navy a more desirable career and so lessen the need for either impressment or physical punishment. Radicals managed to make impressment and flogging the subject of debate in the House of Commons four times between 1824 and 1829, but failed to obtain any real reform in the Navy.[36] The Admiralty was impregnable, given the comparative lack of interest in the issue by the Tory government and the fact that lords of the Admiralty wished to adhere to traditional, tested methods. For example, on 9 June 1825 there was a widely reported Commons debate on the more effectual manning of the Navy, which Admiral Sir George Cockburn, a junior lord in the Admiralty and a trusted spokesperson for the Navy, used as an opportunity to explain that punishments at sea were declining both in number and severity. He ably defended impressment as a necessary evil, and the motion against it was defeated by 45 to 23.

Penrose had argued in his observations on the Navy that 'a great moral, social and intellectual improvement' had taken place in the service, largely due to the benevolent energies of naval officers supported by the government.[37] Yet in pre-Victorian Britain there was still public concern about the lack of naval chaplains. Indeed, there were not even enough for the post-war Navy's shrunken requirements. In 1825 there were 56 names on the list of chaplains, of whom only 22 were at sea, despite the Admiralty's efforts to encourage more clergy to enter the Navy during the French wars and a clear demonstration that the influence of religion could support legitimate authority at sea.[38] The Navy's attitude to religion was partly kept in the public eye by cheap religious tracts, originally written for circulation among warship crews. The tracts proved popular with officers and were eventually published for Christians on shore. They were evidence of zealous interest in the moral condition of the Navy, if not positive proof that seamen themselves had an increasing regard for religion.[39] In 1825, one ex-seaman was still warning parents not to send their sons to sea against their will and certainly not before they had acquired a proper grounding in moral thinking as there was a risk that the boys would be led astray by bad example.[40] The French Revolution had deeply frightened the propertied classes, strengthening their belief that society was a divinely-ordered hierarchy, and there was much support from this quarter for instilling a proper religious spirit into the Navy.

One arena in which the activities of the Navy did win public acclamation was that of Arctic exploration. In 1817, the Act originally offering a reward to any British subject who discovered a North-West passage from the Atlantic to the Pacific through the Hudson Strait was further altered to provide a sliding scale of rewards for expeditions approaching the pole and for reaching certain meridians of longitude. This prompted the first of the great nineteenth-century British Admiralty expeditions to the Arctic when Commodore John Ross was dispatched in April 1818. As the *Gentleman's Magazine* reported later that year, Ross penetrated Davis Strait and Baffin Bay but found no passage. For the first time in years, though, daring naval endeavours had caught the public's imagination and obtained wide coverage in the press. Ross returned with some curiosities from Baffin Bay, including a whip and sledge of bone used by newly discovered 'exquimaux', and 'some very remarkable star fish'.[41] The ensuing controversy about the geography of the area intrigued many and, the following year, Ross's former lieutenant, William Edward Parry, was dispatched to Lancaster Sound. He left on 11 May 1819 and did not return until October 1820. He found no passage but penetrated as far as Melville Island and was the first to winter in those northern latitudes. When he returned, it was clear that such expeditions were now firmly tied to a sense of national honour. The *Gentleman's Magazine* commented that to attempt a discovery of the North-West passage was 'every way worthy a great maritime power' and concluded that success would redound highly to national honour.[42]

It was determined that Parry would be sent on a second expedition with the *Fury* and *Hecla* in 1821. While the *Fury* was fitting out at Deptford, public interest again ran high. Officers accompanying Parry were mentioned by name in the press and in magazines. Natural curiosities from Parry's earlier expedition were deposited in the British Museum for inspection by the public. Parliament distributed the appropriate rewards in 1819–20 to the officers and men who sailed to such high latitudes, and since prize money was no longer attainable in peacetime, these rewards were enviable. The competition for awards were in themselves interesting to the public, as were the terrible conditions the men suffered in the hope of winning fame and fortune. The first to reach the Pacific by a North-West passage would win £10 000 on top of the usual rewards for pushing westwards in high latitudes. Officers on the Parry expedition were astute enough to see that they could harness public interest to boost their own reputation and prospects of preferment. While the ships were fitting out, they were opened to public inspection. The captains issued orders that 'no decent persons were to be refused admission' and officers attended the visitors to explain the various parts of the vessels.[43] Even after Parry departed on his second expedition, public interest was kept at a high level because later in 1821 the journal of Alexander Fisher, surgeon on the 1819–20 expedition, was published and extensively reviewed. Soon afterwards Parry's own journal of his first expedition was published, and on his second voyage he was at least able to send the occasional letter home giving an account of his progress. Even the very lack of news occasioned anxious interventions from well-wishers concerned about the fate of the expedition. When at length Parry returned in 1823, sightseers of all ranks flocked to Deptford in the hope of being permitted to go on board to find out about arctic novelties at first hand. Naval rules demanded that official permission was required before strangers were allowed on board, however, so many were disappointed. Parry's journal of the second expedition was duly published and promoted, and he was sent on a third expedition in 1824. This time, while the vessels were fitting out at Deptford, even more attention was shown to visitors. They came to see various ingenious adaptations to the ships including 'the means of conducting warm air through the vessels, and the contrivances for drawing off the moisture from the steam, breaths, &c'. They were politely received on board and the names of all were inserted in a book. These voyages therefore became part of the fabric of social life in the 1820s, providing excursions, reading matter and subjects for conversation. They were carried out at great expense but at little cost of life until the *Fury* was wrecked in the 1824–25 expedition. The dream of a commercially feasible North-West passage was not to be realized but many felt that these perilous expeditions deserved the gratitude of both the world of science and the maritime world. The exploits of 'enterprizing navigators' did much to restore the standing of the Navy in the public estimation.[44]

III

In 1823 the Painted Hall of the Greenwich Naval Hospital, which had been unsuitable for further use as a refectory ever since the painter Thornhill had finished his masterpiece there, was set up as a national gallery of marine painting, commemorating the public services of the Royal Navy. George IV backed the scheme and donated 31 portraits from the Royal Collection. Later he added de Loutherbourg's great canvas, 'Battle of 1 June 1794' and Turner's 'Trafalgar', painted in 1823. Other donations followed and before long the gallery at Greenwich was drawing crowds of up to 50 000 visitors a year.

At this period, retired seamen were gently ridiculed in various media for their tendency to live in the past, and the anniversaries of naval victories were no longer depicted as occasions of heartfelt thanks. A gap had opened up between the old seafaring culture and the evolving entreprenurial culture of pre-Victorian Britain. In this context, representatives of that earlier culture appeared peripheral to the main business of life. George Cruikshank's caricature of 1 July 1825, *The Battle of the Nile*, is without a trace of respect for the service that former seamen had given to the nation (see Plate 16). He depicted a group of veterans, much the worse for drink, reliving their exploits. Their mutilated condition – most are missing arms, eyes or legs – is used to make the scene more humourous, since the gestures that accompany their dramatic reconstruction of the battle seem incongruous and extravagant given their obvious incapacity to wield arms. Cruikshank's print is one of a number illustrating a publication entitled *Greenwich Hospital, a series of Naval Sketches, descriptive of the Life of a Man-of-War's Man* (1827). The work comprises a series of reminiscences apparently written by a 'Plain Blunt Old Sailor', now an inmate of the hospital. Written in conversational prose speckled with sea terms, these perpetuate the image of the careless but brave and generous tar. Yet in 1827 such figures seem less valued for their bravery than for the sentiment they might evoke in the observer. Of the 'assemblage of old blue-bottles' recounting their exploits at the Nile, we are told, 'It would do your heart good to hear them, and afford a fine subject for the pencil of Wilkie, could he but take a sly glance when the enthusiastic crisis is on, in the description of an engagement.'[45] The concept of naval service had become excessively sentimentalized in peacetime. An indication of the attitude contemporaries were being encouraged to adopt towards ex-seamen is given in the following extract from a sketch in the book called 'I have Done my Duty'.

> 'I dearly love a sailor!' exclaimed the beautiful and fascinating Mrs. D—, as she stood in the balcony of her house, leaning upon the arm of her affectionate and indulgent husband, and gazing at a poor shattered tar, who supplicated charity by a look that could not fail to interest the generous sympathies of the heart: 'I dearly love a sailor, they are so truly the children of nature; and I never feel more disposed to shed tears, than when I see a hardy veteran, who has sacrificed his youth, and even his limbs, in the service of his country.'[46]

The veteran has a tale of utter woe to tell, but his one consolation, repeated many times, is that he has always done his duty. These whimsical sketches, which rehearse many of the themes once powerfully associated with naval life in wartime: partings, reunions, lost loves and comradeship, are now firmly rooted in Greenwich Hospital by the narrator. Oddly, because of the whimsical tone, these themes have the effect of diminishing the status of the Hospital. It becomes less a symbol of national honour and more of a curiosity which, if visited, might offer interesting encounters with sundry ancient mariners. The ethos of naval service and discipline infused in all the narrator's stories, shows how, with hindsight, the order of the Navy might have seemed to provide a sound social model with a reliable framework of authority and hierarchy. But the stories relate to the past and lack the immediacy of everyday life in entrepreneurial, pre-Victorian Britain. In this context, visiting the pictures in the Painted Hall becomes a fashionable leisure activity rather than an act of heartfelt patriotism.

Several other publications in the 1820s sentimentalized both the Navy and the qualities it was presumed to uphold. *The Sailor Boy*, written with the avowed aim of encouraging the lower ranks to aspire to be naval heroes, tells of a schoolboy who ran away to sea after being beaten for giving his pocket money to a mendicant seaman. Honest, generous and brave, he wins fame and later makes a good marriage. The story is aimed at the young and creates an image of the Navy which can be held up as an example of moral behaviour. It also conveniently suggests that adherence to these values will bring money and happiness. The Religious Tract Society continued to use the much-publicized story of James Covey to support its message as late as 1830. As outlined in Chapter 5, Covey, a hardened seaman, had both his legs shot off in battle and subsequently converted to Christ.[47] Popular songbooks continued to feature naval themes and again appealed heavily to sentiment. A collection published around 1820, for example, included 'The Post Captain', a song which praised the character of seamen and implied that if they continued to act in so generous a manner they would be assured of eternity or promotion – either reading might apply.

> Priz'd be such hearts, for aloft they will go,
> Who always are ready compassion to shew
> To a brave conquer'd foe.[48]

In the same collection, a song called 'The Shipwrecked Sailor Boy' features a worthy young seaman who begs for money to journey back to his heartbroken parents:

> I've been in many battles and fought for you all,
> And glad would I have died my country to save:
> Then let me not perish, as surely I shall
> Unless some relief I quickly shall have. (p. 4)

The victory at the Battle of Navarino, 1827, offered an opportunity for more wholehearted praise of the British Navy along traditional lines. In the Strand, a panorama of the battle was opened to public view 'with surprising promptitude, but not at the sacrifice of beauty of execution'. The reviewer in the *Gentleman's Magazine* went on to say that, although some people had formerly complained that panoramas of naval actions had a monotonous similarity (further evidence of the declining interest in naval matters), no such objection could apply to the panorama of Navarino.[49] But more personal accounts of the action were less enthusiastic. A Scot who went to sea against his parents' wishes in the 1820s prefaced his account of the battle with a description of life on board a warship. He appreciates the food, especially hot cocoa for breakfast, but regrets the petty tyranny that so often found an easy home in the Navy.

> This instance of arbitrary power did not add to my good opinion of the service. I plainly saw that a seaman had no chance against an officer, even allowing him to be in the right; and I determined, within myself, to steer clear of every thing that should place me at either the mercy or the justice of my superiors.[50]

He is critical of the arrogant captain who is assigned to the ship when their former, much-loved captain is killed in battle, and asserts that good captains were all too rare in the fleet. In his account of Navarino, he does not flinch from recording instances of cowardice among the seamen, as well as great bravery. He dwells on the horror of battle and the tragic waste of young life – which was perhaps easier to do when the very sovereignty of the nation was no longer at stake as it had been in the French wars. He also revealingly repudiates the kind of heroics that had been so much publicized formerly. A marine called Hill lost both arms in the battle. The author found him in the cockpit, affecting nonchalance and singing so vigorously that he was in danger of opening his amputation dressings.

> I doubted much that this was an endeavour to re-enact an old story that I had heard years before, and could not help attributing such a piece of wretched affectation to the influence of Dibdin's songs, and of many of the melo-dramas of our small theatres, which put into the mouths of our sailors so much false heroism and nauseous sentimentalism. (p. 159)

By the time that the fleet returned home and the ship was paid off, the author had seen enough of the service and returned to Scotland.

In spite of Navarino, which in any case obtained a mixed reception after it was made public that no letter of ultimatum had been delivered to the Turks before the allies opened fire, the Navy was increasingly regarded only for what it had done in the past. It was now connected to a range of leisure activities enjoyed by the public that had nothing to do with maintaining morale in wartime. Naval spectacles still performed an important function in the life of the nation, encouraging national pride and fostering social cohesion, but in some media naval references descended to tokenism. Naval and military themes continued to be popular in music and martial illustrations often decorated nineteenth-century sheet-music covers. These tunes had titles like 'The English Mariner' or 'Old England's Men of War' and the covers featured stereotypical seamen. One example is 'The Old Commodore', a popular song by Dibdin that continued to be reproduced as sheet music. Later, when the price of pianos was lowered, thus placing the instrument within the reach of more people, sheet music with naval themes became if anything more sentimental. Typical titles include, 'The Pride of the Ocean', a quadrille featuring on the cover a priggish-looking midshipman looking across an extremely tidy deck (1862), and a little later 'The Powder Monkey Polka', with a cover illustration showing a rosy-cheeked youth sitting on the barrel of a gun. This format uses naval themes to suggest national character and to imply that young boys sent to sea were following a strong national tradition. Yet class-consciousness dogged the Navy in this later period. One piece, 'The Self-Made Man, a Humorous Song', reflected the ongoing controversy about the difficulties of obtaining promotion without interest but ridiculed those forced to rely on their own merit. It displayed the following verse on the front cover:

> There was a naval officer whose name was capt.[n] Cranks,
> Who bragg'd he was a self-made man, had risen from the ranks;
> Through every grade his character had been without a speck,
> Till from being powder monkey he rul'd o'er the quarter deck

The image of the captain alongside this text presented an unflattering picture of a social climber evidently more concerned with his own status than the well-being of his ship.

In the years after the Napoleonic War, multi-volume naval histories focusing on Britain's great struggle against France helped to reinforce the apparent link between the sea and the national character, which continued to be pursued in later decades. William James's five-volume *Naval History of Great Britain, from the Declaration of War by France in 1793 to the Accession of George IV*, was compiled with the approval of the Tory Admiralty immediately after the Napoleonic War and published in two editions in 1822–24 and in 1826. James preferred detailed description to illustrative plates, complaining that 'of the scores of engravings of sea-fights that have been published, very few will bear close investigation'.[51] He clearly thought that good marine art had to be factually correct and was disappointed to find that contemporary artists made many errors. He noted that some of the best drawings of single-ship actions came from the pencils of those officers who had taken part, not least because they were expert at delineating ships. Yet if officers attempted to draw actions in which they had not been present, they too made errors of fact. No wonder, he thought, that drawings of battle scenes exhibited in shop windows had often been the cause of bitter dispute between rival captains, each claiming that their part in the battle had been misrepresented. James began his work unpropitiously with the words, 'The value to England of her navy is an almost exhausted theme' (p. 1). This apparent awareness of the public mood did not dissuade him from an exhaustive examination of the Navy's part in the French wars. Hard on the heels of James's multi-volume work, in 1823–25, Captain Edward Brenton published his great, five-volume, *The Naval History of Great Britain*, of 1783–1822, which also presented a Tory view of the conflict. Illustrated with maps and portraits of naval heroes, his volumes stood as a testament to Britain's naval strength and recent achievements. Brenton was consciously aiming at the improvement of 'the rising generation' and hoped that the young would seek to emulate the courageous deeds found in his pages.[52] This led him, out of a sense of public duty, to draw attention to acts of misplaced courage and even to criminal acts performed by men of honour who had failed to control their passion. Brenton emphasized the responsibilities of a captain of a ship of war, who controlled a weapon capable of great destruction but also one capable of supporting political negotiation. He asserted that, in future, a discerning public would be more critical of indecisive naval operations than they had been in the days of Keppel and was particularly critical of the mistakes made in the battle of the Glorious First of June, 1794. Although careful to say that sea battles were so confused that no officer could be master of all that took place, his judgemental approach in the treatment of recent history inevitably offended some: the publication of his volumes prompted individuals to correct his version of events or rebut apparent slurs on their honour. In contrast to these detailed naval histories which tended to analyse the recent performance of the Navy, in 1825 Captain William Goldsmith published a naval history of Great Britain that was much more uncritically patriotic in tone. His one-volume work (which included plates of battles and naval heroes), was aimed at those who could not afford the more expensive editions but whose simple patriotism remained untainted by the cynicism that had affected the more sophisticated classes.[53] Goldsmith's narrative is extremely concise, confined to action rather than opinion and includes brief biographies of notable officers. Although he pledged himself to strict impartiality in his preface, he is partial by omission. A comparison of the ways in which these three historians treated the battle of the Glorious First of June serves as an example of this. While James noted that in fact the French had claimed the battle as a strategic victory and Brenton at least regretted that the British had not pursued the French fleet and captured the convoy it was protecting, Goldsmith made no attempt at a balanced view. He ended his account of the battle when the smoke cleared away and Howe was able to depart with his captured enemy vessels.

By the end of the 1820s, whatever place the Navy held in the heart of the nation, it had become a constant target for Whig reformers who wished to see a change in the administration of naval affairs and a reduction of the bureaucracy beneath the Admiralty that seemed such an impediment to transparent accounting. The aim was to achieve savings in official salaries and to remove those who obstructed any reduction in dockyard establishments or alterations to the way in which the fleets were maintained. When the Whigs came to power in 1830, these reforms were quickly driven through. Yet, despite the difficulties of the Navy in these peacetime years, the British remained keenly aware that their security depended upon a strong Navy. Any experiments carried out to improve the sailing quality of warships, including attempts to preserve ships at sea from lightning, were counted newsworthy items. At this period Britons were utterly confident in the country's naval superiority. The sentimentalism the Navy attracted reveals a degree of complacency but its continued representation in various media also indicates a determination to ensure that Britain's Navy remained strong and able to recruit the men it needed. The place that the Navy held in the public consciousness was set to endure in differing forms for another hundred years and more, but it would never again be so central to public discourse or so fine an indicator of public relations.

Notes

1 *GM*, 85 (1815), 335.
2 *An Inquiry into the Present State of the British Navy. Together with Reflections on the Late War with America … by an Englishman* (London, 1815).
3 *Loyal Effusions! A Selection of Odes, Songs, &c. written during the last Twelve Years, by an Old Naval Officer* (London, 1819).
4 J. Austen, *Lady Susan, The Watsons, Sanditon* (Harmondsworth, 1974), p. 169.
5 *The Times*, 28 February 1817, p. 3.
6 *The Naval Chronicle*, 34 (1815), p. 395.
7 [R. Marks], *Nautical Essays: or, a spiritual view of the ocean and maritime affairs: with reflections on the battle of Trafalgar and other events* (London, 1818), pp. 77–8.
8 *The Times*, 2 November 1818, p. 3.
9 *The Appeal of Britannicus, to the British Public, on behalf of the Royal Navy. By an Officer* (Plymouth, 1819).
10 *The Times*, 2 August 1816, p. 3. Cf. *The Times*, 2 June 1819, p. 2.
11 *The Black Book; or, Corruption Unmasked! Being an account of places, pensions, and sinecures, the revenues of the clergy and landed aristocracy*, 2 vols (London, 1820), vol. I, p. 2.
12 *The Times*, 7 February 1816, p. 3; *The Times*, 13 February 1816, p. 4.
13 *The Times*, 18 March 1818, p. 2.
14 *GM*, 87, Pt I (1817), 320.
15 *Things as they were. 1783, Things as they are. 1823*, lithograph by F.W. Ommanney (artist) and C.J. Hullmandel (Printer). NMM PAF3721.
16 *Things as they were, 1757. Things as they are, 1827*, lithograph by H.W. (engraver) and S.W. Fores (publisher). NMM PAF3724.
17 *A mid on half pay*, by C. Hunt (engraver and publisher), 1 June 1825. NMM PAF3722.
18 B. Lavery, *Nelson's Navy. The Ships, Men and Organisation* (London, 1989), p. 94.
19 *GM*, 95, Pt II (1825), 386.
20 *An Inquiry into the Present State of the British Navy*, pp. 58, 75–6.
21 *The Times*, 17 April 1822, p. 3.
22 *The Times*, 21 June 1823, p. 3.
23 *GM*, 93, Pt I (1823), 195.
24 *The Times*, 2 December 1819, p. 2.
25 *The Times*, 14 August 1821, p. 2.
26 A. Burton pseud. [i.e. J. Mitford], *The Adventures of Johnny Newcome in the Navy; A Poem in Four Cantos: with plates by Rowlandson* (London, 1818). Written in 1816.
27 W.F. Sullivan, *Pleasant Stories; or, Histories of Ben the Sailor and Ned the Soldier* (London, 1818), p. 12.
28 Ibid., pp. 38, 46.
29 *A Friendly Address to the Seamen of the British Navy* (Bodmin, 1820), pp. 11–12.
30 Sir C.V. Penrose, *Observations on Corporal Punishment, Impressment, and other Matters Relative to the Present State of His Majesty's Royal Navy* (Bodmin, 1824), p. 52.
31 Ibid., pp. 58–9, 65.
32 *An Address to the Officers of His Majesty's Navy. By an old Naval Surgeon* (Dublin, 1824), p. 8.
33 *GM*, 86, Pt I (1816), 580. Cf. ibid., Pt II, 402–4.
34 *The Times*, 1 October 1823, p. 2.
35 Penrose, *Observations*, p. 15.
36 R. Morriss, *Cockburn and the British Navy in Transition. Admiral Sir George Cockburn 1772–1853* (Exeter, 1997), p. 153.
37 Penrose, *Observations*, p. 65.

38 *The Times*, 23 October 1825, p. 2. Cf. *An Inquiry into the Present State of the British Navy*, pp. 136 – 7.

39 [R. Marks], *Nautical Essays; or, a Spiritual View of the Ocean and Maritime Affairs; with Reflections on the Battle of Trafalgar, and other Events*, 2nd edn (London, 1820), p. 195.

40 H.B. Gascoigne, *Gascoigne's Path to Naval Fame, the Second Edition with an Index of Nautical Terms and Phrases* (Warwick, 1825), pp. 27–8.

41 *GM*, 88, Pt II (1818), 460, 559.

42 *GM*, 90, Pt II (1820), 548.

43 *GM*, 91, Pt I (1821), 81–2, 272, 370.

44 *GM*, 93, Pt II (1823), 355, 595; and *GM*, 94, Pt I (1824), 329–34, 363.

45 *Greenwich Hospital, a series of Naval Sketches, descriptive of the Life of a Man-of-War's Man. By an old sailor* (London, 1827), p. 87.

46 Ibid. p. 67.

47 *The Brave British Tar; or, the True History of a Sailor who had both his legs shot off in Lord Duncan's Victory*, The Religious Tract Society (London, [1830?]).

48 *A Collection of New Songs, containing The Post Captain, The Shipwrecked Sailor Boy, (etc.)* (Newcastle, [1820?]), p. 3.

49 *GM*, 98, Pt I (1828), 71.

50 *Life on Board a Man-of-War: including a full account of the Battle of Navarino. By a British Seaman* (Glasgow, 1829), p. 33; cf. p. 186.

51 W. James, *Naval History of Great Britain, from the Declaration of War by France in 1793 to the Accession Gorge IV*, 5 vols (London, 1822–24), vol. I, p. xxxiii.

52 E.P. Brenton, *The Naval History of Great Britain, from the Year MDCCLXXXIII to MDCCCXXII*, 5 vols (London, 1823–25), vol. I, pp. vii–viii.

53 W. Goldsmith, *The Naval History of Great Britain, from the Earliest Period: with biographical notices of the admirals, and other distinguished officers* (London, 1825), p. vi.

Bibliography

The place of publication is London, unless otherwise stated.

Newspapers and Periodicals

The Annual Register, 1803–04
Cobbett's Weekly Political Register, 1804
Edinburgh Evening Courant, 1777
Gentleman's Magazine, 1747–1825
The Ladies Magazine; or, Polite Companion for the Fair Sex, 1750
The Lady's Magazine, 1760
London Chronicle or Universal Evening Post, 1763, 1803
London Magazine, 1756
The Morning Chronicle, 1803–04
The Morning Post, 1803–04
The Naval Chronicle, 1810, 1815
Navy News, 2001
The Sunday Times, 2001
The Times, 1794–1825, 2001
The True Briton 1803–04

Books, Pamphlets and Articles

Ackermann, R., ed., *The Repository of Arts, Literature, Commerce, Manufactures, Fashions and Politics*, 14 vols (1809–15)
Adams, J., *On Morbid Poisons*, 2nd edn (1807)
An Address to the Hon. Admiral Augustus Keppel, containing candid remarks on his defence before the Court Martial … By a seaman (1779)
An Address to the Landowners, Merchants, and other Principal Inhabitants of England, on the Expediency of entering into Subscriptions for augmenting the British Navy (1782)
An Address to the Officers of His Majesty's Navy. By an old Naval Surgeon (Dublin, 1824)

An Address to the Right-Honourable the First Lord Commissioner of the Admiralty, upon the Decreasing Spirit, Splendour, and Discipline of the Navy ... by an Officer (1787)

Admiral Byng's Defence, as presented by him to the Court, on board his Majesty's Ship St George, *January 18, 1757*

Alexander, W., MD, *The History of Women from the Earliest Antiquity, to the Present Time*, 2 vols (1779)

Altick, R.D., *The Shows of London: a panoramic history of exhibitions, 1600–1862* (Camb, MA, and London, 1978)

The Anti-Gallican; or Standard of British Loyalty, Religion and Liberty; including a Collection of the Principal Papers, Tracts, Speeches, Poems, and Songs, that have been published on the Threatened Invasion; together with many original pieces on the same subject (1804)

The Appeal of Britannicus, to the British Public, on behalf of the Royal Navy. By an Officer (Plymouth, 1819)

An Appeal to the Candour and Justice of the People of England, in behalf of the West India Merchants and Planters (1792)

An Appeal to the Head and Heart of every Man and Woman in Great Britain, respecting the threatened French invasion (1798)

An Appeal to the People: Containing the Genuine and Entire Letter of Admiral Byng to the Secr[etary] of the Ad[miralty], 1756

Armstrong, J., *The Art of Preserving Health: a poem* (1744)

Aspinall-Oglander, C., ed., *Admiral's Wife. Being the Life and Letters of the Hon. Mrs Edward Boscawen from 1719 to 1761* (1940)

Atkins J., *The Navy-Surgeon: or a Practical System of Surgery*, 2nd edn (1737)

Austen, J., *Jane Austen's Letters*, ed. D. Le Faye, 3rd edn (Oxford, 1995)

——, *Mansfield Park* (1814), ed. T. Tanner (Harmondsworth, 1966)

——, *Persuasion* (1818), ed. D.W. Harding (Harmondsworth, 1965)

——, *Lady Susan, The Watsons, Sanditon* (Harmondsworth, 1974)

Barker, H., *Newspapers, Politics and English Society, 1895–1855* (Harlow, Essex, 2000)

Barker, H. and Chalus, E., *Gender in Eighteenth-Century England: Roles, Representations and Responsibilities* (London and New York, 1997)

Barker, J.T., *The Ship Launch. The Substance of a Sermon, preached at Deptford, on Occasion of the Launching of the Queen Charlotte. July 17th 1810* (1810)

Baugh, D.A., *British Naval Administration in the Age of Walpole* (Princeton, NJ, 1965)

—— *Naval Administration 1750–50* (NRS. Vol. 120, 1977)

Beawes, W., *Mercartoria Rediva: Or the Merchant's Directory. Being a Complete Guide to Men in Business* (1761)

Bindman, D., and M. Baker, *Roubiliac and the Eighteenth-Century Monument: Sculpture as Theatre* (New Haven, CT, and London, 1995)

Bermingham, A., and J. Brewer, eds, *The Consumption of Culture 1600–1800. Image, Object, Text* (London and New York, 1995)

The Black Book; or, Corruption Unmasked! Being an account of places, pensions, and sinecures, the revenues of the clergy and landed aristrocracy, 2 vols (1820)

Blackhouse, W., DD, *God the Author of Peace and Lover of Concord. A Sermon preached at the Parish Council of Deal, on Thursday, July 29, 1784* (Canterbury, 1784)

Blake's Remarks on Com. Johnstone's Account of his Engagement with a French Squadron under the Command of Mons. De Suffrein on April 16, 1781 in Port Praya Rd, in the Island of St Jago. A new Edition (1782)

Blane, G., *A Short Account of the Most Effectual Means of Preserving the Health of Seamen, particularly in the Royal Navy* (n.p., 1780)

———, *Observations on the Diseases incident to Seamen* (1785)

———, *Select Dissertations on Several Subjects of Medical Science* (1822)

The Block and Yard Arm. A New Ballad, on the Loss of Minorca, and the Danger to Our American Rights and Possessions. To the Tune of Whose E'r Been at Baldcock (1756)

Bradley, J.E., *Religion, Revolution and English Radicalism. Nonconformity in Eighteenth-Century Politics and Society* (Cambridge, 1990)

Braham's Whim; Or songster's Delight: comprising all the modern fashionable and sea songs now singing at the theatres of London and convivial clubs (1812)

The Brave British Tar; or, the True History of a Sailor who had both his legs shot off in Lord Duncan's Victory, The Religious Tract Society (1830?)

Brenton, E.P., *The Naval History of Great Britain, from the Year MDCCLXXXIII to MDCCCXXII*, 5 vols (1823–25)

Brewer, J., *Party Ideology and Popular Politics at the Accession of George III* (Cambridge, 1976)

———, *The Pleasures of the Imagination: English Culture in the Eighteenth Century* (1997)

———, *The Sinews of Power: War, Money and the English State, 1688–1783* (1989)

A Brief Inquiry into the Present Condition of the Navy of Great Britain, and its Resources (1804)

Britannia Triumphant ... by a society of naval gentlemen (1766)

The British Navy Triumphant! Being copies of the London Gazettes Extraordinary; containing the accounts of the Glorious Victories obtained through the blessing of Almighty God, over the French Fleet ... (1798).

Broadley, J., *Pandora's Box, and the Evils of Britain* (1801)

Brown, A., *Dr Brown's Sermon on the Dangers and Duties of the Seafaring Life* (Boston, MA, 1793)

Brown, F., *The Evils of War. A Fast Sermon, delivered at North Yarmouth, April 7, 1814* (Portland, OR,1814)

Burton, A., pseud. [i.e. J. Mitford], *The Adventures of Johnny Newcome in the Navy; A Poem in Four Cantos: with plates by Rowlandson* (1818)

Bynum, W.F., and R. Porter, eds, *William Hunter and the Eighteenth-Century Medical World* (Cambridge, 1985)

Cameron, A. and R. Farndon, *Scenes from Sea and City. Lloyd's List 1734–1984* (Colchester, Essex, 1984)

Candid Reflections on the Expedition to Martinico, by J.J. a Lieutenant in the Navy (1759)

Cannon, J., *The Oxford Companion to British History* (Oxford, 1997)

The Case and distressed Situation of the Officers of the Navy, Explained in a Letter from a Captain of the Navy to a Member of Parliament (1775)

The Case and distressed Situation of the Widows of the Officers of the Navy, Explained in a Letter from a Captain in the Navy to a Member of Parliament (1775)

Carmichael, Revd J., *A Self-Defensive War Lawful* (Philadelphia, 1775)

Carmichael Smyth, J., *An Account of the Experiment made at the desire of the Lords Commissioners of the Admiralty, on board the Union Hospital Ship* (1796)

Carpenter, K.J., *The History of Scurvy and Vitamin C* (Cambridge, 1986)

Chauncy, C., *A Sermon preached the 18th of July, 1745. Being a day set apart for Solemn Thanksgiving to Almighty God, for the Reduction of Cape-Breton ...* (Boston, MA, 1745)

Clarke, J.A., 'Collectors and Consumerism: The British Print Market 1750–1860', in *The Martial Face. The Military Portrait in Britain, 1760–1900* (Providence, RI, 1991)

Clarke, J.S., *Naufragia; or Historical Memoirs of Shipwrecks and of the Providential Deliverance of Vessels* (1805)

———, *Sermons on the Character and Professional Duties of Seamen* (1801)

———, *The Progress of Maritime Discovery, from the Earliest Period to the Close of the Eighteenth Century, Forming an Extensive System of Hydrography* (1803)

Cleghorn, G., *Observations on the Epidemical Diseases in Minorca, from the year 1744–1749* (1751)

A Collection of New Songs, containing The Post Captain, The Shipwrecked Sailor Boy, (etc.) (Newcastle, 1820?)

A Collection of Several Pamphlets, very little known ... relative to the Case of Admiral Byng (1756)

Colley, L., *Britons: Forging the Nation, 1707–1837* (New Haven, CT, and London, 1992)

The Conduct of the Admirals Hawke, Keppel, and Palliser, Compared (1779)

The Conduct of the Ministry impartially Examined. In a Letter to the Merchants of London, 2nd edn (1756)

Considerations on the Present Peace, as far as it is relative to the Colonies and the African Trade (1763)

Conway, S., *The British Isles and the War of American Independence* (Oxford, 2000)

Cookson, J.E., *The British Armed Nation 1793–1815* (Oxford, 1997)

Cootes, R.J, *Britain Since 1700* (Harlow, Essex, 1982)

Cope, K.L., ed., *Compendious Conversations: The Method of Dialogue in the Early Enlightenment* (Frankfurt, am Main, 1992)

Cordingly, D., *Heroines & Harlots. Women at Sea in the Great Age of Sail* (2001)

Corfield, P.J., *Power and the Professions in Britain 1700–1850* (London and New York, 1995)

Crimmin, P.K., 'The Sick and Hurt Board and the Health of Seamen, c. 1700–1806', *Journal for Maritime Research* (December, 1999), p. 10.

The Cruise; a Poetical Sketch, in eight cantos, by a naval officer (1808)

Cupid Wounded: or, the Mischievous Bee: Being a Collection of entire New Songs sung at all the Places of Public Amusement (1815? and 1820?)

Curtis, Sir R., *The Means Used to Eradicate a Malignant Fever, which raged on board his Majesty's Ship Brunswick, at Spithead in the Spring of the Year 1791* (1794?)

Dailey, B.R., 'The Visitation of Sarah Wight: Holy Carnival and the Revolution of the Saints in Civil War London', *Church History*, 55 (1986), 455

Dale, J., *Nelson and the Navy. A Sonata for the Piano Forte – in commemoration of the Glorious 1st August, 1798*, 2 vols (1798)

[Davis, J.], *Letters from a Mother to her son: written upon his return from his first voyage at sea* (Stockport, 1801)

Derry, J.W., *Politics in the Age of Fox, Pitt and Liverpool* (Basingstoke, 2001)

A Description of Several Pictures presented to the Corporation of the City of London by John Boydell, Alderman … (1794)

Devine, T.M., *The Tobacco Lords. A Study of the Tobacco Merchants of Glasgow and their Trading Activities c.1740–90* (Edinburgh, 1975)

Dibdin, T., *Songs by Charles Dibdin*, 2nd edn (1881)

Dickson, P.G.M., *The Financial Revolution in England* (London and New York, 1993)

The Disabled Sailor (1800)

Donald, D., *the Age of Caricature. Satirical Prints in the Reign of George III* (New Haven, CT, and London, 1996)

Dr Brown's Sermon on the Dangers and Duties of the Seafaring Life; preached before the Protestant Dissenting Congregation, at Halifax (Boston, MA, 1793)

Dugaw, D., 'Balladry's Female Warriors: Women, Warfare, and Disguise in the Eighteenth Century', *Eighteenth-Century Life*, 9(2) (1985), pp. 1–20

Dunne, C., *The Chirurgical Candidate; or, Reflections on Education: indispensable to complete Naval, Military, and Other Surgeons* (1801)

Eagleton, T., *The Rape of Clarissa* (Minneapolis, MN, 1982)

Earle, P., *Sailors, English Merchant Seamen 1650–1775* (1998)

Ehrlich, C., *The Piano, A History*, revised edn (Oxford, 1990)

Estwick, S., *Considerations on the Present Decline of the Sugar-Trade* (1782)

Evans, I., Revd, *A Discourse, delivered in New-York … on 11th December 1783* (New York, 1783)

A Fair Statement of the Real Grievances experienced by the Officers and Sailors in the Navy of Great Britain; with a Plan of Reform ... By a Naval Officer (1797)

Falconer, W., *The Shipwreck*, 6th edn (1785)

The Female Soldier; Or, The Surprising Life and Adventures of Hannah Snell (1750)

Fielding, J., *A Brief Description of the Cities of London and Westminster* (1776)

Fischer, L.R. and H.W. Nordvik, eds, *Essays in International Maritime Economic History* (Pontefract, 1990)

Fissell, M.E., *Patients, Power, and the Poor in Eighteenth-Century Bristol* (Cambridge, 1991)

Fletcher, C., *The Naval Guardian*, 2nd edn, 2 vols (1805)

Fordyce, J., *The Character and Conduct of the Female Sex and The Advantages to be derived by Young Men from the Society of Virtuous Women. A Discourse in Three Parts* (1776)

A Form of Prayer and Thanksgiving to Almighty God to be used at Morning and Evening Service ... (1762)

A Form of Prayer to be used ... upon ... the Day appointed by Proclamation for a General Fast and Humiliation (1782)

A Friendly Address to the Seamen of the British Navy (Bodmin, 1820)

Gascoigne, H.B., *Gascoigne's Path to Naval Fame, the Second Edition with an Index of Nautical Terms and Phrases* (Warwick, 1825)

The Genuine Speech of the truly honourable Adm[ira]l V[erno]n, to the Sea-Officers, at a Council of War, just before The Attack on C[artagen]A (1741)

[Glascock, W.], *Naval Sketch-Book; or, the Service Afloat and Ashore, by an Officer of Rank*, 2 vols (1826)

Glasse, S., *A Sermon Preached before the President, Vice-Presidents, and Governors, of the Marine Society* (1774)

Goldsmith, W., *The Naval History of Great Britain, from the Earliest Period: with biographical notices of the admirals, and other distinguished officers* (1825)

Grainger, J., *The Sugar Cane* (1764)

Greenwich Hospital, a series of Naval Sketches, descriptive of the Life on a Man-of-War's Man. By an old sailor (1827)

Greig, J. ed., *The Farington Diary by Joseph Farington, R.A.*, 8 vols (1922–28)

Habermas, J., *The Structural Transformation of the Public Sphere: An Inquiry into a Category of Bourgeois Society* (Cambridge, 1989)

[Hacket, M.], *A Popular Account of St. Paul's Cathedral: with a Description of The Monuments and other interesting particulars* (1816)

Hamlin, C., 'Predisposing Causes and Public Health in Early-Nineteenth-Century Medical Thought', *Social History of Medicine*, 5 (1992), pp. 43–70

Hancock, D., *Citizens of the World. London Merchants and the Integration of the British Atlantic Community, 1735–1785* (Cambridge, 1995)

Hanway, J., *An Historical Account of the British Trade over the Caspian Sea*, 2 vols 1754)

———, *The Seaman's Faithful Companion* (1763)

————,*The Seaman's Christian Friend: Containing Moral and Religious Advice to Seamen* (1779)

Haven, S., *A Sermon … Occasioned by the Remarkable Success of His Majesty's Arms in the Late War* (Portsmouth, NH, 1763)

Heathcote, G., *A Letter to the Right Honourable The Lord Mayor; the Worshipful Aldermen, and Common-council; the Merchants, Citizens, and Inhabitants of the City of London* (1762)

Hoare, P., *Academic Correspondence, 1803, containing … a description of the Public Monuments voted by the Parliament of Great Britain, to the Memory of Naval and Military Officers, since the Year 1798* (1804)

Horsley, S., *The Watchers and the Holy Ones. A Sermon on Thursday December 5, 1805* (1806)

Hutchison, C.A., *Practical Observations in Surgery: more particularly as regards the naval and military service*, 2nd edn (1826) first published 1816.

Huxham, J., *An Essay on Fevers* (1750)

Ignatieff, M., *A Just Measure of Pain: The Penitentiary in the Industrial Revolution, 1750–1850* (1978)

Impartial Reflections on the Case of Mr Byng, as stated on an appeal to the people, etc and a letter to a member of parliament, etc (1756)

An Inquiry into the Present State of the British Navy. Together with Reflections on the Late War with America … by an Englishman (1815)

Ireland, W., *The Sailor Boy. A Poem in Four Cantos; illustrative of the Navy of Great Britain*, 2nd edn (1822)

Ives, E., *A Voyage from England to India in the Year MDCCLIV and an Historical Narrative of the Operations of the Squadron and Army in India under the command of Vice-Admiral Watson and Colonel Clive* (1773)

James, W., *Naval History of Great Britain, from the Declaration of War by France in 1793 to the Accession George IV*, 5 vols (1822–24)

Jemmat, C., *The Memoirs of Mrs. Catherine Jemmat*, 2 vols (1762)

Jenyns, S., *Thoughts on the Causes and Consequences of the Present High Price of Provisions* (1767)

J.M., a Lieutenant in the Fleet, *The Maritime Campaign of 1778* (London, 1778)

Jones, J.G., *Sketch of a Political Tour* (1796)

Kelly, V., and D.E. Von Mücke, *Body & Text in the Eighteenth Century* (California, 1994)

Kowaleski-Wallace, E., *Consuming Subjects: Women, Shopping, and Business in the Eighteenth Century* (New York, 1997)

Lavery, B., *Nelson's Navy. The Ships, Men and Organisation* (1989)

————, ed., *Shipboard Life and Organisation, 1731–1815* (Aldershot, 1998),

Lawrence, C., *Medicine and the Making of Modern Britain, 1700–1920* (1994)

Leech, S., *Thirty Years from Home, or A Voice from the Main Deck* (Boston, 1843)

The Legal Claim of the British Sugar-Colonies to enjoy an Exclusive right of supplying this Kingdom with sugars … (1792)

A Letter from A Captain of a Man of War, to a Member of Parliament (1773)

A Letter from a Merchant in London to his Nephew in North America (1766)

Letter from a Sea-Officer of France to the Honourable Admiral Keppel (1778)

A Letter to the Right Honourable The Earl of Sandwich, on the Present State of Affairs. By a Sailor (1779)

Life on Board a Man-of-War: including a full account of the Battle of Navarino. By a British Seaman (Glasgow, 1829)

Lincoln, A., 'What Was Published in 1798', *European Romantic Review*, 10 (1999), pp. 137–58

Lincoln, M., 'Naval Ship Launches as Public Spectacle, 1773–1854', *Mariners Mirror*, 83 (November,1997), pp. 466–72.

Lind, J., *An Essay on the Most Effectual Means of Preserving the Health of Seamen in the Royal Navy* (1757)

A List of the Society for the Encouragement of Arts, Manufactures and Commerce (1763)

Lloyd, C. and J.L.S. Coulter, *Medicine and the Navy 1200–1900*, Vol. III (Edinburgh and London, 1961)

Loudon, I.S.L., 'The Origins and Growth of the Dispensary Movement in England', *Bulletin of the History of Medicine*, 55 (1981), pp. 322–42

Love Elegies, by a Sailor, Written in the Year MDCCLXXIV (1780)

Lowe, J., *An Inquiry into the State of the British West Indies* (1807)

Loyal Effusions! A Selection of Odes, Songs, &c. written during the last Twelve Years, by an Old Naval Officer (1819)

Lyon, D., *The Sailing Navy List* (1993)

Macleod, E.V., *A War of Ideas: British Attitudes to the Wars against Revolutionary France, 1792–1802* (Aldershot, 1998)

MacPherson, D., *Annals of Commerce*, 4 vols (1805)

[Marks, R.], *Nautical Essays: or, a spiritual view of the ocean and maritime affairs: with reflections on the battle of Trafalgar and other events* (1818)

Marshall, P.J., ed., *The Oxford History of the British Empire*, 5 vols (Oxford, 1998–99), Vol. II (1998)

Mason, W., *Ode to the Naval Officers of Great Britain, written immediately after the trial of Admiral Keppel, February the Eleventh, 1779* (1779)

Maurice, T., *The Crisis of Britain: a poem* (1803)

Mayhew, J., *Two Discourses Delivered October 9th, 1760* (Boston, MA,1760)

Memoirs and Adventures of Mark Moore, Late an Officer in the British Navy (1795)

McKendrick, N., J. Brewer and J.H. Plumb, *The Birth of a Consumer Society: The Commercialization of Eighteenth-Century England* (1982)

Millar, J., *Observations on the Management of the Prevailing Diseases in Great Britain, particularly in the Army and Navy* (1779)

———, *Observations on the Change of Public Opinion in Religion, Politics, and Medicine on the Conduct of the War; on the Prevailing Diseases in Great Britain; and on Medical Arrangements in the Army and Navy*, 2 vols (1805?)

Miller, D. and P. Reill, *Visions of Empire: voyages, botany and representations of empire* (Cambridge, 1996)

Monks, S., 'National Heterotopia: Greenwich as Spectacle, 1694–1869', *Rising East: The Journal of East London Studies*, **2**(1) (1998), pp. 156–66

More Birds for the Tower, or who'll Confess First (1756?)

More, H., *Cheap Repository Shorter Tracts*, new edn (1799)

———, *The Loyal Sailor; or No Mutineering* (1800?)

Morgan, K., *Bristol and the Atlantic Trade in the Eighteenth Century* (Cambridge, 1993)

Morrice, D., *The Young Midshipman's Instructor* (1801)

Morriss, R., *Cockburn and the British Navy in Transition. Admiral Sir George Cockburn 1772–1853* (Exeter, 1997)

———, *The Royal Dockyards During the Revolutionary and Napoleonic Wars* (1983)

Mr. Reeve's Evidence before a Committee of the House of Commons on the Trade of Newfoundland (1793)

Murray, J., *The Happy Voyage Compleated, and the Sure Anchor Cast* (Newbury-Port, Mass.,1785)

Museum Rusticum et Commerciale: or Select Papers on Agriculture, Commerce, Arts and Manufactures, 6 vols (1764)

Namier, Sir L. and John Brooke, *The History of Parliament. The House of Commons 1754–1790*, 3 vols (1964)

The Narrative of Strictures upon Naval Departments ... by a Sailor (1785)

Naval Administration 1715–50, Navy Records Society, vol. 120 (1977)

The New Art of War at Sea now first practis'd by the English ships, under the Command of the Prudent Admiral Bung (1756)

A New Edition of the Appeal of a Neglected Naval Officer (1785)

A New Form of Worship for the 27th of July (n.d.)

[Nickolls, J.], *Remarks on the Advantages and Disadvantages of France and Great-Britain with Respect to Commerce and to other means of encreasing the Wealth and Power of the State* (1754)

Nicol, J., *The Life and Adventures of John Nicol, Mariner* (Edinburgh, 1822)

Observations and Instructions for the Use of the Commissioned, the Junior, and other Officers of the Royal Navy ... by a Captain in the Royal Navy (1804)

Oman, C., *Nelson* (1947)

Opie, J., *Lectures on Painting, delivered at the Royal Academy of Arts with a Letter on the Proposal for A Public Memorial of the Naval Glory of Great Britain* (1809)

Parsons, Mrs., *The Convict, or Navy Lieutenant. A Novel*, 4 vols (Brentford, 1807)

Peck, J., *Maritime Fiction. Sailors and the Sea in British and American Novels, 1719–1917* (Basingstoke, 2001)

Penrose, Sir C.V., *Observations on Corporal Punishment, Impressment, and other Matters Relative to the Present State of His Majesty's Royal Navy* (Bodmin, 1824)

Pinckard, G., *Notes on the West Indies written during the Expedition under the Command of the late General Sir Ralph Abercomby*, 3 vols (1806)

Plan of National Improvement ....to which are added ... Bonaparte's grand project to conquer Great Britain and Ireland (1803)

Pointon, M., *Hanging the Head* (London and New Haven, 1993)

Pope, D., *Life in Nelson's Navy* (1987)

Porter, D. and R. Porter, *Patient's Progress: Doctors and Doctoring in Eighteenth-Century England* (Oxford, 1989)

Porter, R., *Doctor of Society: Thomas Beddoes and the Sick Trade in Late-Enlightenment England* (London and New York, 1992)

——, 'Lay Medical Knowledge in the Eighteenth Century: the Evidence of the *Gentleman's Magazine*', *Medical History*, 29 (1985), pp. 138–68

Pratt, S.J., *Gleanings in England; descriptive of the Countenance, Mind and Character of the Country*, 2 vols, 2nd edn (1801)

A Practical Discourse to Sea-Faring Men (Boston, 1771)

A Prayer for the Safety of Our Fleets, by His Majesty's Special Command, March 9th, 1796 (printed on card. MOD(N)L–P(NS)184)

Prentice, R., *A Celebration of the Sea* (1994)

Price, J.M., *Overseas Trade and Traders. Essays of Some Commercial, Financial and Political Challenges Facing British Atlantic Merchants, 1660–1775* (Aldershot, 1996)

Pringle, J., *Observations on the Diseases of the Army, in Camp and Garrison* (1752)

The Proceedings at Large of the Court-Martial, on the trial of the Honourable Augustus Keppel ... (1779)

Proofs that Great Britain was Successful against each of her Numerous Enemies before the Late Victory of Sir George Brydges Rodney (1782)

Radcliffe, M.A., *The Female Advocate; or An Attempt to Recover the Rights of Women from Male Usurpation* (1799)

Ramsey, J., *Objections to the Abolition of the Slave Trade* (1788)

Ramsay, Revd J., *Sea Sermons, or a Series of Discourses for the use of the Royal Navy* (1781)

Randall, A.F., *A Letter to the Women of England, on the Injustice of Mental Subordination. With Anecdotes* (1788)

Redford, A., *Manchester Merchants and Foreign Trade, 1794–1858* (Manchester, 1934)

Reinhartz, D., 'Interior Geographies. Map Screens from the Age of Exploration, Expansion, and Trade', *Mercator's World*, 5 (Sept./Oct., 2000), pp. 32–5.

A Reply to a Pamphlet intituled 'A Brief Enquiry into the Present Condition of the Navy of Great Britain' (1804)

Richardson, R., *The Dolphin's Journal Epitomized in a Poetical Essay* (1768)

Ring, J., *Reflections on the Surgeons' Bill: in answer to three pamphlets in defence of that bill* (1798)

Robinson, C.N., *A Pictorial History of the Sea Services or Graphic Studies of the Sailor's Life and Character Afloat and Ashore*, 11 vols (1911),

Robinson, M., *The Poetical Works of the late Mrs Mary Robinson: including many pieces never before published*, 3 vols (1806)

Robson, Joseph, *The British Mars* (1763)

Rodger, N.A.M., *The Wooden World: An Anatomy of the Georgian Navy* (1986)

Rose, G., *A Brief Examination into the Increase of the Revenue, Commerce, and Manufactures, of Great Britain from 1792 to 1799*, 2nd edn (1799)

Rouquet, Revd J., *Thanksgiving Sermon, on account of the Victory … 21st October 1805* (Bristol, 1805)

Rush, B., *Medical Inquiries and Observations: containing an account of the yellow fever, as it appeared in Philadelphia in 1797*, Vol. V (Philadelphia, 1798)

Russell, G., *The Theatres of War. Performance, Politics, and Society, 1793–1815* (Oxford, 1995)

Sailor's Letters, [signed R- B-] (Nettleton, Plymouth, [1800?])

Scott, A.F., *Every One a Witness* (1970)

A Second Genuine Speech Deliver'd By Adm[ira]l V[erno]n on board the CAROLINA *to the Officers of the Navy After the Sally from Fort St Lazara* (1741)

A Sermon, on the Present Situation of the Affairs of America and Great-Britain. Written by a Black (Philadelphia, 1782)

Seward, A., *The Poetical Works of Anna Seward; With Extracts from her Literary Correspondence*, ed. W. Scott, 3 vols (Edinburgh, 1810)

The Sham Fight: or, Political Humbug. A State Farce, in Two Acts, 2nd edn (1756)

Short Strictures on a Brief Examination into the Increase of the Revenue, Commerce, & Manufactures, of Great Britain, from 1792 to 1799. By a Merchant (1800)

Sinclair, J., MP, *Thoughts on the Naval Strength of the British Empire* (1782)

Smith, A., *An Inquiry into the Nature and Causes of the Wealth of Nations*, ed. R.H. Campbell and A.S. Skinner, 2 vols (Oxford, 1976),

Smith, C., 'Sonnet XII. Written on the Sea Shore. – October, 1784', in *Elegiac Sonnets and Other Poems*, 3rd edn (1786)

Smith, T., *A Practical Discourse to Sea-Faring Men* (Boston, MA, 1771)

Solkin, D., *Painting for Money. The Visual Arts and the Public Sphere in Eighteenth-Century England* (New Haven, CT, and London, 1993)

Some Further Particulars in Relation to the Case of Admiral Byng (1756)

Some Remarks on the late Conduct of our Fleet in the Mediterranean. In a letter to a Member of Parliament. By an Englishman (1756)

The Son of Commerce, An Original Poem, in Thirty-four Cantos, Written by a Sailor (1806)

The Sorrowful Lamentation and last Farewell to the World, of Admiral Byng (1757)

Spavens, W., *The Narrative of William Spavens a Chatham Pensioner Written by Himself* (1998), first published 1796

Speech of Lord Grenville in the House of Peers, on the motion of the Duke of Bedford for the Dismissal of Ministers, Thursday, March 22, 1798 (1798)

A Speech, which was spoken in the House of the Assembly of St. Christopher … for presenting an Address to His Majesty, relative to the Proceedings of Admiral Rodney and General Vaughan at St. Eustatius (1782)

Spilsbury, F.B., *Account of a Voyage to the Western Coast of Africa performed by His Majesty's Sloop Favourite, in the Year 1805* (1807)

'Steady as she Goes', *The Young Men and Maids Delight, Being an entire new and choice collection …* , (n.d.)

Stevens, R., *The Complete Guide to the East-India Trade, addressed to all commanders, officers, factors, etc in the Honourable East-India Company's Service* (1766)

Stone, L., ed., *An Imperial State at War: Britain from 1689 to 1815* (1993)

The Story of the Learned Pig, by an officer of the Royal Navy (1786)

Stout, N.R., *The Royal Navy in America, 1760–1775* (Annapolis, MD, 1973)

Strictures upon Naval Departments … By a Sailor (1785)

Substance of an Address to a Parochial meeting held at Chiswick, in the County of Middlesex on Tuesday, the 20th Feb. 1798 (1798)

The Substance of the Evidence on the Petition presented by the West-India Planters and Merchants to the Hon. House of Commons (1775)

Sullivan, W.F., *Pleasant Stories; or, Histories of Ben the Sailor and Ned the Soldier* (1818)

Sutton, S., *An historical Account of a New Method for extracting the foul Air out of Ships etc., 2nd. edn … to which are annexed … A Discourse on the Scurvy by Dr Mead* (1749)

Sykes, N., *Church and State in England in the XVIIIth Century* (Cambridge, 1934)

W. Tench, *Letters from Revolutionary France*, ed. G. Edwards (Cardiff, 2001)

Thompson, Captain, *The Syrens, a Masque, in two Acts, as performed at the Theatre Royal, Covent-garden* (1794)

Thompson, E., *Sailor's Letters written to his select Friends in England during his voyages and Travels in Europe, Asia, Africa and America from the year 1754 to 1759*, 2 vols (Dublin, 1766)

Three Letters relating to the Navy, Gibraltar, and Port Mahon (1757)

Thorne, R.G., *The History of Parliament. The House of Commons 1790–1820*, 5 vols (1986)

Thursfield, H.G., ed., *Five Naval Journals, 1789–1817*, Navy Records Society, vol. 91 (1951)

The Trial of Richard Parker ….Taken in Shorthand on board the Neptune *by Job Sibly* (Boston, MA, 1797)

The Trial of Vice-Admiral Byng, at a Court-Martial, held on Board his Majesty's ship the St. George in Portsmouth Harbour for An Enquiry into his Conduct, while he commanded his Majesty's fleet in the Mediterranean, and particularly on the 20th of May 1756. Together with the Admiral's Defence ….Taken down in Short-Hand (1757)

Trotter, T., *Observations on the Scurvy*, (1786)

———, *Medicina Nautica* (1797)

———, *An Essay, Medical, Philosophical, and Chemical on Drunkenness* (1804)

———, *A Practicable Plan for Manning the Royal Navy and Preserving our Maritime Ascendancy without Impressment* (Newcastle, 1819)

Turnbull, W., *The Naval Surgeon* (1806)

Tweedie, A., *The Naval Achievements of Admiral George Lord Brydges Rodney. To which is added throughts on the conduct of the late minority, now the present Ministry of Great Britain* (Edinburgh, 1782)

Vale, B., *A Frigate of King George: Life and Duty on a British Man-of-War 1807–1829* (London and New York, 2001)

Verity L., *Naval Weapons*, Maritime Collections Series (1992)

Vernon, E., *A Second Genuine Speech Deliver'd by Admiral Vernon on board the* Carolina *to the Officers of the Navy After the Sally from Fort St Lazara* (1741)

Vernon, E., *Some Seasonable Advice from an Honest Sailor, To whom it might have concerned for the Service of the C[row]n and C[ountr]y* (1746)

Vickery, A., *The Gentleman's Daughter: Women's Lives in Georgian England* (New Haven, CT, and London,1998)

A View of the Naval Force of Great-Britain ... by an Officer of Rank (1791)

The Voice of the People: A Collection of Addresses to His Majesty and Instructions to Members of Parliament by their Constituents upon the Unsuccessful Management of the Present War both at Land and Sea (1756)

Walsh, J., C. Haydon and S. Taylor, eds, *The Church of England c.1689–c.1833: From Toleration to Tractarianism* (Cambridge, 1993)

Warner, O., ed., *Jack Nastyface, Memoirs of a Seaman* (1973)

Wendeborn, G.F.A., *A View of England Towards the Close of the Eighteenth Century*, 2 vols (1791)

Wheatley, P., *The Poems of Phillis Wheatley*, ed., J.D. Mason Jr (Chapel Hill, 1966)

Whitefield, G., *A Short Address to Persons of all Denominations, Occasioned by the Alarm of an intended Invasion*, 3rd edn (1756)

Whitefield, G., *Sketches of the Life and Labours of the Rev. George Whitefield, with two discourses preached in the year 1739* (Edinburgh, [1849])

———, *Sketches of the Life and Labours of the Rev. George Whitefield, with two discourses preached in the year 1739* (Edinburgh, 1849)

The Whole Duty of Woman, By a Lady [William Kenrick] (Exeter, 1794)

Williams, E., *Mr Williams's Thanksgiving Sermon* (New 1760)

Willyams, Revd C., *An Account of the Campaign in the West Indies in the Year 1794* (1796)

Wilson, J., *Letter, Commercial and Political, addressed to ... William Pitt* (1793)

Wilson, K., 'Empire, Trade and Popular Politics in Mid-Hanoverian Britain: the Case of Admiral Vernon', *Past and Present*, 121 (1988), pp. 74–109

——, *The Sense of the People: Politics, culture and imperialism in England, 1715–1785* (Cambridge, 1995)

Winterbottom, T. M., MD, *Medical Directions for the Navigators and Settlers in Hot Climates*, 2nd edn (1803)

The Wisdom of Plutus (1757)

Wonderful escape from shipwreck. An account of the loss of His Majesty's Ship CENTAUR, *Cheap Repository Tract* (Bath and 1795)

Woodward, J., *The Seaman's Monitor; or, Advice to Sea-Faring Men*, 15th edn (1801)

Yarrington, A., *The Commemoration of the Hero 1800–1864: Monuments to the British Victors of the Napoleonic Wars* (New York and London, 1988)

Unpublished Dissertations

Blake, R.C., 'Aspects of Religion in the Royal Navy c.1770–c.1870' (MPhil thesis, University of Southampton, 1980)

Land, I., 'Domesticating the Maritime: Culture, Masculinity, and Empire in Britain, 1770–1820' (unpublished PhD thesis, University of Michigan, 1999)

Neff, E.B., 'John Singleton Copley: The Artist as "Realist" and London Impresario' (PhD thesis, University of Texas at Austin, 1997)

Tröhler, U., 'Quantification in British Medicine and Surgery 1750–1830; with Special reference to its Introduction into Therapeutics' (PhD thesis, University of London, 1978)

Index